THE CARR'S
CONNOISSEUR'S CHEESE GUIDE

THE CARR'S
CONNOISSEUR'S CHEESE GUIDE

Judy Ridgway

MARTIN BOOKS

MARTIN BOOKS

Published by Martin Books

Simon & Schuster International Group

Fitzwilliam House, 32 Trumpington Street
Cambridge CB2 1QY

in association with UB (Biscuits) Ltd, Syon Lane,
Isleworth, Middlesex TW7 5NN

First published 1989

Design: Patrick McLeavey & Partners

Photography: The Food Studio (except pages 7,
11, 14, 19, 23, 26, 31, 34)

Typesetting: Hands Fotoset, Leicester

Printed and bound in Italy by
Arnoldo Mondadori Editore

CONTENTS

— The —
HISTORY *of* CHEESE-MAKING

Exactly when and where cheese was first made is not known: like many inventions, cheese-making was probably discovered by a number of different communities at around the same time. Sheep were domesticated some 12,000 years ago, and some time later both sheep and cows were raised in Sumeria and ancient Egypt. Animals were milked into containers of leather, porous pottery or wood and, as it would have been difficult to clean these containers, the new milk must often have soured very quickly. The next step would have been to drain the whey from the curds to make a primitive kind of fresh cheese, and this may be how the first cheese came to be made. However it happened, the first cheeses would have been fairly sharp and acidic.

Using rennet to curdle the milk without souring was therefore a big advance in cheese-making. It is not known when this discovery was made, but by a few centuries BC, cheese had long passed the primitive stage.

The Romans certainly had quite sophisticated techniques of cheese-making, and as their empire spread these techniques became widely diffused. Trade within the empire was one important factor, another was the presence of Roman garrisons throughout the provinces. Soldiers received a daily ration of cheese along with staples such as bread, wine and salt, so wherever a fort was established, cheese-making would follow.

After the fall of the Roman empire in the west, there was a period of social and economic disintegration to a greater or lesser extent in all the former Roman provinces. During this time, cheese-making techniques – along with most aspects of Roman culture – were preserved mainly by the church, although simple cheese-making probably continued in most places.

As the middle ages wore on, religious foundations became great centres of agricultural as well as cultural activity, being major landowners. They were responsible for the development of many different kinds of cheese and many of today's well known cheese names were originally associated with a monastery or convent. As well as having the wealth and time to devote to the art of cheese-making, religious foundations had a particular interest, because of the many meat-free days they observed. Monks of the Cistercian order, who renounced meat-eating completely, were especially important in the history of cheese-making.

From the late-medieval period to the late-nineteenth century, cheese-making in the various European countries continued to develop along distinctive lines, producing the wide choice we have today. With the growth of trade and the increasing urban population, cheese became a highly-thought-of and economically important commodity. When Europeans colonised the New World, they took their traditions with them, and cheese-making industries flourished along European lines in many new countries.

The last hundred years of so have seen the formalising of techniques, based on scientific understanding of the processes involved in making cheese: a parallel trend has been the development of factory-produced cheeses, in line with the development of food processing techniques generally. Cheese-makers in many countries have copied some of the world's most successful cheeses and are mass-producing them on a grand scale.

Left: *Stirring Parmesan curd while it cooks. 'Grana' cheeses date from the eleventh century or earlier.*

GREAT BRITAIN

Little is known of cheese-making in Britain before the Roman period but it is most unlikely that the Romans introduced it. Britain was certainly producing cheese in Roman times and Cheshire cheese is recorded as being on sale in Rome itself. This was probably of a type which the British were already making and which appealed to Roman tastes. Cream cheeses may also have been made, in shallow pottery bowls called *mortaria*. Milk could have been left in such bowls to curdle and the whey poured off through the spout or the rim. The grits on the inner surface of the pottery would have retained the curd-forming bacteria from one day to another, thus removing the need for rennet, herbs or old whey to set the milk working. Cream cheese is still made in this way in some parts of France.

During the dark ages, cheese-making techniques were fairly primitive and mainly produced soft sheep and goat's milk cheeses. However, the more sophisticated techniques known to the Romans, such as the use of rennet, moulding and pressing, were not entirely lost, and the Celts of Wales and Ireland probably continued to make hard cheese.

With the spread of Christianity and the growth of monasteries, cheese-making flourished once again, although it was confined to the summer months. Until the sixteenth century, ewe's milk cheeses were as widespread as cow's milk cheeses and even Cheddar was probably originally made with both ewe's and cow's milk. Medieval cheeses were classified by their texture, not by their place of origin, because most cheeses remained largely in their own districts. With little trading activity and travelling, the various local techniques of cheese-making had a chance to become very firmly established, hence the continuing strength of regional cheese-types up to the modern period.

Medieval cheeses fell into three distinct types: firstly, hard cheeses made of skimmed milk which were rendered still harder by long keeping. These cheeses were destined for the servants, farm workers and peasants and were known as 'white meat', but they were poor in flavour and texture. It was well known that the worst of these cheeses came from the butter-producing areas of Suffolk and Essex. A rude little rhyme about Suffolk cheeses ran:

> *Those that made me were uncivil,*
> *They made me harder than the devil.*
> *Knives won't cut me, fire won't sweat me,*
> *Dogs bark at me, but can't eat me.*

Secondly, the soft cheeses made from whole or sometimes semi-skimmed milk and ripened for a time were much pleasanter. Thirdly, there were fresh cheeses for immediate consumption. Most of this full-cream-milk cheese was a luxury product destined for the table of the lord of the manor.

In lowland Britain cow's milk cheese virtually superseded all other kinds during the seventeenth century, and it was around this time that Britain's traditional cheeses gradually became established. With increased popular mobility and greater trade in foodstuffs, the better quality hard cheeses became more widely known. Hard cheese began to lose its bad reputation, and merchants, factors, and pedlars would buy up cheeses at the country markets and fairs to re-sell elsewhere. Towards the end of the seventeenth century, the London cheese-mongers formed themselves into an unofficial guild and began to ship cheeses by sea, river and canal over relatively long distances.

Cheddar cheese first became popular in the seventeenth century. At first, it appeared only on the tables of the rich, but when the farmers banded together into cheese-making cooperatives, they were able to make more cheese and sell it at a lower price. Cheshire cheese was also made on a cooperative basis, but was not so well thought of.

Stilton was first referred to in 1725 by Daniel Defoe; on tour through England and Wales he passed through Stilton. There are no obvious references to blue cheese specifically before that, though there must always have been some cheeses which naturally turned blue, e.g. Blue Wensleydale, made by monks and perhaps brought over by the Normans (see page 49).

Stilton became well known in the early eighteenth century. In those days, it was allowed to ripen far beyond what would be acceptable today. Defoe records that it was brought to the table with mites or maggots around it so thick that a spoon was brought to eat the mites with the cheese. Gloucester and Wensleydale also began to develop at this time.

Scotland made little cheese, preferring to turn its milk into butter (skimmed-milk cheese was no longer acceptable to most people with the availability of quality hard cheeses). Suffolk and Essex cheeses began to die out for the same reason. Cheese-making in Ireland continued with a small production of a mixture of fresh and mature cheese.

The nineteenth century saw a great expansion in British cheese-making, as scientists began to understand the process of fermentation. Heat treatments developed and new techniques were introduced. By the end of the century, cheese-making had become an up-to-date industry and the mechanisation of production swept away many of the old farmhouse traditions.

The late-twentieth century has seen a great revival of small-scale cheese-making, and many new cheeses made from cow's, goat's and ewe's milk are appearing every year. It is now possible to find local cheeses in most areas.

FRANCE

France has had a reputation since Roman times for producing some of the best cheeses in the world. Cheeses from the Roquefort and Cantal areas were taken to Rome, though it is not known how closely these resembled modern-day cheeses of these areas. During the sixth and seventh centuries cheese-making traditions were continued in the monasteries, as elsewhere in Europe. Charlemagne, King of the Franks and later Holy Roman Emperor, encouraged cheese-making throughout his vast empire in the eighth century. There are numerous stories of this enlightened monarch trying new cheeses and demanding to be sent a yearly supply.

Specialist cheese-making on any scale was confined to relatively few places during the medieval period, but Roquefort, Brie, Cantal and Comte were well known. The monasteries were developing cheeses like Munster and Pont l'Évêque. Local cheese-making by the peasant farmers was also on the increase and ewe's and goat's milk cheeses were more important than cow's milk cheeses for them. By the late-fourteenth century, there were enough cheeses on sale in Paris for the anonymous author of *La Ménagerie de Paris*, a compendium of maxims and recipes, to include a little verse setting out the attributes of a good cheese.

> *Not at all white like Helen.*
> *Nor weeping, like Magdalene.*
> *Not Argus, but completely blind,*
> *And heavy, like a buffalo.*
> *Let it rebel against the thumb,*
> *And have an old moth-eaten coat,*
> *Without eyes, without tears, not at all white,*
> *Moth-eaten, rebellious, of good weight.*

Cheese-making and an appreciation of cheese were encouraged in France by the courtly custom of sending a gift of cheese to those one admired or wanted to impress. Blanche of Navarre is reputed to have sent 200 cheeses to Philippe Auguste every year, and the poet Charles d'Orléans sent cheese to ladies he admired.

As time went on, new techniques of cheese-making were introduced, and the variety of types increased. Local cheese-makers jealously guarded their secret methods and many of them successfully protected their products by legal means – they are still protected today by the *Appellation d'Origine* system (see page 16).

Up to and during the Renaissance period, the place of cheese in the diet depended largely on one's place in the social hierarchy. The poor ate fresh and briefly-aged cheese as a staple part of their diet. The rich enjoyed a variety of cheese, for they could afford to wait for a cheese to mature for six months or even a year. Cheese was served as a novelty item, to titillate the palate at the end of a large meal, rather than as a staple food. People believed that well aged cheese had digestive properties which stimulated a stomach already filled with diverse foods.

In the fifteenth and sixteenth centuries fresh (unmatured) cheeses became much more fashionable among the rich and the very rich. Not only were they served at the cheese course, but also used in the elaborate desserts and fancy pastries which were served at the end of the great banquets of the time.

The French have always enjoyed the good things in life and to the average Frenchman, this means his food and drink. So, it is not surprising that local cheeses have not only survived for centuries but have also given rise to many new cheeses, and that more are being invented all the time. There are currently more French cheeses than there are days of the year. This deep interest in and concern for local cheeses is perhaps part of the reason why the subtle differences between French local cheeses have not become blurred. Nor have they been totally overcome by the increase in factory-produced cheese, as has happened in other countries.

ITALY

Cheese-making had a good start in Italy. The early Romans had an aversion to fresh milk, preferring to turn it into cheese. The milk came mainly from goats and ewes and fig juice was used to curdle it. Cheese-making techniques became more sophisticated and the use of rennet was introduced; in fact, by the first century BC, there was a wide variety of cheese to choose from. Fresh cheeses – which were often flavoured with herbs or spices, or smoked – were extremely popular and served day or night, as snacks or as part of a more formal meal.

Rennet, spun and dried cheeses, and the grainy-textured *grana* cheeses, like Parmesan, were becoming established, as well as a variety of imported cheeses including, English Cheshire, a Greek ewe's milk cheese called Cynthos and probably some French cheeses. Roman soldiers were given an ounce of cheese a day as part of their rations and the Romans used cheese a great deal in cooking; characteristic dishes include cheese and honey baked in pastry, bread and cakes made with cheese and even cheesy sweetmeats.

During the dark ages, religious communities and travelling monks passed on cheese-making knowledge and advice to local people. The Po Valley was an area where the religious orders carried on making cheese and by the thirteenth century this area, which was a centre for trade with the rest of Europe, was one of the main production areas, making Gorgonzola and Parmesan.

Cheese-making remained part of a pattern of general mixed farming all over Italy and both cows and sheep flourished in the north. However, as the monks extended the use of water meadows to provide lush grazing, cows gradually took over, and today Piedmont, Lombardy and the Po Valley are renowned for their cow's milk cheeses.

The rest of Italy does not have such sweet meadowland, and so in the central part of the country and in the south there are approximately twice as many sheep as there are cows. This has been the

Right: *Weighing Gouda cheese in the ancient open-air market at Alkmaar, Holland.*

pattern for many centuries and, as a result, Tuscany, Lazio, Campania, Sardinia, Puglia and Sicily are renowned for their ewe's milk cheeses, known under the general name Pecorino.

The geography of Italy is so diverse that the range of cheeses produced begins to rival that of France. In the north, alpine meadows produce their own particular type of cheese, whereas the swamps of the south are an ideal climate for the water buffalo, whose milk has traditionally been used for cheese. There are even reports that buffalo were exported to France in the middle ages so that their milk could be used for cheese-making. Real Italian Mozarella is still made partly from water-buffalo milk.

As in France, the local strength of Italian cheese-making traditions, and the high regard in which the Italians hold good cheese, have ensured that quality cheese production continues, despite the advance of factory-based production methods.

NETHERLANDS

Archaeological finds suggest that cheese-making went on in the Netherlands soon after the end of the Roman period, but the first known records are from the ninth century. These show that butter and cheese for the court of Charlemagne were made in Frisia. During the middle ages, cheese-making became extremely well established, with special cheese weigh-houses or *kaaswaag* in Haarlem, Linden and Leeuwarden. The geography of Holland is very suitable for dairy farming and cheese-making was an important activity from an early period.

These early Dutch cheese-makers developed cheeses which had exceptional keeping qualities. They were extremely reliable and easy to transport. The cheeses were exported overland to Germany and later by sea to the far corners of the Baltic and the Mediterranean. The style of Dutch cheese was already defined at this time, and the majority were similar to the Edam and Gouda familiar to us today. Though few in number and not very varied, Dutch cheeses have become so successful that Holland is – to many people – synonymous with cheese.

Modern Dutch cheese-making is entirely factory-based and has to use pasteurised milk. For this reason there is less interest in traditional farmhouse-based cheeses than in, for example, the United Kingdom.

SCANDINAVIA

Cows, milk and cheese are probably not the first items that spring to mind on hearing mention of the Vikings; in the ninth century, however, Vikings caught by the Moors of Spain are said to have been asked to pass on everything they knew about cheese-making to their captors. The Vikings were also instrumental in introducing new breeds of cattle into Europe, some of which provided the bloodlines for modern breeds, like the large brown cow of Normandy, Guernsey cattle and Gloucesters. The Vikings travelled with their bulls and cows on-board their longships, and these interbred with native cattle where they settled.

The earliest cheeses to make any impact in Scandinavia were probably made in Denmark, where archaeological finds show that the primitive tribes kept goats, sheep and cows. Later, Denmark was the home of many of the Viking bands and they carried these cheese-making traditions to other countries. In Norway and Sweden the earliest cheeses were the strongly flavoured, long-lasting cheeses like Gammalöst which kept through the long dark winters and sustained the Norsemen on their long sea voyages.

The monks of the middle ages were the next to exert an influence, as in other European countries.

At the same time, trade was flourishing between the Scandinavian countries and Holland. An early Norwegian cheese which dates from that time is a semi-hard spiced cheese called Nokkelost or 'key cheese'. It bears some resemblance to a Dutch cheese called Leiden, which used to carry the mark of St. Peter's crossed keys, the arms of the city of Leiden, and this suggests a strong influence from the Netherlands on medieval cheese-making in Scandinavia.

Because of the need to preserve food, particularly through the winter, the Scandinavians early developed a taste for smoked and spiced cheese. In Finland, fresh cheeses were smoked over a straw or hay fire and there are many examples of highly-flavoured cheeses spiced with cumin seed and cloves.

Even in the sixteenth and seventeenth centuries, foodstuffs were commonly used in both Denmark and Sweden as currency and to pay the taxes levied by the church, and cheese was a particularly important exchange commodity. In areas where pastures were owned by the church, milk or cheese was the required payment. The vicar then made more cheese with the milk and traded his cheese for other commodities. These cheeses became known as *Prästost* or 'parsonage' cheese.

In Denmark, cheese-making was an occupation to be proud of: the larger the cheese, the greater the professional skill of the maker. Some cheeses were so large that several men could hardly lift them. During the reign of King Christian II of Denmark at the beginning of the sixteenth century, there was a church edict to forbid the eating of cheese during Lent. King Christian had something of a dilemma as the upholder of the faith but also a champion of Danish cheese. So, for a suitable fee, he offered his people special letters of dispensation which reconciled religious observance and the eating of cheese.

Despite its early start in cheese-making, Denmark did not establish individual cheeses; most of its cheese-making was, and still is, derivative. Cheese-makers were invited in from other countries and leading Danish cheese-makers, like Hanne Nielsen in the early nineteenth century, travelled abroad to perfect their craft. Denmark is a major exporter of cheese today, but all its production is factory-based using pasteurised milk. For this reason Denmark still does not have any really distinctive local cheeses. The same is true of the other countries of Scandinavia.

GERMANY AND SWITZERLAND

Home-made, non-renneted cheeses have been made for many, many hundreds of years in Germany and Quark, the modern name for this type of cheese, still accounts for half the total German cheese production.

By the middle ages, rennet cheeses were established and in the castles of the Teutonic Knights cheeses were made in various qualities; *Herrenkäsen* for the nobility and *Gesindekäse* for the commoners. Cheese became so popular that it had to be imported from Holland and Switzerland.

Today, there are very few indigenous German cheeses, most are copies of cheeses from other lands. Limburg cheese, for example, originally from Belgium, is now almost a German cheese. Münster has a similar history, originating in the French Vosges, and Allgäu Emmenthal is based on the Swiss original. All German cheeses must be made with pasteurised milk and most of today's production is in factories.

Swiss cheeses have been renowned since Roman times. The Swiss are another nation who once used their cheeses as currency: artisans, workers and priests were paid partly in cash and partly in fine Swiss cheeses. Cheeses were also bartered across the frontiers for rice, spices and wine.

The Swiss farmers have always been proud of their cheese-making skills and cheeses like Emmenthal and Gruyère have developed international reputations. There are also some less-well-known that are excellent, such as Tête de Moine. Unpasteurised milk is used in Swiss cheese-making and the tradition of fine farmhouse cheeses has weathered the introduction of factory-production more succesfully than is the case in Germany.

UNITED STATES OF AMERICA

The United States is now the largest producer of cheese in the world, yet the cheese industry started only in 1851, when Jesse Williams opened the first Cheddar cheese factory in Oneida County, New York State. Many more factories have opened since then, but Cheddar or Cheddar-based cheeses account for 80 per cent of all cheese produced.

Many of the native American cheeses, like Colby, Monterey Jack, Tillamook and Pineapple are variations of Cheddar. Colby originates from Vermont, and Monterey Jack was first made around 1892 in California.

Liederkranz cheese is one of the few American cheeses which does not conform to the pattern; it was invented by a New York delicatessen owner in 1850 and named after his choral society. It is a soft, mould-ripened cheese and is now produced mainly in Ohio.

As a result of successive waves of immigration, Americans also enjoy a good many European-style cheeses. Many of these have to be home-made because the United States will not allow cheeses made with unpasteurised milk to be imported.

AUSTRALIA AND NEW ZEALAND

The early British settlers in Australia found no dairy tradition and had to rely on knowledge from the old country. Cheese-making began in New South Wales during the early part of the last century and it was Cheddar which was made. Other States soon followed New South Wales's lead and for a hundred years or more, Cheddar to various states of maturity was made on the farms and homesteads.

As immigrants from countries other than Britain arrived in Australia, so different cheese-making techniques were introduced and today there are more than fifty different cheeses produced by Australia's vigorous dairy industry. They include copies of Mozzarella, Provolone, Parmesan, Feta, Emmenthal, Gouda, Edam, Brie and Camembert

New Zealand also has a flourishing cheese-making industry and in terms of exports is second only to the Netherlands. As in Australia, the British settlers started off making English cheeses. Cheddar was paramount, but in recent years New Zealanders have turned to making all kinds of cheese including Danbo, Gouda, Edam, Gruyère, Colby, Feta and Parmesan.

OTHER COUNTRIES

Cheese-making is essentially a European tradition, and there are few European countries which have not had a flourishing cheese producing industry. Spain, for example, has a long history of cheese-making and today makes quite a large number of good cheeses, but the quantities made are not very large and the cheeses have not been exported. Belgium and Austria have also always produced good cheese, but they have tended to be rather over-shadowed by their neighbours. Belgium seems to have given up all claim to Limburg, but is now busy producing a new range of modern cheeses.

Cheese is quite important in Greece and some small quantities are produced in the Middle East. Further north, Russia produces considerable quantities of cheese.

The knowledge of simple cheese-making techniques did find its way east as well as west from

Left, above and below: *Emmenthal cheeses are cleaned on a revolving table. These cheeses are three and a half months old, and nearly ready for sale.*

Asia Minor. India makes a simple curd cheese known as Panir, and China produces a surprising 126,000 million tonnes of cheese a year. Cheese is also made in other parts of the East and Far East, but it never became a particularly important part of the diet. On the whole, cheese-making in the East remains relatively simple.

On the other side of the world, cheese-making was unknown to the indigenous peoples of both North and South America. Sheep and cattle were shipped to South America by settlers, but they did not thrive and those that did survive were bred for meat rather than for milk. Cheese is made in countries like Argentina, but they tend to be copies of long-keeping cheeses like Gouda and Edam, or of some of the Italian cheeses like Mozzarella and Parmesan.

In Central America and Africa and in some parts of South East Asia, the climate is too hot for successful cheese-making. This, coupled with the fact that the cattle are not good milkers, means that cheese is not part of the normal diet.

PROTECTED NAMES

Certain cheeses have nationally and sometimes internationally agreed protection for their names. In France, the *Appellation d'Origine* system is applied to cheeses in much the same way as the *Appellation Contrôllee* system is applied to wine. The twenty-seven cheeses affected may only be produced in certain designated areas of the country. Entries in the A–Z of Cheeses indicate if a cheese is protected by this system.

A similar system is run on a smaller scale in Italy and in Spain. In the latter country, only five cheeses are involved. In the United Kingdom, Stilton is the only cheese to have similar protection.

The labels of origin only apply in the country which runs the system. However, a measure of international agreement was achieved among European countries with the publication of the Stresa Convention in 1951. This gave complete protection to a very small number of cheeses such as Gorgonzola. These cheeses may not be produced anywhere in Europe other than their areas of origin.

A much larger number of other cheeses have limited protection, in that versions produced outside their own countries must be labelled as such, e.g. Danish Port Salut or French Sbrinz.

— MILK *and* CHEESE —

Milk is the raw material from which cheese is made; differences from one batch of milk to another will manifest themselves in the finished product – the cheese. It is possible to standardise the milk to fit a specific process and, indeed, this is what the large automated cheese manufacturers do. The result is a standardised product, consistent, clean and pleasant, but to my mind devoid of any real character in comparison with a farmhouse cheese.

Milk is in fact a very variable commodity. Obviously the animal from which the milk comes will be one of the major factors, but the food that the animal has been eating, the soil on which its pasture is growing and the weather on the day it is milked will all affect the milk itself. Before the advent of scientific methods in cheese-making the flavour of the cheese depended almost entirely on where the cows had been grazing and, to some extent, it still does.

SOURCES OF MILK

Milk from different animals has some quite marked differences, but even within the same group of animals, different breeds produce very differently flavoured milk.

Most of the world's cheeses are made from cow's milk. Dairy cattle produce milk for up to ten months after the birth of their calves. This is usually followed by a two-month dry period. By staggering calf production in a large herd, milk is available all year round.

The milk changes in character during the lactation period. The first milk to be produced is full of nourishment for the newborn calf and contains colostrum or 'beestings'. This is followed by the 'new milk', which is rich in fats and proteins. As the lactation period progresses, so the yield and the fat content decrease, until the end of the period when fats increase once again. Milk produced towards the end of the milking is higher in fats than the first flow and there is also a difference between morning and evening milk, the latter being richer. Summer milk is reputed to produce better cheese, because it tends to be richer than winter milk.

Sheep can live in countryside which is unsuitable for cattle and the use of their milk allows cheese to be made in areas where it would not otherwise be possible. The ewe's lactation period is short, however, the yields are low and the availability of the milk seasonal – usually from mid-January to mid-May. The availability of ewe's milk cheeses depends on how long they need to mature.

Goats, too, provide milk in regions where cattle are scarce. Goats have a high milk yield, but their lactation period is very short and so, again, the milk is seasonally available. Pure goat's milk cheeses are usually available from the beginning of spring to the end of the autumn. Goat's milk has a very high fat content and because it is free from many of the pathogens (agents that cause disease) that affect cow's milk, it is rarely pasteurised. Goat's milk imparts an unmistakeable flavour to cheese produced from it. Many people who are allergic to cow's milk can eat goat's milk, and sometimes ewe's milk, products without any problems. Milk from other animals is not widely used, though the water buffalo has been important in southern Italy. Yaks, reindeers and camels are sometimes milked for cheese, but nowadays only in a few remote areas.

The fodder and the nature of the grazing will affect the character and content of the milk from all these animals. Some authorities believe that even the stage at which hay is cut, or the use of artificial or organic manure on pastureland can affect the flavour of the milk.

— *The* —
PRINCIPLES *of* MAKING CHEESE

The principles of cheese-making are the same for all cheeses, but within them there is room for endless variety. The cheese-maker's skill has resulted in hundreds of different cheeses. Indeed, the process is so complex, and the treatment of each cheese so critical, that even two cheeses, which started off from the same batch of curds and have undergone the same processes, will not necessarily taste exactly the same. Only the mass manufacturer aims to make all cheeses of a certain type taste the same, and the unpredictability of cheese is considered to be part of its attraction by many connoisseurs.

Milk is turned into cheese by extracting the water (whey) from the milk, leaving the milk solids (curds) behind. There are five basic steps to achieve a finished cheese.

1. Preparing the milk.
2. Coagulating the milk into curds and whey.
3. Cutting the curds.
4. Moulding, salting and pressing the cheese.
5. Ripening the cheese.

Each of these stages is crucial in producing a good quality cheese, but also in determining what *kind* of cheese is produced. There are countless variations at each stage to produce the huge variety of cheese made around the world.

PREPARING THE MILK

Some cheeses are made with milk from a single milking, either morning or evening, but more often the evening milk is kept overnight and mixed with the morning milk straight from the cow. Cream may be added to the milk to make a richer mix or, conversely, the milk may be partly or even fully skimmed to make lower fat cheese.

Pasteurisation In the past, only raw milk and cream were used for cheese-making on the farm. Today, the vast quantities of milk used for factory-produced cheeses are heat-treated by pasteurisation before being made into cheese, as is some milk used in 'farmhouse' cheeses. Milk is pasteurised by heating to just over 70°C/160°F for 15 seconds. This is designed to sterilise the milk partially and kill off all the potentially harmful bacteria in it. Pasteurisation is useful for large producers, for it allows them to mix milk from different herds and achieve a standardised product. It also kills off any fault-producing organisms and enables the manufacturers to exert more control over the cheese-making process, by using their own carefully developed starter cultures.

The disadvantage of pasteurised milk is that it tends to destroy the individuality of the cheese and makes a blander product. Most connoisseurs will tell you that the contrast between cheeses made from unpasteurised milk and those made from pasteurised is like the difference between fine wine and table wine. They argue that pasteurisation inactivates the natural enzymes in the milk which would normally help the final flavour of the cheese to develop. Also it retards the action of the rennet, which means the curd needs much longer ripening before the full flavour and texture of the cheese is

Left: *Rich Swiss Alpine pasture gives a special flavour to the milk, and to the cheese made from it.*

achieved. Nor do they believe that pasteurisation is necessary on health grounds. There have been far fewer problems associated with cheese made from unpasteurised milk than with that made from pasteurised milk. Even the few recorded cases of listeria caused by cheese have nearly all been traced back to pasteurised, not unpasteurised, milk.

Unpasteurised milk used to make cheese in modern dairies is not a health hazard. The standard of hygiene is very high and is likely to remain so. In addition, many of the pathogens which might be present are destroyed by the cheese-making process itself, particularly when making hard and semi-hard cheese. Soft and semi-soft cheeses may be more at risk, as they do not have time to develop the lactic acid levels which protect hard cheese.

The use of raw milk continues in certain soft cheeses, such as Brie de Meaux and some Camemberts, and other French creameries are following suit. Plenty of small-scale producers in a variety of countries make genuine farmhouse cheeses.

While some countries, like Denmark and the United States, demand that cow's milk cheese is made from pasteurised milk, British farmhouse cheese-makers are resisting a suggestion that a similar requirement should be introduced into the United Kingdom. I hope that commonsense will win and the growing choice of British cheeses will continue unchecked.

Additives to milk   Some cheeses have natural dyes such as annatto added to the milk to colour them. The different cheese-producing countries vary in their laws on the addition of food colours, but Denmark, for example, bans all colouring agents in home-produced cheeses, except that used in Danish Cheddar.

Moulds may be added to promote veining or to grow a mould rind; these include *penicillium Roquefortii* for blue mould cheeses and *penicillium candidum* for white mould rind cheeses. Propolonic acid bacteria may be added to create holes inside the cheese. This bacterium lives on the lactic acid given off by the other bacteria and in turn gives off massive amounts of carbon dioxide, which collects in pockets or 'eyes'.

However, the most important additives are usually a starter or lactic acid culture and rennet. Starter cultures usually consist of lactic streptococci and lactobacilli, which occur naturally in milk once it has left the cow. Rennet is an enzyme extracted from the stomach of a young calf or lamb and from micro-organisms. Plant rennets occur, too, such as the juice of fig leaves, thistle seeds, ladies bedstraw, safflower and melon. The effect of these additives is to begin the process of coagulation.

COAGULATING THE MILK

If left to itself, raw milk will sour naturally. This is due to the action of bacteria like lactobacilli and lactic streptococci which ferment the lactose (the sugar that naturally occurs in milk) to lactic acid. These bacteria usually outgrow the other microbes which may have contaminated the milk and it is this dominance that made it possible to produce cheese in the past without decay caused by other micro-organisms. If left to sour long enough, the milk solids will coagulate and separate from the liquid or whey. This process is fairly unpredictable, however, if the cheese-maker allows it to occur naturally.

Today, pure cultures of lactic-acid-forming bacteria are added to the milk in the form of starter cultures. This means that the cheese-maker has much greater control over this important stage in the process. The bacteria chosen for the culture are preferred because they produce very little besides lactic acid and carbon dioxide and give the cheese a sharp, clean taste.

Once the starter culture has been added to the milk, the acidity of the curds will gradually increase. Some cheeses, known as lactic-curd or acid-curd cheeses, for example Quark and Fromage Frais, are coagulated entirely by the lactic acid formation. Other cheeses need rennet as well.

After the starter culture has been added, the cheese-maker constantly tests the acidity in the milk so that he knows just when to add the rennet. Once this has been added, the casein molecules lump together, the curd is allowed to set into a junket-like gel, and settle for an hour or two at an even temperature. The temperature used ranges from 21°C/70°F to 35°C/95°F and depends upon the kind of cheese being made. Low temperatures result in soft, jelly-like curds suitable for making soft cheeses; and high temperatures lead to the hard, rubbery curds needed for hard cheeses.

CUTTING AND TREATING THE CURDS

Separating the curds from the whey and concentrating them is the next stage. How this is done will affect the moisture content and the texture of the finished cheese. Cutting the curds releases the whey, so for softer cheeses they are cut sparingly – and ladled into moulds to be drained naturally – and for harder cheeses, they may be cut vertically and horizontally into tiny pieces, or combed into thin strands.

As the small pieces of curd fall to the bottom of the vat, they cling together again to form a solid mass and this is cut again. In cheddaring (the process developed for Cheddar cheese), the curds are piled in blocks one on top of the other so as to expel the maximum amount of whey. They may remain in this position for a few minutes, or a few hours, depending on the kind of cheese that is being made. For other types of hard cheese the curd is cut and turned and the result is more crumbly, and less fine and smooth in texture than Cheddar cheese.

As well as cutting the curds, the cheese-maker may also heat the curds. Heat causes the curds to become denser, more compact and to release more whey. Temperatures vary from 41°C/105°F to 54°C/130°F. Soft cheeses are cooked or scalded at lower temperatures than hard ones, yet some soft and crumbly cheeses, like Roquefort and Stilton, are not cooked at all. Other cheeses, like Provolone and Mozzarella, are cut and heated until the curd can be pulled into tender strings. The curd is then kneaded and stretched in order to accentuate the fibrous structure and compact it further. These cheeses are known in Italy as *pasta filata* and elsewhere as spun-curd or plastic-curd cheeses.

Once the whey has been drained off it, too, can be used to make cheese, and Swedish Mesost is one example; Italian Ricotta used to be another, but now it is more likely to be made from full milk. Today whey is mostly used in other products: as an additive in animal feed and as an ingredient in products such as margarine.

Cheeses flavoured with herbs, spices or wine now have them added to the curds. Once cheddaring and mellowing are complete, the curd is milled again. Kneaded curds are not milled.

MOULDING, SALTING AND PRESSING THE CHEESE

Salting All cheeses, except the softest cream and cottage cheeses, are salted. The salt may be added to the milled curds, as in cheddar cheese, or it may be rubbed on to the surface of the formed cheese, as in the manufacture of Parmesan. Alternatively, the cheese may be soaked in brine after moulding: many Swiss and Danish cheeses are made in this way. Salt dehydrates the curd so that more whey can be removed by subsequent pressing, it changes the Ph (acidity/alkaline level) of the cheese and slows down the activity of the starter bacteria, thus controlling the rate at which the cheese later ripens. Salting also helps to suppress the growth of spoilage bacteria.

A few cheeses, like Greek Feta cheese, are so heavily salted that all bacterial activity is stopped, in fact it is 'pickled' and will not benefit from further ripening. As well as being salted, the cheese may now be sprayed with mould-forming spores, to form a bloomy white rind; washed with alcohol, to slow down the effect of mould or bacteria; buried in ashes to give it a coating; or washed with bacteria to create the distinctive aroma of some very pungent cheeses.

Moulding The prepared curds are ladled into perforated moulds and now the cheese-making process really begins to vary between types. The moulds can be almost any shape or size and may be made of stainless steel, wood, basketware or, indeed, any kind of suitable material. Alternatively, hand-moulding in cheese cloth may replace rigid moulds.

Pressing The curds may be left to firm naturally, or they may be lightly or heavily pressed.

RIPENING

This stage takes place in special storage rooms where the temperature and humidity are carefully controlled. The temperature is kept fairly low at about 10°C/50°F to ensure that the desirable micro-organisms grow at a slow and steady rate, thus guarding against uneven maturing and the production of the unwanted chemical by-products of rapid growth. The relative humidity is quite high at around 80 per cent for hard cheeses and 95 per cent for soft and mould-ripened cheeses. This prevents the surface of the cheese drying out.

Blue cheeses ripen from within because of the action of the starter bacteria and the veins of mould. Cheddar and Swiss-type cheeses also ripen from within as a result of the evenly dispersed starter bacteria. However, cheeses like Brie and Camembert ripen by the action of their surface mould which was sprayed on, from the outside in, as do cheeses like Pont l'Évêque and Munster, which ripen through the action of the bacteria which grow on their surfaces after being washed on.

During the ripening, cheeses start to take on their own special characteristics of taste. The various bacteria which were included in the starter cultures or added to the curd, or the moulds which were added to the curd or sprayed on, now begin to work. The blue veining starts to appear in blue cheeses; the holes form in Emmenthal-style cheese and the moulds form on the outsides of cheeses like Brie.

Ripening is a very involved and complicated process in which the microbes and enzymes in the cheese slowly change their chemical compositions from complex organic molecules into simpler ones. Each of these changes contributes to the flavour and texture of the ripened cheese. How long the ripening takes is critical, but the time varies from cheese type to cheese type. Soft cheeses, like Camembert, may be ripened for only a few weeks, whereas a cheese like Parmesan may be ripened for two or three years. Even within the same cheese type the ripening may vary considerably, and judging how a cheese is proceeding is part of the cheese-maker's skill.

Turning cheeses at regular intervals during ripening ensures even development. This is not the only attention they get; cheese-makers check the colour, odour, shape, texture and even the sound of their cheeses, too, and a cheese iron may be used to check a sample from the centre. The iron is inserted in the cheese and removes a 'plug' from inside.

Once the cheese has ripened, it is coated to prevent moisture loss, spoilage and physical damage. Cloth, wax, fat, foil and plastic are all used for this purpose.

BLUE CHEESES

The very first blue cheeses were probably the result of accidental contamination by microbes naturally occurring in a particular area. The Roquefort caves, for example, harbour one predominant mould and the Brie region another. These microbes act upon the cheeses when they are stored in the caves to ripen. Until comparatively recently, blue cheeses could be made only where these moulds

Right: *Using a cheese 'harp' to cut the curds into small pieces before they are cooked.*

were present. Nowadays, cultures of *penicillium Roquefortii* can be prepared and sent anywhere in the world. Even in the original regions, pure cultures are used to start off the mould growth, and only occasionally are the naturally-occurring moulds allowed to flourish alone.

Cultures may be added to the milk at the very beginning of the cheese-making process or they may be added to the curd. There are many different strains of the major varieties of mould and the cheese-maker may choose how mild or how strong a strain he wants. The growth of the mould within the cheese can be unpredictable, but the cheese-maker can delay the development of the mould by sealing the cheese and withholding air. Then, when he or she is ready for the mould to start growing, the cheesemaker will pierce the cheese with stainless steel needles to aerate the paste and so help the veins to spread. Young veins are usually very light blue in colour, these brighten as the cheese ripens and may turn green or even disappear as the cheese ages.

SUMMARY OF VARIABLE FACTORS WHICH AFFECT THE FINISHED CHEESE

1   The type and mix of milk or milk and cream used.
2   The use, or not, of a starter culture and the choice of bacteria included.
3   The use, or not, of rennet and the types used.
4   The use of hole or mould forming bacteria and the specific choice made.
5   The temperature at which coagulation takes place.
6   The length of time the curds are allowed to stand before cutting.
7   The method of cutting the curds, cheddaring, and kneading.
8   The degree to which the curds are cut.
9   The temperature to which the curds are raised: scalding and cooking.
10   The degree and method of salting.
11   The size and shape of moulds and the degree of pressing.
12   The choice of rind and finish.
13   The method and period of ripening.
14   The choice of coating.

CHEESE-MAKING PROCESSES

Cheeses are sometimes classified by the way in which they are made. These are not all clear-cut methods for there is often some overlap, but they can act as a useful guide.

Fresh cheeses These are unripened cheeses or cheeses which are not ripened for more than a few days. Some, like fresh goat's and ewe's milk cheese and Feta cheese, are lightly pressed or moulded by hand, others are just packed into tubs or crocks. They may be coagulated with the use of lemon juice or an acid culture at low temperatures (Quark) or high temperatures (Ricotta), or with rennet (curd cheese).

Ripened unpressed cheeses The curds are cut as little as possible and allowed to drain naturally. They may be quick-ripened with surface moulds or bacteria (Camembert, Brie, Pont l'Évêque) or for two to three months with natural moulds (Stilton), or for four to twelve weeks with starter cultures (Esrom).

Pressed uncooked cheeses which are ripened These cheeses may be lightly or heavily pressed and may be ripened for anything from two to eighteen months (Samsoe).

Pressed cooked cheeses which are ripened The curds are 'cooked' in the whey before being milled, moulded and heavily pressed (Cheddar, Parmesan) and may be matured for as long as four years.

Pasta filata cheeses The curd is immersed in hot water and kneaded either by hand or by machine. The cheeses may be eaten at once (Mozzarella) or ripened (Provolone).

Whey cheese Strictly speaking these are not cheeses at all as they are made from the whey. They may be fresh (Ricotta) or pressed and dried (Mesost).

TEXTURE OF CHEESE

The texture or consistency of cheese is often used as a means of classifying it. The hardness or softness is directly related to the cheese's water content: the softer the cheese the higher its water content. The problem with this kind of classification is that one group overlaps another to such an extent that it can be difficult to decide in which section to include a particular cheese. It becomes more complicated because many cheeses lose moisture as they mature. The distinction between semi-soft and semi-hard cheeses can be a particularly difficult one to draw. I have usually given the producer's description if there is one, or that given by the Dairy Board or cheese authority of the country concerned. Here are the descriptions for the categories used in this book. The percentage of water is only a rough guide.

Very soft (80 per cent water) These cheeses are spoonable and include almost all fresh cheeses, except Mozzarella and Feta. Cream cheese or fresh goat's cheese are good examples.

Soft (50–70 per cent water) These are spreadable cheeses like Brie and Camembert.

Semi-soft (40–50 per cent water) Often crumbly or springy, these cheeses can be difficult to slice. Many blue cheeses come into this category along with many 'monks' cheeses'.

Semi-hard (40–50 per cent water) What the Germans call sliceable cheese; they include Tilsit and Gouda, and cheeses like Caerphilly and Cheshire.

Hard (30–40 per cent water) Very firm and dense, these cheeses are quite grainy. They may be sliceable when young, but very hard and barely grateable when old. Parmesan is a prime example of this type; Cheddar is a less hard 'hard' cheese.

RINDS

Fresh cheeses do not usually have any rind, but in other cheeses the rind is very distinctive. The rind is important because it controls the progression of moisture from inside the cheese to the outside and of air into the cheese. It also regulates the escape of gases released by the cheese during the ripening period. Cheese-makers monitor the condition of the rind carefully because it is so important. Most rinds fall into the following categories:

Dry natural rinds The rind is formed by the curds at the edges of the cheese drying out. They may be brushed or scraped, as in the case of Stilton, bandaged to make them coarse or grainy, or oiled to become smooth and shiny. They are generally tough, hard and thick and moulds may grow on the coarser ones; these rinds are not usually eaten.

RINDS *continued*

Soft bloomy white rinds These cheeses have a thin or thick white mould on the surface. The most frequently used mould is *penicillium candidum*. This is sprayed on to the cheese after brining. The white mould may be left to grow unhindered in fast-ripening cheeses or it may be brushed off from time to time to produce a thicker rind. The mould is pure white, fluffy and dry to the touch when the cheese is young (the fluffiness will be flattened by any wrappings), and it may darken with age. The rind may be eaten. A typical example is Camembert.

Washed rinds Cheeses washed with water, brine, wine or beer, or with a culture of *breyibacterium linens* develop a thin yellowish-red bacterial growth. The rind is usually soft and damp to the touch, but should not be slimy. These cheeses tend to have a pungent smell, but are not necessarily strongly flavoured. The rind is not eaten. Pont l'Évêque is a typical example.

Artificial rinds These are rinds which do not occur as an integral part of the cheese. They may be organic or inorganic, but they are added by the cheese-maker. Organic rinds include herbs or leaves and inorganic ones include wax, ashes or plastic wraps. The latter tend to be used in the larger manufacturing operations where cheese technology is very advanced. The method tends to avoid heavy curing costs and ensures that more of the cheese is available to eat.

Plastic-wrapped cheeses do not ripen in the way that natural rind cheeses do: the air-tight seal means that there is no gas or water exchange. The cheeses are also usually stored at fairly low temperatures which means that they are likely to be mild in flavour and the taste will come from the action of the starter used. Wax-coatings do not have the same restrictions, since they are used to seal the cheese after it has finished ripening.

Organic coatings may be eaten, but are more usually discarded, as are inorganic rinds.

SMELLY CHEESES

The fermentation of milk is a process of controlled spoilage. As the microbes and enzymes in the cheese degrade the original food, the fats and proteins break down and can produce highly odorous molecules. For example, an aged Camembert will have roughly half its nitrogen-containing compounds converted to small water-soluble compounds and of these one quarter may be ammonia. Soft cheeses ripen more quickly and often more extremely than hard cheeses because they are moister and, therefore, more hospitable to microbes. A really smelly Camembert is actually over-ripe, but some people like it that way! Other smelly cheeses, like Munster and Pont l'Évêque, owe their odour to the bacteria which live on their surfaces, and their flavour is often much less pungent.

The ten smelliest cheeses from France are:

Époisses	Maroilles	Boulette d'Avesnes	Langres	Dauphin
Munster	Livarot	Camembert	Chaumes	Carré de l'Est

Left: *Cheeses in the second maturing phase, in the caves of Roquefort.*

— CHEESE *and* NUTRITION —

Milk is composed of over 75 per cent water, with other constituents held in suspension. These constituents are fats, proteins, minerals and vitamins. The proportion of these constituents in a finished cheese depends partly on the type of milk or milk mixture used and partly on how hard or soft the cheese is. Soft cheeses hold more water than hard cheeses, which have had much of the liquid pressed out of them.

FAT IN CHEESE

There are a number of different fats in whole milk, including both saturated (60 per cent) and unsaturated (40 per cent) fatty acids. During cheese-making, most of these fats, which are held in suspension in the milk, are deposited in the curd. The fat content of a cheese is not only important nutritionally, but also legally. Legislation in many countries lays down certain minimum percentages of fat for each type of cheese. These percentages are based on the dry weight of the cheese, that is, after all the water has been removed. Thus the figure of 45 per cent given in the A–Z section for both Camembert and Emmenthal refers to the dry weight. However, the actual fat content of these two cheeses is not the same: Emmenthal has a higher *fat content* ounce for ounce or gram for gram because it contains less *water*. Do bear this in mind if you are trying to keep the fat or calorie content of your diet down. It also means that seemingly 'creamier' cheeses, like Camembert, are less fattening than Emmenthal, if eaten in the same quantities.

The fat content of a cheese is an important indicator of the levels of vitamins A and D which are both fat soluble. Vitamin A, particularly, is lost in cheeses made from skimmed milk. 'Low-fat' versions of cheeses like Cheddar tend to have slightly less of vitamins A and D than the conventional version.

PROTEIN IN CHEESE

Casein is the basic and most important milk protein and this is present in cheese together with the simpler proteins which result from the ripening process. Other milk proteins are water-soluble and are lost in the whey during cheese-making. (They are the proteins in whey-based cheeses.) 'Low-fat' cheeses have about 4–5 g more protein per 100 g than the conventional ones.

When cheese is overcooked, the casein coagulates to a tough stringyness and this can be harder to digest.

The amount of cheese protein which is immediately usable by the body is quite high, at around 70 per cent, and this compares very favourably with meat and poultry at around 67–68 per cent. Even more of this protein can be utilised if cheese is eaten with cereal products, so bread or biscuits and cheese do make a very nutritious meal. Other complementary mixes include cheese and potatoes and cheese and pulses, such as peanuts or beans.

This works because cheese is rich in the amino-acid lysine and beans, cereals and so on are low in it. Thus the mix releases more of the protein from the other items. However, the real picture is not quite as simple as this, as other amino-acids are also involved.

VITAMINS AND MINERALS IN CHEESE

As well as vitamins A and D, cheese also contains some of the B vitamins and vitamin E, but no vitamin C. Minerals include calcium and phosphorous and as a rule, the harder the cheese, the greater the concentration of minerals. 'Low-fat' cheeses have slightly more calcium.

FOOD VALUES FOR 100 g OF COMMON CHEESE TYPES

	kCal	protein g	fat g	water g	sodium mg	calcium mg	vit. A μg	vit. B (niacin) mg
Camembert-type	300	23	23	48	1400	400	250	1.00
Cheddar	400	26	34	37	600	800	400	0
Cottage	100	14	0.5	79	450	60	30	0
Cream	440	3	47	45	300	100	450	0
Danish Blue	360	23	29	40	1400	580	300	1.00
Edam	300	24	23	44	1000	750	300	0
Parmesan	400	35	30	28	750	1200	400	0.30
Stilton	460	26	40	28	1200	350	450	0.20

Source: Food Tables *Bender and Bender, Oxford University Press, 1986*

— A —
GUIDE *to* ENJOYING CHEESE

BUYING CHEESE

The information you get from your eyes and nose is the best guide when buying cheese. If you are buying from a specialist cheese shop you may be able to back up this information with a tasting.

Cheese should usually smell good. Those which smell very strongly of ammonia are usually over-ripe. Some of the washed-rind cheeses, however, have very strong farmyardy smells and this is perfectly normal for these cheeses.

Cheese should look good. It should not be beaded with sweat, nor show blobs of fat – nor should it be very tight and 'closed' looking. Both states are the result of bad handling and overheating or overchilling.

Any cut surface should have a fresh look. Hard and cracked surfaces, or surface mould, usually means that the surface has been left uncut for a day or so.

STORING CHEESE

In an ideal world everyone would buy enough cheese for their needs that day and buy again the next. To encourage this cheese-mongers, specialist cheese shops and some supermarkets go to great lengths to bring their cheeses to the peak of condition and maintain them there until they are sold or discarded. Most people do not shop daily but instead buy food at the weekend or during a marathon week-day shop. In these circumstances cheese must be stored at home. However, if you have a special dinner or party when you will serve cheese, it is worth trying to buy it on the same day.

Temperature Cheese has its own individual nature and should be treated with care. It does not like extremes of cold or heat and should be kept at around, or just over 10°C/50°F. This is easy if you have a cellar or an old-fashioned food larder, but more difficult if you live in a centrally-heated home with either a wall cupboard or a refrigerator to choose from.

The domestic refrigerator, which should be set at under 10°C/50°F, is really too cold to store cheese for any length of time, but if it has to be pressed into service – as indeed it does for most of us – place the cheese in the warmest section, like the salad crisper or the door compartments. Protect the cheese by placing it in a plastic bag or wrapping it in cling film or foil and then placing it inside a plastic box. Never wrap small pieces of cheese together, their flavour will mingle and they will lose their individuality.

If you have a storage place at the correct temperature then closely cover the cut surface of the cheese and wrap it in a clean tea-towel or some greaseproof paper which will allow the cheese to breathe, rather than foil or film. Soft cheeses can be stored in their original boxes or, if they are cut, with the cut side against a flat surface. Cheese which has been stored in a cool place must be brought to room temperature before being served; this takes at least an hour, and could take longer, depending on the size of the piece and how long it has been chilling.

Right, above: *Parmesan curd is collected in muslin before moulding.*
Right, below: *Whole Parmesan cheeses are tested for maturity.*

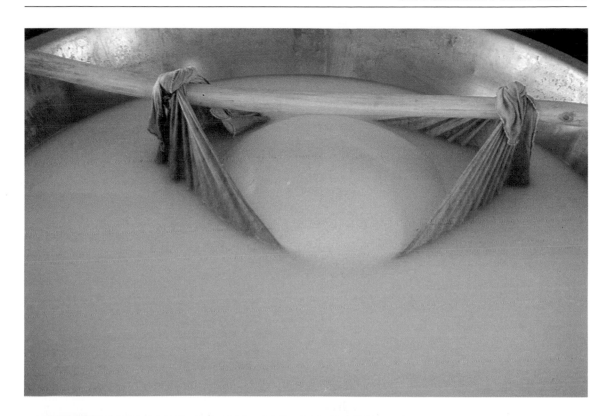

How long? Storage times will vary, depending on the type of cheese you buy and its maturity. It is best not to keep any cheese for too long, and fresh cheeses should be eaten on the day they are bought or the next. Semi-hard and hard cheeses can be kept if you have the right conditions and sometimes it is worth buying a large piece or a whole cheese – it will almost certainly be cheaper. If you do buy a whole cheese, turn it at least once a week, cut off only as much as you think you will need and bring that piece to room temperature. Do not keep bringing a whole cheese to room temperature.

Soft cheeses are much more sensitive because of the higher moisture content and the continuing ripening action of their surface mould or bacteria. Cheeses with a fairly firm paste such as Reblochon and Pont l'Évêque can be kept for a few days, but cheeses with a marked tendency to go runny, like Brie, Camembert and Liederkranz, should be eaten as soon as possible. Once these cheeses are past their peak, they deteriorate very quickly.

Foil and vacuum-packed cheese can be kept for quite long periods, within the 'sell-by' date, provided the pack is not opened. Once it is, treat it as you would any other cheese.

Wrongly treated cheeses need not be discarded. Wipe the droplets of fat off sweating cheese, or cut off a thin layer to expose the cleaner cheese inside. If it is too dry, grate it and use on toast or in cooked dishes. Hardened cheese may be softened for cooking by wrapping and keeping it for a while in a cloth soaked in white wine.

Freezing Connoisseurs probably won't freeze cheese, but it can be done. Hard cheeses tend to go crumbly after they have been frozen so it is best to grate the cheese first. Pack manageable amounts of grated cheese into bags, expel the air, seal the bags and freeze. Defrost just before using or sprinkle on to dishes in its frozen state. Use as quickly as possible after defrosting.

In theory, softer creamier cheeses take better to freezing than hard cheeses, but in practice they just lose their flavour. Fresh cheeses, like Quark, freeze reasonably well, but they should be thawed slowly and *not* refrozen.

SERVING AND PRESENTING CHEESE

Cheese can be eaten at any meal or as a snack, but certain types suit different times of the day. Roquefort or Munster do not usually accompany breakfast, whereas Edam is mild enough not to assault the palate early in the morning. Piquant cheeses like Feta and the Spanish Cabrales make good appetisers, and the traditional English cheeses go well with bread and pickles for lunch.

A cheese course usually forms part of a formal meal and the question arises whether to serve it before or after the dessert course. In Britain, the tradition is to finish the meal with cheese, because cheese goes well with port which is served at the end of a meal.

In France and Italy, the cheese is served after the main course and before the dessert. This is probably because the palate cannot appreciate the wine the French serve with their cheese if it has just had a sweet dessert. It does make sense, if you have been drinking a good red wine, to continue with it through the cheese course before moving on to a sweeter wine at the end of the meal.

How cheese is served varies from country to country and from cheese to cheese. Semi-hard cheeses lend themselves to thin slicing, and this is best done with a special hand-held continental cheese slicer. Other cheeses may be cut into chunks, wedges or served whole.

THE CHEESE COURSE

When entertaining it is tempting to rush out and buy a whole range of interesting looking cheeses, but once home you may find that the selection does not look quite so good on your board. A few really good cheeses will probably look better than a haphazard array, and one cheese in first class condition is also worth considering. If you do want to serve a selection, consider the following points:

The menu The cheese should not clash with the wines you are planning to serve and should be in harmony with the rest of the meal. Spicy food is best followed by young, refreshing soft-textured cheeses. Richer cheeses can follow plainer roasts or grills. Young refreshing cheeses to follow spicy foods include Young Banon, Kernhem, Caciotta, Pyramid or Fromage Frais, or Ricotta flavoured with fresh herbs or chopped nuts.

Richer cheeses to follow roasts or grills, could be Cotherstone, Saint Agur, Brillat-Savarin, Devon Garland, Bavarian Blue, Roncal, Caprice des Dieux, Rambol or Boursault.

Cheeses to follow rich sauces: hard goat's and ewe's milk cheeses come into their own here, such as Sainte Maure, Carolina, Ribchester, Pecorino, Acorn or Valençay. Also traditional English cheeses, such as Wensleydale, Caerphilly and Lancashire.

Colours Offer some colour contrast; a selection of cheeses which look very similar in colour will not be as attractive as one which offers variety. For example, choose one well-coloured cheese, or one or two with brightly coloured rinds. Garnishes of grapes, parsley and other herbs also add colour. Unusually-coloured cheeses like Sage Derby and Windsor Red and layered cheeses, like Roulé, Huntsman and cream cheese loaf with Danablu are very popular for providing colour.

Textures Add interest with different textures both in the rind and the cheese itself. Include at least one hard cheese, maybe one with holes, and a softer, creamier cheese. Different shapes and sizes of cheese can also look attractive so include a rolled Caboc, a pyramid-shaped goat's cheese or small cheeses like Langres, Baby Bel or Mini Bleu de Bresse.

Flavours Choose a variety of flavours as everyone has their favourites. It is a good idea to arrange the cheeses in order of strength of flavour with the mildest at one side and the strongest at the other. The 'smelly' cheese list on page 27 gives some ideas from one end of the spectrum. Garlic and other flavoured cheeses like Gaperon, Boursin, Boursault and Roulé, add interest to a range of flavours. Really mild cheeses include many of the French factory-made cheeses, such as Belle des Champs, Chamois d'Or, Neufchâtel, Petit Suisse and Pyrénées. The Italian Provolone-style cheeses are also fairly mild.

Presenting the cheese course Avoid a board that is too large or too heavy to easily pass around. One that will hold three or four cheeses will be sufficient. Make sure you have at least two cheese knives, one with a serrated edge for cutting hard cheeses and one keen sharp knife for sticky or crumbly cheese.

Other surfaces or containers on which to serve cheese include wicker, bamboo, basketware, marble, decorative plates and ceramic dishes.

For special occasions consider any of the following:

A terracotta plate lined with leaves and decorated with tropical fruits.

A wooden board with soft summer berry fruit and fresh herbs.

A bed of alfalfa sprouts for a selection of hard cheeses decorated with cherry tomatoes.

Nasturtium and dandelion leaves on a marble base with nasturtium flowers.

Vine leaves and grapes and olives for a selection of Italian or French cheeses.

Evergreens, dried fruits and nuts for a Christmas board.

Marble base with fresh bay leaves and tangerines.

A bed of lettuce leaves with dill pickles and fresh dill for an English selection.

Accompaniments The cheese should be the star of the cheese course and so a good quality, plain water biscuit is one of the best accompaniments to cheese. Choose large or small biscuits according to the time of the day and the size of the meal. Crackers, oatcakes and wheaten biscuits are also good accompaniments, and some people like rice cakes with cheese.

Bread is also good with cheese, particularly if the cheese course is the main course. The bread should be well crusted. If it is a cheese buffet there should be plenty of choice so that guests may choose well flavoured breads like rye, crusty wholemeal and poppy seed bread or mild-flavoured white rolls to go with the cheeses they have selected. You may like to match the style of bread to the nationality of the cheese; for example serve french bread with French cheeses, flat Italian bread with Italian cheeses, or pumpernickel with German cheeses. Home-made or bought olive or onion breads are excellent with full-flavoured mature cheeses. Walnut bread is *de rigeur* in many French restaurants as an accompaniment to their best cheeses. Rich tea breads are good with crumbly, salty cheeses like Lancashire.

Celery is the traditional accompaniment to cheese in the United Kingdom, but all kinds of raw fruit and vegetables go well with cheese, particularly on a cheese buffet. Try radishes, watercress, carrot sticks or chicory. Some cheeses have special accompaniments which have become classic over the years: pears, for example, may be served with Gorgonzola or with Pecorino cheese. In Italy I have seen the latter served with fresh, raw, shelled broad beans. In the United Kingdom, Wensleydale cheese is often served with apple pie or with fruit cake. Caraway seeds are traditional with Munster; mustard with Gruyère and walnuts with Roquefort.

COOKING WITH CHEESE

Some cheeses, such as Gruyère, Parmesan and Mozzarella, are particularly associated with cooking. This is because they have an excellent flavour when cooked and behave in a way which is consistent with the cook's requirements. However, many of these cheeses are also very good uncooked. Equally, cheeses which are not normally associated with cooking, such as blue cheese and goat's milk cheese, can be used to advantage in the kitchen.

The secret of cooking with cheese is not to overcook it and, where possible, it should be added towards the end of the cooking time. The behaviour of cheese when it is cooking depends on the way the protein, casein, reacts to heat. Above a certain temperature, the casein will coagulate and separate from the fat and water in the cheese to produce a tough, stringy mass. Hard, well-ripened cheeses can tolerate higher temperatures than soft cheese because more of the casein has been broken down into other less complex and less easily coagulated proteins. Thus hard cheeses are better for crisp cheese toppings. The tendency to break down is also reduced if it is mixed with a starchy food such as flour or breadcrumbs, hence the popularity of crunchy *gratin* toppings of grated cheese and crumbs.

Cheeses which have a high water and fat content can be quite easily blended with a liquid which is composed mainly of these ingredients, for example blue cheeses will blend into oil-based vinaigrette, and soft creamy cheeses will 'dissolve' into a cream sauce. However, whether it is a flour and stock-based sauce flavoured with hard cheese or a cream-based sauce made with soft cheese, it must not be overcooked. If it is, it will separate into a stringy or grainy mass. Fondue, which is kept bubbling at the table, succeeds because the alcohol in the wine or spirit base lowers the boiling point of the sauce to a point where the casein should not curdle.

Fresh cheeses like Haloumi and Feta, in which the casein has not been broken down, sieze up on the first contact with heat. This is useful if you are making Greek fried cheese or using cheese sticks in a stir fry, for the cheese will not run. However, the cooking process must be extremely speedy or the cheese will be too tough to eat.

If you are planning to use up some blue or goat's milk cheese in cooking, it is worth remembering

Left: *Cheese is a traditional accompaniment to other simple but delicious food and drinks. (Photograph by Graham Kirk; as pictured in* Country Living.*)*

that the former seems to intensify in flavour and should be used sparingly, whereas goat's milk cheese actually loses a little of its musty flavour.

Cheese for salads Traditional English style salads use grated cheese in a mound in the centre or at the side which would be the traditional farmhouse cheeses. You could also use cheeses like Acorn, Edam, Gruyère, Roncal, Tilsit, Spenwood, Canestrato, Colby and Dunlop in just the same way.

In other salads the cheese is diced or cut into thin strips and mixed with ham and other cold meats for a chef's salad or with diced vegetables. The semi-hard cheeses like Gouda, Haloumi and Sbrinz are very useful for this type of salad.

In more modern salads, the cheese is usually sliced and arranged in an attractive pattern with the other salad ingredients. Any kind of cheese that will slice can be used here, but the softer cheeses like Chèvre, Camembert and Brie are the most popular. Try with sliced Fontina, Fourme d'Ambert, Milleens, Cashel Blue or Bonchester. Goat's milk cheese, such as Crottin de Chavignol, is often sliced and toasted on bread before being added to the salad.

Both side salads and salad appetisers have cheese scattered over them. A Greek salad is incomplete without crumbled Feta cheese. Slivers of Parmesan may be served with strips of prosciutto and well-flavoured leaves; and blue cheeses, like Roquefort, Stilton and Bleu d'Auvergne, lend themselves to blue cheese and nut salads.

Snacks with cheese The 'Ploughman's lunch' of bread, pickles and cheese is a popular pub snack, but it can just as easily be served at home. The variations on this theme can be endless.

Wensleydale with apple and oatcakes.
Pecorino with fresh pears and cobnuts.
Chèvre with wholegrain mustard, crispbreads and oranges.
Appenzell with apples and cranberry sauce.
Explorateur with bananas and walnut bread.
Kefalotiri with olive oil, thyme and pitta bread.
Brie with tangerines and chicory spears.
Pipo Crem' with mangoes and watercress.
Ribchester with kiwi fruit and radishes.
Shropshire Blue with pickled walnuts and cress.
Jarlsberg with strawberries and pistachios.

As well as toasted and baked cheese canapés, cheese can be used to make uncooked canapés. Some cheeses, like Grana Pedano and Serra are traditionally shaved into slivers or crumbled into bowls to serve with aperitifs. Others are cubed or cut into slices. Most of the semi-hard and hard cheeses can be used in this way. Diced cheese also looks good on cocktail sticks. Make up some of the following combinations on cocktail sticks and serve stuck into a large melon, pumpkin or marrow.

Pineapple and pickled cocktail onions with Cheddar.
Bacon wrapped round water chestnuts with Austrian smoked cheese.
Cubed smoked chicken and cucumber with Tilsit.
Cocktail gherkins and prosciutto with Caciocavello.

Soft cheeses, like Fromage Frais, Quark and cream cheese, make ideal bases for dips. The semi-soft cheeses, like Brie and Camembert, can also be puréed into the mixture if their rinds are removed, and blue cheeses also work well. Hard cheeses can be grated into the mixture. Unusual ideas are almost limitless but could include some of the following:

Gaperon, Boursin or Boursault and Fromage Frais.
Chèvre and sesame seeds.
Stilton and Quark with chopped walnuts.
Camembert and caraway seeds.
Petit Suisse, finely chopped strawberries and green peppercorns.

CHEESE AND WINE

Cheese seems to have a particular affinity to wine and the two tastes really complement each other. However, you cannot just pick a cheese and a wine at random and expect them to get on well.

Traditionally red wine is the best partner for cheese, and this is very often the case. Start by choosing cheese and wine of the same general character. A young, fresh cheese – like young Brie, small Banon, three-week-old Gubbeen, unpressed goat's cheese or young Pecorino – will certainly partner a young Beaujolais, whereas a powerful Provolone will probably need a good Barolo to match it.

Very often, partnerships are suggested by the region from which the cheese comes. Wines from the same region have an immediate affinity. Try Châteauneuf du Pape, for example, with Roquefort; Barbaresco with Gorgonzola; Nuits St George with Cendré; Barbera with Bel Paese; a light Chianti with Pecorino; cider or calvados with Normandy cheeses like Pont l'Évêque, or Schnapps with Danablu.

Combining cheese and wine from the same region is a useful start, but there are other good combinations. Try English Blue Cheshire with St Emillion or, if it is very mature, with old dry sherry, or with port; mature Gouda with the wines of the Medoc; Limburg with a robust Chianti; a young Brie with Fleury or a more mature version with a Côte du Rhone. Other striking affinities are Danablu and Rhone or Rioja wines; Port Salut with Bergerac or Fitou; Cantal with Morgan and Saint Nectaire with a Côte de Provence.

White wines need not be ignored. Goat's milk cheese marries well with Sauvignon wines like Sancerre or Fumé Blanc, and Munster goes well with Gewürztraminer. Cheshire goes well with a Meursault, Tilsit with Muscadet and Chabichou with Sancerre or Pouilly Fumé.

Sweet wines come into their own with some of the blue cheeses or even with a really mature Cheddar. Other successful partnerships are Gorgonzola and Vin Santo; Roquefort or Lanark Blue with Sauternes; or Dolcelatte with a German Trockenbeerenauslese.

Choosing wine to go with the cheese course This also involves looking at the menu as a whole. Indeed, the choice may have to be made the other way round. If, for example, you are planing to serve Tournedos with a classic Bordeaux, you may want to go on serving the same wine.

Really strongly-flavoured cheeses like Gaperon, Maroilles and paprika-coated Rigotte are so strong that they will swamp many of the classic wines. They would certainly kill a good Burgundy and claret is unlikely to stand up too well either. The only answer for these cheeses is something like a Rioja or perhaps an Australian Shiraz.

Very smelly cheeses do not necessarily have a strong flavour so that you do not need to take so much care with cheeses like Livarot or even Limburg.

At the other end of the scale, the mild cheeses like Explorateur, Devon Garland, Caprice des Dieux and Lymeswold all respond to light wines like Valpolicella, Beaujolais Village and Touraine Rouge. They also show up well with fragrantly delicate white wines like the better QMP German Kabinett and Spätlese wines or the French Vouvray.

HOW TO CUT CHEESE

Small goat's milk cheeses Cut in half

Pyramid or cone shaped cheeses Cut in horizontal slices

Round or square soft cheeses Cut like a cake into triangles, do not cut across the wedge.

Small or large drum-shaped cheeses (such as Cantal or baby Stiltons). Cut into discs and then into wedges like a cake.

Wheels Best cut by the cheese-monger.

Logs Cut into slices.

— The —
A–Z of CHEESES

ABONDANCE

Semi-hard or soft cow's milk cheese.
Fat content 40 or 45 per cent

Two quite distinct French cheeses take their names from the Abondance breed of cows raised in Savoie. One is a semi-hard cheese often known as Tomme d'Abondance (Tomme being the dialect word for cheese); the other is a very rare soft cheese also known as Vacherin d'Abondance.

Availability Only available locally. The semi-hard version is matured for two to three months and is best in the late summer and autumn. The soft version is matured in cold cellars for three months and is best in the autumn and winter.

Description Tomme d'Abondance is produced in wheels which may weigh anything from 5 kg (11 lb) to 20 kg (44 lb). The cheese has a natural grey-brown rind and a firm, supple texture. The aroma is slightly musty, the flavour mild and fruity.

Vacherin d'Abondance is produced in 1.5 kg (3½ lb) discs. It has a washed rind and a soft paste with a tendency to run; the flavour is mild. It is packed in a box tied with a strip of spruce bark.

Manufacture Made in farmhouses from partly-skimmed milk.

Serving Serve either cheese as part of the cheese course or on its own with water biscuits and celery.

ACORN

Hard ewe's milk cheese. Fat content 52 per cent

Hand-made Welsh cheese produced in Dyfed.
Availability Fairly widely available. Can be matured for up to six or seven months.
Description Produced in 2 kg (4½ lb) truckles, the cheese has a natural dry rind. The paste is pale in colour with a tendency to turn blue after cutting and keeping. The flavour is clean and full with a good after taste.
Variation Skirrid is similar, but is marinated in mead, to give a distinctive flavour.
Manufacture Made from whole ewe's milk with vegetable rennet.
Serving Serve as part of the cheese course or on its own with water biscuits and grapes. As a snack, try it with home-made mustard, bread and nuts. Store wrapped in foil or cling film in a cool place or in the fridge.
Cooking Use in soufflés and egg dishes. Cut into slivers and scatter over a rocket and chicory salad.

APPENZELL

Semi-hard cow's milk cheese. Fat content 50 per cent

This distinctively flavoured Swiss cheese is said to have derived its name from the words for 'abbot's cell', referring to the Abbey of St Gallen. The word *Appenzellor* is used for the small family groups who make the cheese in their mountain chalets.
Availability Wide, in supermarkets. The cheese is sold after three to four months. It is best when bought in the autumn and winter.

Cheeseboard: Emmenthal, Caprice des Dieux, Caboc, Vulscombe, Gaperon, Fourme d'Ambert, Barac, Shropshire Blue

Description Produced in wheels weighing between 6 and 8 kg (13 and 18 lb), Appenzell has a hard, fairly thick, tan-coloured rind. The paste is pale yellow in colour, with a number of pea-sized, regularly spaced holes. It has a very distinctive fruity flavour which is a result of washing the cheese in a mixture of spices, white wine and salt. The exact ingredients are contained in a carefully guarded, centuries-old recipe.

Variations Appenzell rass or Rasskass is a version of Appenzell made from skimmed milk and matured for longer. It is usually made in a smaller size and has a lower fat content. The paste has smaller holes and a much more pungent flavour.

Royalp is a Swiss attempt to reproduce Tilsit, but it is more like Appenzell than German Tilsit. The cheese has a firm paste, containing a few pea-sized holes, and a mild flavour, with a spicy, piquant after taste. It is generally made from pasteurised milk, but in eastern Switzerland, it is also made from unpasteurised milk. This version has a red rather than a green label.

Manufacture Produced in much the same way as Tilsit, Appenzell is made from unpasteurised whole milk. The curds are cut much more coarsely than the hard cheeses and the whey is treated to lower temperatures. As soon as the cheeses are made, they are taken to cool storage cellars with high humidity, and rubbed regularly with the special wine and spices mixture. All authentic Swiss Appenzell cheeses carry a label showing a rampant bear – an illustration taken from the arms of the Appenzell canton. The reputation of Appenzell is protected by a special authority which has its headquarters at St Gallen.

Serving Serve as part of a cheeseboard, cut in small chunks with aperitifs or, as the Swiss do, cut in thin slices with fresh fruit or salad. Well-wrapped, it will keep in a cool place or in a fridge for a month or so. If it develops a slight mould on the surface, simply scrape it off before serving.

Cooking Appenzell melts well and can be used in all kinds of cooking when a distinctive taste is required. The Swiss use it to make cheese fritters, frying fancy shapes in a batter of eggs, beer and milk. It can also be sliced into salads or spiced with paprika and speared on to sticks to make cocktail kebabs with pineapple.

History This is cheese with a long history, and it may well have been known to Charlemagne. Originating in the Appenzell region of Switzerland, the cheese is now made in the areas of St Gallen, Thurgau and Zurich. In the middle ages, Appenzell became so popular abroad that there were hardly any cheeses left to sell at home. So, in 1571, a law was passed that required the cheese merchants to export only those cheeses which could not be sold on the home market.

ARAGON

Semi-hard ewe's and goat's milk cheese.
Fat content 45 per cent

Also known as Tronchón, this Spanish cheese is made in the provinces of Castellón and Teruel.

Availability Widely available, in Spain only.

Description Produced in dish-shaped discs, weighing around 3 kg (7 lb), this cheese has a glossy, golden yellow rind and a tendency to sink on the upper surface. The paste is firm and pale yellow, darkening at the edges. The flavour of the young cheese is pleasantly mild and a little salty; it strengthens in flavour as it matures. Matured for a minimum of one week, the cheese may be matured for three to four months.

Serving Slice it and serve with biscuits or bread, or use in place of Mozzarella in a salad with avocado and tomatoes. In Spain, I have seen it cubed and served with a dry Amontillado sherry.

ASIAGO GRASSO DI MONTE

Hard cow's milk cheese. Fat content 30 per cent

This Italian cheese originated in the rocky plateau of Asiago in the foothills of the Dolomites. It is now made throughout the province of Vicente and the Tre-Venezie.

Availability Widely available, in Italy only.

Description Produced in cylinders varying from 9–13 kg (20–29 lb), the cheese has a hard golden yellow rind. The paste is a straw-yellow colour, with many small holes. Even when young, its flavour is rich and full and it matures to an even firmer piquant grating cheese (Asiago d'Allievo). It is matured for a minimum of two months. Some cheeses are matured for six months and some for up to a year.

Variation Asiago Pressato is whiter with small holes and a thin elastic rind. The flavour is very mild and delicate.

Manufacture Asiago is made from whole and partially skimmed cow's milk blended together from both a morning and an evening milking. After coagulation the curds are scalded, pressed and ripened.

Serving Serve the younger cheese on a cheeseboard, as part of a ploughman's platter, or with wholemeal bread, black olives and lollo rosso lettuce.

Cooking Grate the mature cheese and use it to make well-flavoured sauces, soufflés and toppings. Asiago resembles the Cantal of the Auvergne and can be used in provincial recipes from that area.

AUSTRIAN SMOKED CHEESE

Processed cow's milk cheese. Fat content 45 per cent

Smoked cheeses are made in a number of countries and they vary both in the way that they are produced and processed and in the way that they are smoked.

Availability Widely available. Immediately after processing and smoking.

Description These cheeses are usually packed in plastic covers in sausage shapes of various sizes. The paste is pale cream in colour, very dense and almost rubbery in texture. The flavour is mildly smoky.

Manufacture Austrian smoked cheeses are usually made by blending a mixture of Gouda and Emmenthal-type cheeses. The smoking is done over oak wood shavings. However, some cheeses are smoked by rubbing with 'smoked salt' or by adding a so-called liquid smoke in the form of a chemical flavouring – so check the labels.

Serving Serve as part of a cheeseboard or on its own with celery and biscuits. Cube and serve it on cocktail kebabs with fruit or cut into slices and serve on pumpernickel with sweet pickles. Its smoky flavour goes well with bacon kebabs and bananas. Unopened cheeses will keep for a few months in the fridge. Once opened the cheese should be eaten within a week.

BABY BEL

Semi-hard cow's milk cheese. Fat content 45 per cent

This bland factory-made cheese was invented in France in 1931. It is made in much the same way as Edam and has a paste and texture like a very mild Gouda. Despite the fact that it is a rather boring cheese, it has proved extremely popular and the Bel fromageries have factories in Spain, Algeria, Japan and Denmark. One of their cheeses, produced under licence in Kentucky, is called Albany.

Availability Widely available.

Description Produced in small 250 g (9 oz) flattened balls, Baby Bel has a distinctive red wax coating and a pale yellow, dense paste. The flavour is very mild indeed.

Serving Serve as a snack with salad or with bread and pickles.

In its wax coating Baby Bel will keep for three to four months, but once cut the cheese should be eaten within a week or so because it dries out quite quickly.

Cooking Grate or slice it and use in any dish that requires a mild-flavoured cheese. Try it in Welsh Rarebit with sprigs of mint or use it sliced with hamburgers.

BANON

Soft cow's, goat's or ewe's milk cheese.
Fat content 45 per cent

This delicious French cheese from Provence is immediately recognisable by its small size and its wrapping of chestnut leaves tied with raffia. Farmhouse versions are made with either sheep's or goat's milk, but dairy made cheese uses cow's milk.

Availability Widely available. The cheeses may be ripened for anything from two weeks to two months. Goat's and ewe's milk versions are best in summer and autumn, and spring and summer, respectively.

Description Produced in small 100–200 g (3½–7 oz) discs and wrapped in leaves, the cheese has a slightly sticky rind which tends to blue with age. The paste is white and soft with a faint lactic smell and the flavour mild and slightly sour. Aged cheeses are often larger in size with a dark greyish-brown rind and a dark yellow paste. The flavour is stronger than in the young cheese.

Variation Banon Poivre d'Ane or Banon au Pebre d'Ai is a similar cheese which is rolled in the herb summer savory.

Manufacture The chestnut leaves used to wrap the cheese are first soaked in eau-de-vie and grape marc. Once the cheeses are wrapped they are placed in terracotta jars and left to ferment.

Serving Serve on a cheeseboard or with crusty bread or plain biscuits. Stored in a cool place, the cheese will keep for up to two weeks. However, if it smells or starts to sweat it is past its best.

History The peasants of the Alpine region of Vancluse have made these cheeses for hundreds of years and their recipes have been very jealously guarded. The cheese takes its name from the local town with the most important market.

Banon is an important ingredient in a local speciality called Fromage Fort du Mont Ventoux. The cheese is washed and liberally sprinkled with salt, pepper and vinegar, or marc may also be added. The mixture is placed in an earthenware pot. Over a period of time the cream rises to the surface, is stirred back into the cheese and the longer the mixture is left the stronger the flavours become.

Banon

BARAC

Semi-hard cow's or ewe's milk cheese.
Fat content not available

Named from an old Scottish word for milk-maid, this is an unpasteurised cheese made at Annan, Scotland.
Availability Specialist cheese shops. Matured for three months.
Description The cheese is made in 625 g and 1.5 kg (1¼ lb and 3½ lb) rounds with a natural unwaxed or a waxed crust. The paste is very pale in colour with a lightly tangy flavour.
Variation Baby Baracs 500 g (1 lb) are available at Christmastime.
Serving Serve as part of the cheese course or in a ploughman's lunch, or cut it into cubes and serve with aperitifs. Also good as a snack with walnuts and tangerines.

BARAKA

Semi-soft cow's milk cheese. Fat content 60 per cent

This is one of the French manufacturers' responses to the steadily growing demand for Brie and Camembert-style cheeses. Its most outstanding feature is its shape – a horseshoe. The name is Arabic for 'good luck' and the rumour is that it sells well at Christmas, New Year and Easter.
Availability Specialist cheese shops or ethnic shops. Eaten fresh or matured for a month or so.
Description Produced in small 300 g (10 oz) horseshoe shapes, the mature cheese has a white bloom rind and a soft creamy paste. The flavour is very mild.
Manufacture This is a factory-produced cheese made from pasteurised milk.
Serving Serve on its own or as part of the cheese course, and brighten up with dried fruit and nuts. Served this way it goes very well with a light spätlese Moselle.

Bavarian Blue

BAVARIAN BLUE

Semi-soft cow's milk cheese. Fat content 70 per cent

This is a German cheese, factory made from pasteurised milk with additional cream. One of the relatively new hybrid cheeses, it has the white mould rind of a Camembert cheese and blue patches in the paste produced by innoculating with *penicillium Roquefortii*.
Availability Widely available.
Description Produced in flat 1 kg (2 lb) discs, the cheese has a white mould rind and is usually wrapped in foil. The paste is creamy white in

colour, sometimes with a few small holes; it has patches rather than veins of pale blue mould, and the texture is very creamy. The flavour is very mild and gentle.

Variations Cambozola, the brand name of one version of Bavarian Blue, was the first soft blue cheese to be made in Germany. The name is said to have been coined to suggest a combination of the two famous names of Camembert and Gorgonzola. Bla Castello is the Danish version of this cheese.

Serving Serve on a mixed cheeseboard or spread straight on to bread rolls, biscuits or crusty bread.

Wrap in foil and store in the salad compartment of the fridge for up to ten days. Remember to remove it from the fridge at least an hour before serving or the mild flavour will disappear altogether.

Cooking Use to flavour vegetables, such as cauliflower, celeriac or broccoli, or in soups.

BEAUFORT

Hard cow's milk cheese. Fat content 50 per cent

This French Gruyère-style cheese has been made in the mountain chalets of the Savoie for hundreds of years and maybe even as long ago as Roman times. It has a higher fat content than other Gruyère-style cheeses, a distinct fruity aroma and flavour and is probably the best of the French Gruyère-style versions. There are different types of Beaufort depending on the time of the year when it is made. All the cheeses are protected by the French *Appellation d'Origine* laws.

Availability Specialist cheese shops. Matured for a minimum of six months, the best cheeses are Beaufort de Montagne or Beaufort Haute Montagne. The names are legal descriptions restricted to cheeses made from summer milk in certain specific areas. They are at their best between September and May.

Description Produced in large, flattened concave cylinders weighing 20–60 kg (44–132 lb) Beaufort has a thin natural rind and a smooth paste with very few holes or cracks. The flavour is rich, fruity, salty and quite strong.

Manufacture Beaufort is a cooked, pressed cheese made in a similar way to Gruyère. It is ripened in cool, humid caves or cellars.

Serving Serve on a cheeseboard, a ploughman's platter or as a snack with fruit or salad. Slice and use in open or closed sandwiches or cut into cubes and serve with aperitifs.

Cooking Beaufort is widely used in local cooking in fondues, gratin dishes, pies and flans. Try it in any recipe which calls for Gruyère.

BEAUMONT

Semi-hard cow's milk cheese. Fat content 50 per cent

This is a French factory-made cheese invented in the town of the same name in the Haute-Savoie area.

Availability Specialist cheese shops and french delicatessens. Matured for one and a half months, the best cheeses are made during the summer and autumn.

Description Produced in 1–5 kg (2–11 lb) discs, the cheese has a smooth, light yellow rind. The paste is mild and creamy.

Serving Serve as part of the cheese course or on its own with wafer biscuits. Beaumont goes very well with home-made tea breads like date and walnuts, marmalade and raisin, and banana and cashew nut. Add an apple or a pear for a snack.

BEAUVOORDE

Semi-hard cow's milk cheese. Fat content 50 per cent

In its present form, Beauvoorde is a very modern cheese produced in a modern dairy in Passendale, Belgium.

Availability Specialist cheese shops. Matured for four to five weeks before being sold.

Description Produced in hexagon shapes in two sizes, weighing 3 kg (7 lb) and 6 kg (13 lb), the cheese has a natural greyish-yellow rind. The paste is yellow with a few pea-sized holes in it. Beauvoorde has a milky aroma and a delicate flavour.

Serving Serve sliced with a continental hand-held slicer as the Belgians do at any meal. Or use it in open or closed sandwiches, or on a ploughman's platter with mild pickles.

Cooking This cheese toasts well and can be used with breadcrumbs for a crunchy topping or on toast in onion soup. The Belgians use the cheese in the soup itself.

History Beauvoorde was first made in the village of the same name around 1904. A local innkeeper named Arthur Djes began to make cheese with milk from the Polders to a tradi-tional recipe. The cheese did well and, with only a short disruption during World War I, Arthur Djes and his family continued to produce the cheese up to the thirties. Production stopped again during World War II, but restarted and is now produced under modern conditions by the Belgian dairy industry.

BEENLEIGH BLUE

Semi-hard blue ewe's milk cheese.
Fat content not available

A fairly new English cheese made in Devon from the unpasteurised milk of Friesland ewes.

Availability Specialist cheese shops.

Description Produced in 3.5 kg (8 lb) drums, this cheese has a natural crust. It is light textured and has a fairly strong flavour.

Manufacture The cheese is made to a tradi-tional recipe and matured for seven months underground.

Serving Serve as part of the cheese course or with biscuits and watercress. This type of blue cheese has a special affinity with pears.

Cooking Crumble over a mixed leaf salad with walnuts and olive oil. Grate and use to flavour sauces for pasta and fish.

BELLE BRESSANE

Soft blue cow's milk cheese. Fat content 50 per cent

This is a new cheese probably prompted by the success of Bleu de Bresse. It is factory made from pasteurised milk and moulded in the shape of a ring.

Availability Specialist cheese shops.

Description Produced in 2 kg (4½ lb) rings, the cheese has a white mould rind and is sold wrapped in foil. The paste is very soft and creamy with a blue mould running through it, and the flavour mild but piquant.

Serving Serve as part of the cheese course or on its own with apples or pears. Remove the foil and wrap in clean foil for storing it in a cool place or in the fridge for up to a week.

Cooking Try mashing it with tomato chutney and chopped herbs or spring onion and use for blue cheese on toast or mix it with a soft cheese to make a cheese pâté or a mousse.

BELLE DES CHAMPS

Semi-soft cow's milk cheese. Fat content 50 per cent

One of the many French factory made cheeses which has been introduced in recent years. It is extremely bland and keeps well. The cheese is sold mainly through supermarkets.

Availability Widely available.

Description Produced in 1.75 kg (4 lb) rounds, the cheese has a white bloomy rind and a pale yellow paste containing some small holes. The flavour is sweet and very mild.

Serving Serve as part of the cheese course with well flavoured wheaten biscuits or oatcakes as a snack, or in sandwiches with ham or tomatoes.

Cooking Remove the rind and melt into cream- or flour-based sauces to serve with white fish or shellfish. It can also be sliced to give a mild, cheesy boost to burgers.

BEL PAESE

Semi-soft cow's milk cheese.
Fat content 45–52 per cent

Created by an Italian cheese-maker, Egidio Galbani, in 1906, Bel Paese is named after the popular nineteenth-century young people's geography book written by a friend of Galbani's family, Abbot Antonio Stappani. The Abbot's portrait appears on every Bel Paese package together with a map of Italy. The American version shows a map of the western hemisphere. Egidio Galbani lived and worked in Melzo and the cheese was made in a factory in that town in 1920, but it is now manufactured in Certosa, outside Milan.

Availability Widely available. Bel Paese is matured for about one and a half to two months before going into the shops.

Description Produced in 2 kg (4½ lb) thickish discs, the cheese has a washed, shiny white or yellow rind and is usually wrapped in foil. The paste is pale yellow with a smooth springy texture and the flavour is sweet and buttery.

Variations Smaller half bits, 500 g (1 lb) versions, and small round processed versions called Crema Bel Paese.

Italico is the official name given to a range of semi-soft table cheeses similar to Bel Paese. They are usually made from whole cow's milk, though sometimes skimmed milk is used, and are sold under the brand names of the creameries producing them: for example, Pastorella, Bella Alpina, Bickaud and Vittoria.

Manufacture Bel Paese is made all the year round, usually from pasteurised milk. Lactic acid and rennet are both used to coagulate the milk. The curds are cut and raked for quick drainage; they are not cooked but are pressed into shape. The cheese is fairly quick ripening, and is washed regularly with salt water to prevent the growth of mould and to assist the development of the rind.

Serving Serve as a mild alternative on a cheeseboard or on a ploughman's platter with white rolls or biscuits and fruit – the Italians eat it with figs and apples. Double wrap and keep in a cool place for up to ten days.

Cooking Bel Paese is a useful cheese for cooking because it melts well without becoming tough. Try on cheese croûtes baked in the oven, or in place of Mozzarella on pizzas, lasagne and the like. It does not go stringy, but the result is pleasantly creamy, so try it, too, in soups and sauces.

Bel Paese

Bleu d'Auvergne

BERGKÄSE

Hard cow's milk cheese. Fat content 45 per cent

This German 'mountain cheese' is similar to Allgäu Emmenthal, but the eyes are smaller and the flavour rather stronger. There are a number of different versions of the cheese. Made only in the High Alps of the Allgau district, it can be difficult to find good examples of this cheese.
Availability Locally available in Germany only.
Description Produced in large wheels weighing 50 kg (110 lb) the cheese has a firm, dark yellow rind and a pale yellow paste with eyes the size of large peas. The flavour is delicate, yet piquant, and more aromatic than Emmenthal.
Serving Serve sliced on bread or biscuits or cut into cubes and serve with aperitifs.
Cooking This is a useful cheese for cooking, it melts well and can be used to give a good flavour to all cheese dishes.

BLEU D'AUVERGNE

Soft blue cow's milk cheese. Fat content 45 per cent

This is one of twenty-seven French cheeses protected by *Appellation d'Origine* status. The cheese is made in the department of Cantal and Pay-de-Dôme and in the mountains of Cantal, Autillac and Vic-sur-Cere. It was originally made on the farms, and some still is, but a great deal is also creamery made with pasteurised milk.
Availability Widely available. The cheese is matured for about three months. The farmhouse cheese is best during the late summer and autumn months.
Description Produced in 2.5–5.5 kg (5½–12 lb) flat cylinders, the cheese is foil-wrapped and has a fairly soft, creamy paste with a few holes in it; the greenish blue veining should be well distributed. The flavour is very sharp and piquant.
Manufacture Bleu d'Auvergne started its life as an imitation of Roquefort, but using cow's milk in place of ewe's. The cheeses are traditionally matured in humid cellars and pierced with needles after two months, and the creamery process closely follows the traditional method. The mould used is *penicillium glaucum*.
Serving Serve on a cheeseboard or on its own with biscuits and celery. Remove the foil covering and double wrap in fresh foil. Store for seven to ten days in a cool place.

Cooking Bleu d'Auvergne can be used very successfully in cooking but remember that the flavour does intensify when it is heated. It makes a very good cheese soufflé or use it in a salad with hard-boiled eggs, green beans and potatoes or in a blue cheese salad dressing.

BLEU DE BRESSE

Semi-soft blue cow's milk cheese.
Fat content 50 per cent

Bleu de Bresse started off as a much larger, French imitation of Gorgonzola called Saingorlon which was produced during World War I. Bleu de Bresse was invented in 1950 as a smaller, more easily marketable version. It is made from pasteurised milk in large commercial dairies.
Availability Widely available.
Description Produced in three cylindrical or round-loaf sizes: mini 100 g (3½ oz), moyen 300–400 g (10–14 oz) and maxi 2 kg (4½ lb), the cheeses have a smooth blue rind. The paste is pale in colour with greenish blue veining and the flavour is quite piquant.
Serving Serve as part of a cheeseboard or on its own with water biscuits. Bleu de Bresse is good with celery or other salad ingredients. It is very good mixed with soft cheese and used as a stuffing for raw vegetables. The little cheeses look lovely sliced into salads – toasted pine kernels are a good partner.
Cooking This cheese can be used in any recipe which calls for blue cheese.

BLEU DES CAUSSES

Semi-soft blue cow's milk cheese.
Fat content 45 per cent

Rather similar to Bleu d'Auvergne this French cheese is made from unpasteurised milk in commercial dairies in Aquitane.
Availability Specialist cheese shops. The cheese is matured for three months before being sold.

Description Produced in 2.5 kg (5½ lb) flat drums, the cheese is sold wrapped in foil. It has a thin natural rind and the paste is fairly firm with well-distributed blue veins. The flavour is sharp and pungent but not as full as Roquefort.
Manufacture The cheese is matured in limestone caves with humid spore-bearing 'fleurines' or draughts rather like those in the Roquefort caves.
Serving Serve on its own or as part of the cheese course with pears or grapes. Excellent with olive bread or mild black bread.
Cooking Use in the same way as Bleu d'Auvergne or Bleu de Bresse.

BLEU DE GEX

Semi-soft blue cow's milk cheese.
Fat content 45 per cent

This is another of the twenty-seven French cheeses protected by the *Appellation d'Origine*. It is also known as Bleu de Haute Jura and is made in the Saint Germain-de-Jaoux in small co-operative dairies.
Availability Specialist cheese shops. Matured for two to three months before going on sale, it is best in the summer and autumn.
Description Produced in 6–8 kg (13–18 lb) drums, the cheese has a natural brushed rind which is dry, rough and grey in colour. The paste is dense and white with well-defined deep blue veins and a full flavour.
Serving Good as part of the cheese course or as a 'blue' Ploughman's lunch, with pickled walnuts, celery and home-made bread.

BLUE CHESHIRE

Semi-hard blue cow's milk cheese.
Fat content 48 per cent

Occasionally a Cheshire cheese will blue naturally, but it is said that this only happens to one in 10,000 cheeses. Today, science lends a hand and penicillium Roquefortii is usually added to the milk. The result is a first class blue cheese with an exceedingly rich flavour. Blue Cheshire is quite expensive and hard to find, because it needs extra ageing and is only made on one farm.

Availability Specialist cheese shops. It is sold after about two months' maturation.

Description The cheese, made in 9 kg (20 lb) or 2.5 kg (5½ lb) drums, has a thick hard rind. The paste is a very deep reddish-yellow with greenish-blue veining running from the centre to the edges. It is quite soft in the centre and more crumbly at the edges. The flavour is pungent without being too strong.

Manufacture Blue Cheshire, made with un-pasteurised milk, is a tastier, more acid cheese than ordinary Cheshire. It is different in other ways, too: the curd is less finely cut and the cheeses are not so heavily pressed. They are dyed with annatto and produced in calico-lined hoops. The cheese must be kept at just the right temperature until it is pierced by compressed air jets which replace the conventional needles. A really blue cheese is achieved in two months.

Serving Serve on its own with kiwi fruit or on a cheeseboard garnished with celery. Crumble into low fat soft cheese to make an unusual dip, or have as snack with crusty rolls, banana and watercress.

Cooking Use in any recipe which calls for blue cheese, but do remember that the colour will be different.

History Cheshire cheeses which had turned blue were not popular with the cheese-makers of the past. The phenomenon was called green fade and the cheese was usually thrown away, although sometimes a little was kept to treat sores and infected wounds. Some was sold cheap and found its way to the Yorkshire miners, who also used it medicinally. Attempts were made to exploit green fade in the last century, but no-one could be sure that the selected cheeses would turn blue. The present-day Blue Cheshire was invented by Mrs Hutchinson Smith of Hinton Bank Farm, Whitchurch. *See also Cheshire.*

BLUE WENSLEYDALE

Hard cow's milk cheese. Fat content 48 per cent

This is the traditional Wensleydale cheese, the white variety really only came into vogue this century. Some cheeses are made at the Hartington Stilton creamery in Derbyshire. Others are made on farms in various parts of the country-side.

Availability Specialist cheese shops. The blue version of Wensleydale is matured for up to six months.

Description Made in 5 and 8 kg (11 and 18 lb) drums, the cheese has a thick rind. The paste is a creamy white with blue veining running through it. The flavour is quite distinctive. It is fairly delicate and honied when young and develops to a stronger, more definite flavour as it matures.

Manufacture Cheese-makers will tell you that Blue Wensleydale is almost more tempera-mental than Stilton and this is why so few people now make it. It is made in the same way as white Wensleydale, but *penicillium Roquefortii* is added to the milk. The cheese is pressed for only 24 hours before being transferred to the cheese store where it is turned regularly.

Serving Serve as part of the cheese course or simply with bread or biscuits and celery. It is good with dessert wines like Jurançon or Sauternes.

Cooking Blue Wensleydale can be used in cooking, but it should be used sparingly as the flavour seems to intensify on heating. Try as an egg stuffing with watercress, in a sauce for broccoli or in a soufflé.

History Tradition has it that Wensleydale cheese was brought to Britain at the time of the Norman Conquest by the Cistercian monks who built the abbey of Jervaulx. In those days, the cheese was made from ewe's milk and probably resembled Roquefort much more than it does today. With the dissolution of the monasteries under Henry VIII, the recipe was lost, though farmers continued to make blue cheese from cow's milk. *See also Wensleydale.*

Blue Cheshire (page 48)

Blue Wensleydale (page 49)

BONCHESTER

Soft cow's milk cheese. Fat content 44 per cent

This is a first class Brie or Coulommiers-style cheese from the border counties of Scotland. The cheese takes its name from Bonchester Bridge where it is made.

Availability Specialist cheese shops. May be seasonally available as the cheese is made with milk only from grass-fed (March to December) Jersey cows. May be eaten young and mild, or matured for up to five weeks.

Description Bonchester is a mould-ripened cheese with a very white mould coating. It is produced in 100 g (3½ oz) and 300 g (10 oz) rounds or discs. The mature cheese may have small brownish flecks in the surface. It is soft to the touch, but not flabby and has a thick buttery texture, soft without being runny. The flavour is fairly strong.

Manufacture Made from full fat, pasteurised milk with no artificial additives.

Serving Serve a large whole cheese on its own or a smaller cheese as part of a selection. Oatcakes and a peaty single malt whisky such as an Islay are good affinities.

BOULETTE D'AVESNES

Soft cow's milk cheese. Fat content 45 per cent

This unusual cheese from northern France is one of the smelliest French cheeses. It was traditionally made by heating buttermilk to precipitate the solids and was eaten mainly by the farmers themselves. Today it is usually made from imperfect and unripened Maroilles cheese.

Availability Specialist cheese shops. Matured for three months before sale.

Description Hand moulded into irregular cones, the cheeses have a red washed rind. Some factory produced cheeses are tinted rather than naturally red. The paste is greyish and rather doughy, the flavour very tangy and the smell strong and penetrating.

Manufacture In traditional cheeses the butter-

milk solids were mixed with herbs and spices, hand moulded into small cones, ripened for three months and regularly washed with beer. Factory made cheeses are made from mashing up the unripe Maroilles cheeses and mixing them with the same herb and spice mixture (including parsley, tarragon and pepper) as was used in the buttermilk cheeses.

Serving Serve on its own at the end of a meal. Only strong wines from the Rhône or Rioja will stand up to this cheese, or perhaps a dry Madeira like Sercial or a dry Oloroso.

BOURSAULT

Soft cow's milk cheese. Fat content 75 per cent

Also known as Lucullus, this small factory made triple cream cheese from France is made in Normandy and the Île de France.

Availability Specialist cheese shops. Matured for three to four weeks, this cheese is at its best in the autumn or winter months.

Description Produced in tiny, 7.5 cm (3½ in) cylinders weighing about 200 g (7 oz), the cheeses have a light bloomy, slightly pinkish rind. The paste is extremely creamy and mildy aromatic. The flavour is a little nutty and not cloying considering the amount of cream used to make the cheese.

Variations Herb and garlic-flavoured versions are also on sale. Le Roi is the brand name for a similar cheese, with a darker rind, made in a creamery in Brittany. The cheese is mild with a stronger after taste.

Buying guide Avoid any cheeses which are very red in colour or runny.

Serving Serve on a cheeseboard or on its own with biscuits and celery or grapes. Spread on to canape bases or mix with fresh herbs and use to stuff raw vegetables. Blend with Fromage Frais to make dips or pile on to open sandwiches with black grapes or cherry tomatoes.

BOURSIN

Fresh soft cow's milk cheese. Fat content 70 per cent

This small round French cheese was one of the first modern flavoured cheeses to become fashionable. It is a triple cream cheese factory made in Normandy.

Availability Widely available. This cheese is ready to eat straightaway.

Description Boursin, usually produced in a miniature drum about 7 cm (3 in) in diameter, may be flavoured, or coated with garlic, herbs or black pepper.

Variations Tartare is a similar double cream cheese which is packed in tubs. It is rather milder and softer than Boursin.

Margotin is a fresh cheese with a lower fat content. It is flavoured with garlic, herbs and black peppercorns and is fairly firm with a peppery flavour.

Serving Serve with bread or biscuits or use as canapé toppings and raw vegetable stuffings. Boursin and its derivatives will keep for about a week after purchase. Store in the fridge.

Cooking Boursin can be used to give an interesting flavour to soups and sauces. Or try using it in savoury biscuit mixtures in place of some of the butter. The runnier Tartare is quite good in jacket potatoes or thinned for salad dressing. Try Boursin or Margotin with grilled steaks.

BRICK

Semi-soft cow's milk cheese. Fat content 50 per cent

This is an original American cheese which for some obscure reason is sometimes called 'the married man's Limburg'. It was first made in Wisconsin in the 1870s and probably owes its name to its shape, however, there is a story that it was originally pressed with bricks.

Availability Widely available, in the United States only.

Description Produced in 2.5 kg (5½ lb) brick-shaped blocks, the cheese has a natural, reddish coloured, washed rind. The paste is very pale in colour and is firm, supple and scattered with numerous holes. The flavour is sweet and spicy with a touch of nuttiness – like a stronger version of Tilsit. It is matured for three months before going on sale.

Variation Some cheeses have their rind removed and replaced with wax.

Manufacture Made from pasteurised milk, the curd is coagulated with a lactic bacteria starter and rennet. The curd is cut and scalded, may be washed in water, then drained for twenty-four hours and put into moulds. The cheeses are salted in brine and during ripening the rind is washed regularly to keep the flavour relatively mild.

Serving Serve sliced on a cheeseboard or in open or closed sandwiches. Cut into cubes and serve with aperitifs or cut into sticks and use in a chef's salad.

BRIE

Soft cow's milk cheese. Fat content 40–50 per cent

A 'king of cheeses', Brie was originally made in the French department of Seine-et-Marne. Today a small quantity is still made from unpasteurised milk in the original area, but much of it is made in cheese factories using pasteurised milk. Brie, like Camembert, is heavily imitated and versions are made in almost all the cheese-producing countries.

Availability Widely available. The best time to buy the speciality Brie is during the late summer, autumn and winter.

Description Produced in flattened discs weighing 1–3 kg (2–7 lb), Brie has a bloomy white rind possibly with some pinkish red spots and a glossy straw-coloured paste which should be smooth and plump. The cheese smells slightly mouldy and the flavour is full, fruity and mild. Cheeses which have a very strong smell have been allowed to ripen for too long.

Variations Brie de Meaux is one of the twenty-seven French cheeses protected by an *Appellation d'Origine*. It is made in the Île de France from unpasteurised milk and is recognisable because there is more red colouration on the rind. It has a full aroma and a much more fruity flavour.

Brie de Mélun is also protected by an *Appellation d'Origine* and made from unpasteurised milk in the same area. It is matured for eight weeks or more and has a very dark red rind with only traces of white. The paste is golden yellow, the flavour extremely tangy and the smell very strong. The mature cheese is known as Brie de Mélun Affiné. The same cheese, sold unripe, is called Brie de Mélun Frais. This version may be coated in powdered charcoal and described as 'bleu'.

Brie de Montcreau is very similar to Brie de Mélun Affiné except that it is only matured for six weeks.

Brie de Coulommiers or Brie Petit Moule, which may be farm or factory made, is cheaper than the other named Bries but is not usually as good.

Brie au Bleu is the French creameries' answer to German Blue Brie and it is as new to the French as it is to the Germans! It has a higher fat content because the pasteurised milk is enriched with cream.

Non-French Brie: There are many countries producing their own versions of Brie. The Danes market a version as Dania and the Germans market theirs usually as flavoured Brie. In the United Kingdom, Lymeswold is the brand name for factory produced Brie. However, there are also some English farmhouse Bries, such as Somerset Brie.

Manufacture Made with unpasteurised milk, the speciality Bries are produced by traditional methods. They are neither cooked nor pressed and the skill is in the even spooning of the layers of curd into the cheese rings and the removing of the whey. It is all too easy to make a dry, chalky cheese. The cheeses are turned and matured on straw mats. After a week they are sprinkled with *penicillium candidum* and matured at a carefully controlled temperature until they are ripe. Factory made Brie is ripened for about three weeks. The small dairies of Meaux and Mélun ripen it for between one and two-and-a-half months.

Buying guide All the speciality Bries will be sold by name. French factory made Brie is known as Brie Latier. If possible buy the Brie freshly cut from a whole cheese. Avoid cheeses with a hard or sticky rind, or which are too red. A strong smell of ammonia is a bad sign, though not so serious in a farm cheese. If the cheese is running across the board it is too ripe! However a chalky texture should also be avoided.

Serving Serve on a cheeseboard, on a ploughman's platter with sweet pickles or honour a whole cheese by serving on its own with water biscuits and grapes. A ripe Brie complements a light, sweet wine like Beerenauslese from Germany. A ripe cheese will only keep for about three days. If storing a cut piece, place a piece of cardboard against the cut edges to prevent the cheese running and store in a cool place.

Cooking Brie is a useful cheese because it melts easily into soups and sauces. It can also be used in croquettes, vol-au-vent fillings, layered potato bakes, fish pies and vegetable casseroles. Spread it on canapés or use it to make cheese biscuits or bread. Cut into slim wedges, coat with egg and crumbs and deep-fry.

History This is one of the oldest French cheeses and its history extends back to the dark ages. In the eighth century Charlemagne is reported to have found the cheese at the priory of Rueil de Brie. Since then successive members of the French royalty have declared themselves to be great lovers of the cheese. Louis XVI went so far as to say to his captors that 'a glass of red wine and piece of Brie' was all that he required from them. The cheese finally gained the accolade of 'the king of cheeses' at a cheese contest organised by Talleyrand to relieve the boredom of the negotations at the Treaty of Vienna in 1814 after the battle of Waterloo. Each representative, and there were thirty in all, was asked to present his national cheese at dinner. When Talleyrand brought in the Brie de Meaux it was unanimously declared the best.

BRILLAT SAVARIN

Soft cow's milk cheese. Fat content 78 per cent

A French triple cream cheese, produced in Normandy, it is named for the man who said 'a meal without cheese is like a beautiful woman with only one eye'.

Availability Specialist cheese shops.

Description Produced in small 500 g (1 lb) drums, the cheese has a light downy white rind and quite a firm buttery paste. Matured for three weeks, it is sometimes ripened for longer, then the rind turns red or the paste becomes soft and oily.

Serving Serve as part of the cheese course, after grills or roasts. Open or closed sandwiches or canapés are good, with fresh herbs and slices of fruit. Tangy fruit like kiwi or orange also accentuate the taste with the cheese course.

BROTHER BASIL

Semi-hard cow's milk cheese. Fat content 45 per cent

Made in Bavaria, this is a new German cheese with a pleasantly smoky flavour which is more delicate than many of the smoked cheeses currently on sale.

Availability Widely available.

Description Packed as a flattish loaf with a mahogany-coloured wax coating, the paste is pale yellow in colour with small holes scattered throughout. The texture is smooth, firm and easily sliced. The flavour is creamy and smoky.

Variations Flavoured with chopped ham.

Manufacture This cheese is made by traditional methods and smoked in real wood smoke.

Raucherkäse is the German generic name for smoked cheese. The word, however, does not always mean that the cheese has been smoked, it may indicate that an artificial smoke flavour has been added to the milk.

Serving Serve as part of the cheese course or on its own in open or closed sandwiches. The ham-flavoured version is good cut into sticks in a salad with celery and apples.

BRUSSELSEKAAS

Soft cow's milk cheese. Fat content 0.5–20 per cent

Produced in an area south west of Brussels, this tangy Belgian cheese is popular in its own country. Also called Fromage de Bruxelles, its production dates back to the sixteenth century.

Availability Widely available, in Belgium only.

Description Produced in 150 g (5 oz) fat, round flats and packed into plastic boxes or cellophane, the cheese has little or no rind. The aroma and flavour are sharp and distinctive and the latter becomes more pronounced as the cheese matures for three to four months.

Manufacture The cheese is made from skimmed milk with varying degrees of fat added. The cheeses, washed regularly throughout their maturation period, form little or no rind. They are then moulded into shape and wrapped for sale.

Serving Serve on its own or on a cheeseboard.

BURGOS

Fresh ewe's milk cheese. Fat content 58 per cent

Made in the Spanish province of the same name, Burgos is really a local cheese.

Availability Widely available, in Spain only. Burgos is best eaten the day it is made or, failing that, the day after.

Description Produced in 1–2 kg (2–4½ lb) flat rounds, the paste is soft and even-textured; the flavour very mild and slightly salty.

Manufacture Made from fresh ewe's milk, the curds are curdled with rennet and then scalded to release the whey. They are then ladled out into moulds to finish draining before being brined.

Serving In Spain, this cheese is often served as a dessert sprinkled with sugar or honey. It also goes well with fruit.

Brillat Savarin

Brother Basil

BUTTERKÄSE

Semi-soft cow's milk cheese. Fat content 50 per cent

A bland and inoffensive cheese, also called Damenkäse ('Ladies cheese'), which is factory made in all parts of Germany and Austria.
Availability Widely available, in Germany and Austria only.
Description A fast-ripening, close-textured, pale yellow cheese which may or may not have small holes, but is fairly creamy. The flavour is very mild indeed. Lower fat versions are more elastic in texture.
Serving Serve sliced in a selection of other cheeses or in open or closed sandwiches. Use fresh herbs to add more flavour and serve with a fruity Beaujolais or hock.

CABECOU

Semi-soft goat's milk cheese. Fat content 45 per cent

These tiny French goat's milk cheeses are made in Aquitaine. The name is a diminutive of *chèvre* or goat. They are occasionally made with ewe's milk or a mixture of cow's and goat's milk.
Availability Specialist cheese shops. They are matured for three to four weeks and are best in the autumn and winter.
Description Produced in 40 g (1½ oz) flat discs, the cheese has a natural, slightly bluish rind and a texture varying from hard to semi-soft. Very hard cheese should be avoided. The flavour is characteristically 'goaty'.
Serving Serve with the cheese course or as a snack with fruit or salad. I particularly like it with fresh figs.

CABOC

Fresh cow's milk double cream cheese.
Fat content not available

This is a revival of a Scottish chieftain's cheese. It is rich, creamy and coated in oatmeal.

Availability Widely available.
Description Produced in small 100 g (3½ oz) logs and 1 kg (2 lb) cheeses, this fresh creamy cheese is rolled in toasted pinhead oatmeal. The rich, buttery but rather bland flavour goes well with the toasted oatmeal.
Manufacture This cheese is made from thick cream.
Serving Serve with the cheese course or mash with the oatmeal coating and a little malt whisky and serve on toast.
History The oldest record of an existing Scottish cheese is a recipe for Caboc which was made by Mariota de Ile, the daughter of a fifteenth-century MacDonald of the Isles. This recipe was passed down the female line to her descendant, Susannah Stone, who now makes the cheese in Ross-shire.

CABRALES

Semi-soft blue cow's milk cheese, sometimes with ewe's and/or goat's milk. Fat content 45 per cent

This is Spain's most important blue cheese and it is covered by the Spanish Denominations of Origin laws. It is hand-made on farms in the Penamellera Alta region of Asturias in northern Spain and takes its name from the town of Cabrales. However, the name Cabrales can also apply to goat's milk cheese generally.
Availability Specialist cheese shops.
Description Produced in cylinders of 7–15 cm (3–6 in) and 1–5 kg (2–11 lb) in weight, the cheese has a grey rind with reddish-yellow patches and is sold wrapped in leaves. The rind is soft and thin to begin with, but becomes more crusty with age. The paste is dull white with bluish-green, irregular veining and may develop yellowish-brown patches. It is quite creamy and can be spread. The cheese has a strong aroma and robust flavour. It is matured for at least two, and up to six, months.
Variations Gamonedo or Gamoneu is similar to Cabrales, but even more strong-smelling. The cheese is also smoked for ten to twenty days. Picon is another very similar cheese.

Manufacture Fresh milk from cows, goats and ewes is mixed in whatever proportions are most convenient, but cow's milk makes up the largest part. The milk is coagulated and after at least an hour the curd is cut into cubes the size of walnuts and drained. It is then packed into cylindrical moulds, drained further and then dry-salted. The maturing process is carried out in two stages: the first dries the cheese and lasts for about eight days and the second is concerned with the ripening through the *penicillium* veining. The best conditions of humidity and ventilation occur in caves carved out of the rock face – inside there are draughts of air called *sopladas* caused by the difference in temperature and pressure inside and outside the caves.

Buying guide Genuine Cabrales is always wrapped in the leaves of the maple or the plane tree.

Serving Serve as part of the cheese course or on its own with rustic bread and fresh salad.

Cooking The Spanish make a variety of fondue by cubing the cheese and beating it together with cider. It is also creamed with brandy or minced black olives and spread on to thin slices of bread or toast.

CACETTO

Semi-hard cow's milk cheese. Fat content 44 per cent

This small Italian spun curd or *pasta filata* cheese, has an interesting pear shape with a lobe created by a raffia string used to hang it for storage or smoking.

Availability Specialist cheese shops. Matured for about eight to ten days before selling.

Description Small pear-shaped cheese with a pale ivory wax coating. The paste is white, with a few scattered holes of various sizes; the flavour is smooth and round.

Variations Cacetti may be smoked. Burrini are very similar in shape and size to Cacetti but the cheese paste is moulded round a large knob of butter. They are ripend for two to three weeks and may also be smoked. They are also known as Manteca, Butirri or Buriella.

Serving Serve with bread. If using Burrini spread with the buttery heart of the cheese.

Cooking Serve toasted with scrambled eggs or use in place of Mozzarella in a salad with sliced oranges, tomatoes or sharon fruit, olive oil and herbs.

CACIOCAVELLO

Hard cow's milk cheese. Fat content 44 per cent

This is one of the oldest of Italian cheeses and no one really knows how it got its name. It may refer to the method of spinning the curd over or astride *(acavallo)* a wooden pole or it may refer to the method of ripening the cheeses by hanging them in pairs over poles as if on horseback *(a cavallo)*. Another theory is that the cheese was once made from mare's milk.

Caciocavello is a spun curd or *pasta filata* cheese which is moulded into a large spindle shape with a bulbous rounded end and an elongated end with a ball above a string tie. It is usually made in southern Italy.

Availability Specialist cheese shops. Ripened for two to three months it produces a sliceable cheese and after six to twelve months it is a grating cheese.

Description A fairly large pear-shaped cheese weighing between 2–3 kg (4½–7 lb), it has a thin, smooth, pale straw-coloured rind which may be smooth or slightly flaky or scaly. The paste is white to pale straw colour and has a few holes scattered through it. The young cheese is sweet and delicate, but it matures to a sharper, more strongly flavoured cheese.

Variation Caciocavello Siciliano is much the same as the mainland version, except that goat's milk may be mixed with the cow's milk, and the cheese is pressed into oblong moulds rather than made into pear shapes.

Manufacture Produced in much the same way as Provolone.

Serving Serve in a ploughman's lunch with bread and tomatoes or with fruit. I like it with green olives or olive bread. Double wrap the cheese and keep it in a cool place or in the fridge for up to two weeks.

Caboc (page 56)

Cooking Grate and use the mature cheese in most kinds of cooking, or try slicing and melting it over pan-fried potatoes. Especially good in meat dishes.

History If the name does refer to mare's milk it would take the cheese back to the nomadic era when mare's milk was an occasional food. It is certain that Caciocavella was known in Roman times. Similar cheeses have been traditionally made in Bulgaria and in nearby Hungary, Romania and Turkey and in each place the cheeses carry a similar name.

CACIOTTA

Semi-soft cow's, ewe's or goat's milk cheese.
Fat content 42 per cent

This is really a term for a small cheese made in the traditional manner from local milk on farms in, mainly, central and southern Italy. For this reason there are many different kinds of Caciotta,

and there is a factory version, but this tends to be rather bland and boring.

Availability Specialist cheese shops or ethnic shops. Caciotta is usually ripened for around ten days, but some may be ripened for a month or more. The best are said to be from Urbino or Tuscany.

Description Produced in small discs weighing from 1–2 kg (2–4½ lb), Caciotta may be white, yellow or golden in colour, and could have a smooth, firm rind or a basketwork imprint typical of Pecorino. The cheeses are usually very creamy with a sweet, mild flavour. Some more mature cheeses are a little sharp.

Variations Caciotta di Pecora, made in Sardinia and central Italy exclusively from goat's milk, is matured for about a month. The paste is dense and the flavour mild.

Chiavara is a Caciotta made from cow's milk in the Genoa region.

Serving Serve with bread or biscuits and salad. In Italy, I saw Caciotta traditionally served with fresh young broad beans.

CAERPHILLY

Semi-hard cow's milk cheese. Fat content 48 per cent

For many years, this Welsh cheese was only made in England, but today it is made at the Dairy Crest creamery in Powys. In addition, one or two smaller producers are also back in business in Wales itself. The cheese used to be very popular with the Welsh miners who would take it to work and eat it like cake. The cheese is very salty and must have seemed ideal for replenishing the salt lost through sweat while working at the coalface.

Availability Widely available. Farmhouse Caerphilly should be eaten very young – traditionally ready within a week to ten days. Creamery Caerphilly is matured for up to two weeks and should be eaten as soon as possible after purchase.

Description Shaped like a millstone or cart-wheel and weighing around 3½ kg (8 lb), the cheese has a thin rind, the texture is moist and crumbly and the paste white in colour. The taste is delicate and mild, but quite salty and slightly acidic.

Variation Romany, with Double Gloucester and onions.

Manufacture Made from full fat milk as soon as possible after the milking, the curd is cut into small cubes, drained quickly and then lightly pressed. The farmhouse cheeses are brined for twenty-four hours and then rubbed with rice flour. This process helps to form a thin rind and gives the cheese its distinctive salty flavour.

Serving Serve in the cheese course or as part of a ploughman's lunch. It is so mild it can be eaten on its own or with a bunch of grapes, an apple or some sticks of celery. A good follow-up to a rich main course.

Cooking Caerphilly gives a very salty flavour to cooked dishes, but it is good crumbled on to toast and grilled with a splash of vinegar over the top. It forms the main ingredient in Glamorgan sausages. Caerphilly cheese is also good in salads and in sandwiches with watercress.

Caerphilly

History Caerphilly dates back to the early eighteenth century when farmers in and around Caerphilly and the Vale of Glamorgan made cheese with milk from Hereford and Somerset. It was known as the 'new cheese', not because it was new, but because of its quick ripening properties. Two batches were made daily throughout the summer months, one from the morning milk and one from the evening milk and each was ready for sale within a couple of weeks.

The Cheddar cheese-makers on the other side of the Bristol Channel saw the advantages in making a quick-ripening cheese, which they could sell while they were waiting for their Cheddars to ripen, and so by the beginning of this century Caerphilly was being made in large quantities in the West country.

During World War II, the production of Caerphilly was stopped and, without Cheddar to fall back on, the Welsh producers went out of business.

CAMEMBERT

Semi-soft cow's milk cheese.
Fat content 45–50 per cent

One of the world's most famous cheeses, it originated in the Pays d'Auge of Normandy, but its production is not restricted to France. It is made in most countries that produce cheese on a large scale and is eaten everywhere – from San Francisco to Saigon.

The very best Camembert still comes from the Pays d'Auge where it is hand made on farms, although the number making it is diminishing and the number of large factory creameries, using pasteurised milk to make it, is increasing.

Availability Widely available. Matured for two months, the factory produced Camembert is available all the year round. Farmhouse Camembert ripens within a month and is available at the end of the spring and during the summer and autumn.

Description Produced in small 250 g (9 oz) discs, the cheese has a white rind which should be smooth and supple. The bloomy white mould may be flecked with red in farmhouse versions. The paste is firm and supple with no chalky patches and it is a lovely pale gold colour. The smell should be clean and fruity with a faint tang of mushrooms. The flavour while not over pronounced is distinctive.

Variations Camembert de Normandy, which is produced on farms, is protected by the French *Appelation d'Origine* laws.

Demi-Camembert and Camembert-en-portions are respectively half cheeses and cheese portions and are factory made.

Manufacture Production starts by gently heating the milk until it is ready for the rennet to be added. Coagulation takes about sixty to ninety minutes. After this time the curds are just about strong enough to go into perforated moulds. The cheeses are drained and then sprinkled with spoonfuls of *penicillium candidum* and dry salted. They are then ripened in high humidity cellars and packed in vegetable parchment and wooden boxes for distribution.

Buying guide A genuine farmhouse Camembert has the words *fromage fermier, lait cru* or *non pasteurisé* and the initials VCN (which stand for *Véritable Camembert de Normandie*) on the label. The very best ones may also be labelled *Pays d'Auge*.

Avoid cheeses which smell of ammonia or which are so soft that the paste is almost gluey: these cheeses are over-ripe. Camembert is not intended to be so strong that you can smell the cheeseboard across the room!

Serving Serve with a cheese selection or on its own. It can be used in a ploughman's lunch with sweet pickles, chunky-cut bread and a glass of cider. I like to serve a single Camembert with a full white Burgundy, such as Meursault; if the cheese is too ripe, though, it will mask the wine's flavour. Store Camembert in its box. If it is not fully ripe it can be ripened at home in a cool cupboard or a wine cellar. Do not place it in the fridge, unless fully ripe, as this will stop the cheese maturing. Once the cheese is cut it should be wrapped in foil and eaten as soon as possible.

Cooking Camembert works very well in the kitchen. It can be used to give an interesting flavour to courgettes, gougères, potato bakes, soups and sauces. Try melting it with cream, wine and herbs for a pasta sauce or use it in soups with celery or Jerusalem artichokes. Mash it together with chopped nuts or sesame seeds for canapé toppings, or use to stuff green peppers together with cooked rice and raisins. Camembert can be deep-fried in breadcrumbs; serve with pickles or sweet and sour jam made by adding onions, vinegar and Worcestershire sauce to any jam.

History Camembert is a young cheese. It is said to have been invented by a Madam Marie Harel in 1702 although there has been a long tradition of this kind of cheese in the area where she lived. The truth probably is that Mme Harel refined the recipe and led the way to a wider appreciation of this cheese in much the same way that Mrs Paulet introduced Stilton to a larger audience. The story goes that a Mme Marie Harel invented the cheese and sold it at the market of Vimontiers. She passed the recipe on to her daughter whose husband, Victor Paynel, presented one of his wife's best cheeses to Napoleon III. History does not relate whether this monarch liked the cheese but it continued to find a wider market. In those days the cheese was packed in paper and straw and could not be transported much further than Paris without getting damaged; it suffered in appearance too, because rinds were often blue. In 1890 a Monsieur Ridel solved the transport problem by inventing the cylindrical chip-wood box and, in 1910, the cheese-makers came up with the idea of spraying the cheeses with *pencillium* mould to make an attractive white downy rind. The cheese never looked back!

CANESTRATO

Semi-hard ewe's milk cheese. Fat content 45 per cent

Traditionally made in Tuscany and Sicily, the name for this Italian cheese is derived from the baskets in which it ripens and the imprint they leave on the rind.

Availability Widely available, in Italy only. Made between October and June.

Description Usually produced in 2 kg (4½ lb) cylinders or discs, Canestrato may vary considerably depending on the variety of milk used, the type of rennet or curdling agent used and the length of the ripening period. The young cheese has a dense, whitish yellow paste with a scattering of holes. It is sometimes known as Pecorino Canestrato or Pecorino Siciliana.

Variations When the words 'Canestrato' or 'Incanestrata' are used, it denotes a hard, matured ewe's milk cheese made specially for grating. The cheese may have peppercorns added to the curd before it goes into the mould.

Manufacture The cheese is sometimes made with a mixture of cow's and ewe's milk or even with cow's milk alone, but ewe's milk is traditional. The production is typical of a scalded curd cheese.

Serving Serve the young cheese as part of a selection or on its own with Italian bread, tomatoes and olive oil and a sprig of basil for aroma.

Cooking The matured cheese is good for grating and cooking, and can be used in place of Parmesan for a milder flavour in *gratin* dishes or sauces.

CANTABRIA

Semi-hard cow's milk cheese. Fat content 45 per cent

Made exclusively from the milk of Friesian cows, this cheese is now made all over the province of Cantabria in northern Spain, and is covered by the Spanish denomination of origin laws.

Availability Widely available, in Spain only.

Description Produced in flat cylinders weighing between 500 g (1 lb) and 3 kg (7 lb), the cheese has a soft greyish-yellow rind. The paste is ivory coloured with a firm, but supple, creamy texture and the flavour is fairly mild.

Manufacture The cheese is made from pasteurised milk and the curds are heated and pressed for twenty-four hours.

Serving Serve sliced with a continental hand-held cheese slicer with the cheese course or as part of a Spanish ploughman's lunch, with olives and large beef or continental tomatoes.

CANTAL

Semi-hard cow's milk cheese. Fat content 45 per cent

Also known as Fourme de Cantal or as Salers, this is one of France's oldest cheeses. It comes from the Auvergne and the best cheese is made in the mountain farms during the summer months. It is one of the twenty-seven French cheeses protected by the *Appellation d'Origine*.

This cheese is sometimes known as French Cheddar, but the comparison is unfair as it has its own mountain herb flavour.

Availability Specialist cheese shops or ethnic shops. Matured for anything from three to six months before sale, the farm cheeses are made in the summer and autumn and are available from about October, but they are difficult to find outside France. They are also known as Cantal Fermier or may be labelled Haute Montagne.

Description Produced in 35–45 kg (77–99 lb) drums, the cheese has a thin, grey rind which is dry and powdery, and darkens with age. The paste is pale yellow in colour, close textured and smooth. The cheese has a milky aroma and a pleasantly nutty flavour. A poet once wrote of Cantal that 'to elaborate on Cantal is an error of taste; it is all simplicity'.

Variations Cantalet or Cantalon is a baby farmhouse Cantal weighing around 10 kg (22 lb). It is made towards the end of the summer when the milk is particularly rich.

Manufacture The production of Cantal follows simple traditional methods. The cheese is not cooked, but the curd is pressed, sliced and pressed again before salting and ripening.

Serving Serve with the cheese course, as a snack or in a ploughman's lunch. Cantal has a tendency to dry out, so it should be stored well wrapped in a humid place. If it has to go into the fridge, store it in a polythene box for no more than a week.

Cooking Cantal grates and melts well and is very useful in cooking. In the Auvergne an unripe version of the cheese, known as Tomme d'Aligot is used in cooking. Try Cantal in soups, sauces, purées and on gratin dishes. An unusual application is in savoury choux buns or bread rolls.

History Almost two thousand years ago Pliny referred to the excellence of Cantal cheese by saying that these cheeses from Gaul were popular in Rome. The cheese has been mentioned, too, in various other tracts through the centuries.

CAPRICE DES DIEUX

Semi-soft cow's milk cheese. Fat content 60 per cent

This is a factory produced double cream cheese with a white bloomy rind which is made from pasteurised milk.

Availability Widely available.

Description This small oval cheese weighing 150 g (5 oz) is packed in small boxes. It has a white rind and a very creamy, mildly flavoured paste.

Serving Serve as part of the cheese course. An individual cheese packed lunch, with mildly flavoured salads or fruit. Try some sliced on a salad with asparagus and orange dressing.

Caprice des Dieux

Capricorn (page 64)

CAPRICORN

Soft goat's milk cheese. Fat content 50 per cent

Invented in 1983 in Somerset, this cheese is made from the milk of a large herd of British Saanen goats by one company.

Availability Specialist cheese shops.

Description This is a small mould-ripened, cylinder-shaped soft cheese 5 cm (2 in) high, weighing 100 g (3½ oz) and coated with a white mould. The flavour is mild, but as the cheese ripens towards the centre, the flavour gets a little stronger, though it never reaches the pungency of some French goat's cheese.

Manufacture The milk is pasteurised before use. The curd is formed by adding a vegetable rennet and it is poured into moulds. After draining and salting, the cheeses are stored for eight to nine days while the mould forms.

Serving Serve whole as part of the cheese course. Once cut, it is best eaten immediately, though it will keep for a day in the fridge.

Cooking Small pieces of leftover cheese can be used to flavour vegetable soups or stuffed mushrooms.

CAPRINI

Cow's or goat's milk cheese.
Fat content not available

These Italian cheeses used to be made from goat's milk, but are today usually made from cow's milk instead.

Availability Widely available, in Italy only. These cheeses are usually made to be eaten immediately.

Description Caprini are small delicate lactic cheeses and may be moulded in almost any shape. They have a fresh, mild flavour.

Variations Caprini di Moulevecchia has a thin covering of brownish mould and is matured for longer than most. Caprini di Semicotto is a scalded, matured cheese from Sardinia.

Serving Try with Italian bread, green olives and cherry tomatoes.

CAROLINA

Hard ewe's milk cheese. Fat content 51 per cent

A traditional hard English cheese made on a farm in Kent from a recipe which originated in Somerset. The milk is unpasteurised and a vegetable rennet is used.

Availability Specialist cheese shops. The cheese is sold after maturing for two months.

Description Made in 500–750 g (1–1½ lb) and 2–2.75 kg (4½–6 lb) drums, the cheese has a dark greyish-brown rind, a firm texture and a slightly farmyardy, quite strong flavour with lemony overtones.

Serving Serve as part of the cheese course or with bananas and crusty rolls or chicory and tabbouleh.

Cooking The cheese can be grated into soups and sauces or used as an unusual stuffing for tomatoes or other vegetables.

History The present producers bought the recipe for Carolina from cheese-makers in Somerset whose pastures may once have been part of the local Cistercian abbey holdings. The cheese is named after these pastures and may be similar to the ewe's milk cheese made in the monks' time.

CARRÉ DE L'EST

Semi-soft cow's milk cheese.
Fat content 40–50 per cent

This is a fairly strong-smelling French factory made cheese from the Champagne and Lorraine districts which is made with pasteurised milk.

Availability Widely available. Matured for three weeks before sale.

Description Produced in 200 g (7 oz) squares, this cheese has a white bloomy rind, a creamy yellow paste and a mild flavour.

Variations Petit Carré is a smaller variety produced for export. There is also a washed-rind version with the same name and this has a much more pronounced smell.

Serving Serve on a cheeseboard with walnut bread and a Rioja or Côte du Rhône. Store in its box in the fridge for up to two weeks, but be sure to remove it at least an hour before eating or its flavour will be lost.

Cooking Carré de l'Est can be used in cooking. Try it in cheese tartlets, toasted sandwiches or melted in soups.

CASHEL BLUE

Semi-soft blue cow's milk cheese.
Fat content not available

This is the only Irish farmhouse blue cheese; it is made from unpasteurised milk and shaped into small rounds.

Availability Specialist cheese shops. Best between six and ten weeks maturation, all cheeses carry the date of manufacture.

Description Produced in small 1.5 kg (3½ lb) cheeses, Cashel Blue is creamy, almost spreadable, and has light blue veining. As it matures, the flavour strengthens and becomes quite piquant, and the rind develops an extensive pink colouring and surface ripening.

Manufacture The cheeses are matured on the farm, until the blue mould is well developed, and then wrapped in foil.

Serving Serve as part of the cheese course or on its own with a sweet wine, such as Coteaux du Layon or Barsac. I like it as a snack with mangoes, salad and rye bread.

Cooking Use in any blue cheese recipe, especially vegetable-based soups or sauces for fish.

CEBRERO

Hard cow's milk cheese. Fat content 50 per cent

Sometimes sold under the Portuguese name of Queixo do Cebreiro, this Spanish cheese is made in Lugio in the Cebrero mountains near to the Spanish/Portuguese border. The cheese has a distinctive shape and a fairly sharp flavour.

Availability Widely available, in Spain and Portugal only.

Description Cebrero is shaped rather like a stubby mushroom or a drum with an overhanging rim. The rind is firm and crusty with white streaks, the cooked paste is firm and close-textured and the taste is creamy and piquant.

Serving Serve with the cheese course or with crusty rolls and watercress.

CECILIA

Hard ewe's milk cheese. Fat content 51 per cent

A traditional hard English cheese farm-produced in Kent and matured in oak barrels on a bed of hops. The milk is unpasteurised and a vegetable rennet is used. The cheese is named after the maker's mother.

Availability Specialist cheese shops. The cheese is sold after maturing for two months.

Description Made in 500–750 g (1–1½ lb) and 2–2.75 kg (4½–6 lb) drums, the cheese has a natural yellowish-grey rind, a firm but moist texture and is made by the same people as Carolina. Cecilia has a creamier flavour.

Serving Serve as part of the cheese course. On its own, try it with peaches and a mixed leaf salad.

CENDRÉ

Semi-soft cow's milk cheese.
Fat content 20–45 per cent

Cendré is the general name for small semi-soft cheeses ripened in wood ash, which often have a very strong flavour and are made locally in Champagne and Burgundy.

Availability Locally available, in France only. Matured for two months.

Description These cheeses vary in size and texture depending on the region where they are made and the type of milk used. They are extremely strong tasting and sometimes almost rank in flavour.

Cashel Blue (page 65)

Variations Cendré d'Aisy, is a 375–625 g (12–20 oz) cheese from Burgundy. Cendré d'Argonne is a small cheese from Champagne. Cendré de Champagne is a small 275 g (9 oz) cheese which can be very strong indeed.
Serving Serve in the cheese course or on its own with a very well flavoured bread.

CERVERA

Fresh soft ewe's milk cheese. Fat content 67 per cent

Made in the Valencia area of Spain, this fresh cheese is also known as Questo Fresco Valenciano.
Availability Locally available, in Spain only. This cheese is ready to eat as soon as it is made.

Description A disc-shaped cheese, varying in weight from 1–2 kg (2–4½ lb), it has the characteristic aroma of sheep's cheese and is very fresh tasting.
Serving Try it with crusty bread, large continental tomatoes and black olives.
Manufacture The shape of the cheese varies because it is usually pressed into a round by hand.

CHABICHOU

*Semi-soft goat's milk cheese.
Fat content 45 per cent*

This French cheese, named after the diminutive for goat in the Poitevin dialect, has various forms of its name, including Cabichou, Chabi and Cabicou. There are farm and creamery versions, both of which are good.

Availability Widely available. Matured for two to three weeks, the cheese is best bought during the summer and early autumn.

Description Chabichou is produced in tiny 100 g (3½ oz) drum shapes. The rind is white and bloomy, the paste firm but not hard and the farmhouse version has a bluish coloured rind with red streaks in it. The flavour is quite strong and goaty. Like other farmhouse cheeses, it is usually labelled 'Fermier'; while the creamery cheese is labelled 'Laitier'.

Serving Serve with the cheese course or on its own with biscuits and celery.

Cooking These small goat's milk cheeses are very useful for people who are allergic to cow's milk. Melt into soups for extra flavour or use in stock-based sauces for fish and poultry. Interesting in quiches, with soy or cow's milk.

CHAMOIS D'OR

Semi-soft cow's milk cheese. Fat content 62 per cent

Despite the leaping goat-like antelope on the wrapping, this cheese is actually made with cow's milk at one of the large French creameries. It has been invented recently to meet the demand for bland, white bloom cheeses. However, this demand may be more from the retailer than the consumer for this cheese has a relatively long shelf life of six weeks.

Availability Widely available.

Description Produced in 2–3 kg (4–6½ lb) wheels, this cheese has a white rind and an ivory coloured, fairly firm paste. The flavour is extremely mild with a certain creaminess in the mouth.

Serving Serve in the cheese course or on its own with water biscuits and grapes. Especially good after a rich main course, such as game or a hearty casserole.

Cooking Chamois d'Or can be used in any recipe that calls for Brie or Camembert.

CHAOURCE

Semi-soft cow's milk cheese.
Fat content 45–50 per cent

A small, dryish cheese, made in the Champagne area of France, it is protected by the French *Appellation d'Origine* laws and made in small dairies from unpasteurised milk.

Availability Specialist cheese shops and ethnic shops. Some cheeses are ripened for two to three weeks, others are sold when they are more mature at one to two months. It is best bought during the summer and autumn months.

Description Produced in small 500 g (18 oz) drums, the cheese has a thin white rind and a dry rather than a creamy texture. The flavour is slightly sour and fruity, but improves as the cheese matures.

Serving Serve as part of the cheese course or on its own with biscuits and celery. The flavour especially complements a good, red Burgundy. Unopened cheese can be kept for up to a week in the fridge. Cut cheese does not keep for more than a day or two.

CHAUMES

Semi-soft cow's milk cheese.
Fat content 50 per cent

When it is fully ripe and farmhouse-made, this French cheese is one of the smelliest, but the flavour is aromatic rather than strong. It is made in the Dordogne from pasteurised milk. Some is factory-produced, and this tends to be sold when young and still quite mild.

Availability Widely available.

Description Produced in 1.5 kg (3 lb) cylinders or discs, Chaumes has a tough yellow-brown rind, a golden yellow paste with a few holes and a firm, rather elastic texture. The flavour is full, creamy and rather nutty. The cheese should look bright and clear in colour.

Serving Serve as part of the cheese course, or on its own with bread or biscuits and celery or grapes. A particularly good 'ploughman's', with coarse French country bread, black olives, and salad: wash it down with a light claret.

CHAVROUX

Fresh soft goat's milk cheese. Fat content 45 per cent

A new goat's milk cheese from France, it is made in the Charentes area of south west France.
Availability Widely available. This cheese is ready to use as soon as it is produced.
Description Chavroux is packed into 250 g (8 oz) truncated pyramid-shaped containers. It is white in colour, soft in texture and the flavour is light, mild and refreshing.
Serving Turn out to serve on a cheeseboard or spread on to bread, biscuits or canapés.
Cooking Blend with lemon juice and water for an unusual dressing for green salad leaves. Use as a base for dips.

CHEDDAR

Hard cow's milk cheese. Fat content 48 per cent

Cheddar is the most widely made cheese in the world and, as a result, it is often known by the derogatory title of 'mousetrap'. In fact, top quality Cheddar is first class, but much of the mass-produced product is boring and bland. There is no excuse for this because even though the remaining west country farms – who produce Cheddar by traditional means – do produce a first class cheese, this can be matched by the large automated factories. Indeed, a cheese from the fully automated Dairy Crest cheese factory at Aspatria, in Cumbria, won top prize in its class at the International Cheese Show, held at the International Food Exhibition in London in the spring of 1989. Some Canadian and New Zealand Cheddars are also produced to an exceedingly high standard.

Cheddar cheese is extremely popular in all English-speaking countries, perhaps because of its immense versatility. It can be enjoyed in its natural state as a snack, or on a cheeseboard and, as it melts so easily, it can be used in virtually every type of cooking.
Availability Widely available. Cheddar is sold at various stages of maturity: the mild Cheddar sold in supermarkets, is between three and five months old; mature Cheddar is over five and up to nine months or, occasionally, up to twelve months old. Farmhouse Cheddar is usually twelve months old and some good cheese is kept for eighteen months, or even two years, before it is sold.
Description The traditional cheese is drum-shaped, weighing about 25–28 kg (55–61 lb) and is bound with a material called grease bandage which ensures that a hard rind forms on the outside of the cheese. Golden yellow in colour, the cheese has a smooth and fairly hard texture and should never crumble when cut. The flavour varies from mild to full, nutty and strong, depending on the age of the cheese.
Variations Most factory and some farm Cheddar is now block shaped. The cheese is vacuum packed in polythene and stored at low temperatures. Ripening in these circumstances is minimised and the cheeses are very mild in flavour.

Smaller versions of the farmhouse drum-shape are called truckles. These weigh from 1–7 kg (2–15 lb).

Scottish Cheddar is often much redder in colour than English Cheddar because it is dyed with annatto. The Scots also produce a black-waxed mature Cheddar.

Flavoured versions are available in the United Kingdom as follows:
Admirals: with port and Blue Stilton cheese
Albany: with cumin seed
Applewood: smoked and coated with paprika
Charnwood: with paprika, and lightly smoked
Cheviot: with chives
Glenphilly: with malt whisky
Ilchester: with beer, garlic and parsley; with sweet pickle; with port wine
Nutcracker: with walnuts
Nutwood: with cider, hazelnuts and raisins
Oakwood: smoked
Penmill: with peppercorns
Rutland: with beer, garlic and parsley

Walton: with Stilton and hazelnuts and with a hazelnut coating
Windsor Red: with elderberry wine

Low fat versions are available in the United Kingdom as follows:
Merlin: smoked cheese

Non-United Kingdom Cheddar A lot of the Cheddar cheese produced in New Zealand is exported. Its noticeable very bright yellow colour is natural and due to the fact that many of the cows in New Zealand's dairy herd are Jersey cows. Most the cheese is matured for rather longer than other factory made Cheddars. There are various styles available including:
Medium: matured for about nine to twelve months
Mature: matured for not less than sixteen to eighteen months
Traditional: prepared in a cylinder shape and matured for not less than eighteen months
Vintage: matured for not less than two years

Canada makes some first class Cheddars. They are known for their good flavour which is due to the longer maturing times. Black Diamond and Cherry Hill are probably the best known.

American Cheddar is sold throughout the United States and is often simply referred to as 'American'. Introduced by the Pilgrim Fathers, it was originally made on the farms, but factory production soon took over and there is no farm cheese now. American comes in all shapes and sizes, much of it heavily dyed and often waxed black, red or orange. The names under which the cheese is sold usually refer to the shape: for example Barrel, Mammoth and Daisy. Others are regional names, such as Coon, a rare Cheddar with a fully matured flavour from New York States; Camosun, a mild Cheddar from Washington State; Cornhusker, a mild springy version with holes in the paste; Pineapple which is hung to ripen in nets which produce a pineapple shape; and Tillamook, a strong Cheddar from Oregon.

Manufacture Cheddar is made from full fat milk. Mostly the milk is pasteurised, but there are a few farms in the west of England which use unpasteurised milk. The cheese is not cooked. The unique process, which separates Cheddar from other hard cheeses, is the way in which the curds are cut and drained. The process is called cheddaring and the result is an extremely even and smooth textured cheese.

Once the rennet has been added and the curd set, it is milled to pieces the size of a pea. These are heated gently and the whey is drawn off. The curd forms into one cohesive mass and is cut into thick blocks which are stacked on top of one another and turned so that more whey is drained out. The curd is then milled again, salted, packed into moulds and pressed. In factory production the cheddaring is done in a cheddar tower and the process is virtually continuous.

Farmhouse Cheddar is packed into cylindrical moulds lined with grease bandage. This ensures that a hard rind forms on the outside of the cheese which prevents moulds getting into it and lets the gases escape slowly so that the cheese matures correctly to give the product its full flavour. Farmhouse Cheddar is graded at the age of sixty to a hundred-and-twenty days then stored for a further nine months or more until it is ready to be sold.

Buying guide Buy only from shops or supermarkets that have a high turnover at the cheese counter to ensure a really fresh cheese. For the best flavours buy cheese which has been freshly cut from a whole cheese. Cheese which has been cut and wrapped by the shop or has been vacuum packed will not taste the same. Check the labelling to see where the cheese comes from and whether it carries one of the relevant cheese marks (see page 148). Look at the cheese carefully and don't buy it if it is hard and dry, or sweating or weeping. The rind should be dry.

Serving Serve good farmhouse Cheddar on a cheeseboard, as part of a ploughman's lunch or simply as a snack. It is good with beer, red wine or port – let the circumstances make the choice.

Store between 5°–10°C (40–50°F). If it has to go in the fridge, wrap it tightly in clingfilm or foil or, for a slightly warmer storage area, wrap it in muslin. Never serve it directly from the fridge or cool store, but bring it slowly up to room temperature.

Cooking Cheddar is an excellent cheese to use, it melts easily and a well-matured cheese gives an excellent flavour to any dish. The better the flavour of the cheese, the more sparingly you can use it. It is usually best to grate the cheese before adding it to the other ingredients. Traditional dishes using Cheddar include Welsh rarebit, panhaggerty, cauliflower and macaroni cheeses, cheese scones and cheese and potato pie. However, it can be used in many more dishes as a topping with breadcrumbs or nuts, in white sauces, layered with vegetables or mixed with pie fillings. Use it raw, too, either grated, cubed or cut into sticks in salads, on cocktail kebabs or in dips.

History Cheese from the Cheddar Gorge region of Somerset was well established in Elizabethan times. Tradition has it that the cheeses were ripened in the vast network of caves that stretch under the Mendip Hills. Cheddar cheeses were so highly prized that they graced only the tables of the rich and, it is

recorded, they were often 'bespoke before they were made'. In the very early days ewe's milk may have been used together with cow's milk. The cheeses were much larger and took much longer to mature than they do now and they may also have had some holes in the paste. There are stories of huge cheeses needing two or three men to lift them.

CHEEDAM

Hard cow's milk cheese. Fat content not available

This mild Australian cheese was inspired by both Dutch and English cheeses and is roughly a cross between Edam and Cheddar.

Availability Widely available, in Australia only.

Description Cheedam is produced in large rindless blocks, the paste is golden yellow in colour and the texture firm but fairly supple. The flavour is very mild.

Serving Serve on a cheeseboard, as part of a

Cheddar

Cheshire 'White' and 'Red'

ploughman's platter with good chutney or pickles, or in open or closed sandwiches. Double wrap and store in the fridge for up to a week or ten days.

Cooking Cheedam can be used in most culinary applications when either Cheddar or Edam is called for.

CHESHIRE

Semi-hard cow's milk cheese. Fat content 48 per cent

The underlying salt deposits of the Cheshire plain give a distinctive salty taste to this oldest of traditional English cheeses. It has been made in Cheshire since pre-Roman times. There is a story that the Roman legions built a wall round Chester, the capital of Cheshire, to protect the city's cheese industry. Cheshire cheeses were transported to Italy and sold in the Roman food markets.

Cheshire is second only to Cheddar in economic importance, but its manufacture is limited to the United Kingdom. The Chester cheese found in France and some other parts of Europe is not the same at all.

Most Cheshire cheese is creamery made, but there are still a small number of farmers in the counties of Cheshire, Shropshire and Clywd who make traditional cheeses on their farms.

Availability Widely available. The cheeses are usually sold after four to eight weeks' ripening, but sometimes a particularly fine one will be kept for longer ripening for anything up to fifteen months.

Description Traditional cheeses are cylinder shaped and weigh around 18 kg (40 lb). They may be cloth-bandaged, but they are more likely to be wrapped in muslin and dipped in wax so the outer surface is smooth and soft. A final layer of cloth is then glued on to the outside of the cheese. Creamery cheeses are often made in block form and matured in plastic. The texture of the cheese is loose and crumbly, much more friable and moist than Cheddar and much paler in colour. It is known as 'White' Cheshire. The taste is mild and salty when young, but acquires more of a tang with age.

Variations 'Red' Cheshire is exactly the same as 'White' Cheshire, but the cheese has been dyed with annatto to a deep peach colour. This does not affect the taste of the cheese. 'Red' Cheshire is said to be more popular in the Midlands and the south of England.

Manufacture Evening and morning milk are mixed and, with the exception of farmhouse Cheshire, pasteurised. The whole cheese-making process only takes two or three hours. After coagulation, the cheese is scalded in the whey for about forty minutes and the whey is drained off while the cheese-maker cuts the curd and tears it into small pieces. It is then milled, salted and put into moulds for pressing.

Buying guide If the cheese looks bright and fresh, it is fresh; if it looks dry and cracked, or is sweating, it should be avoided.

Serving Cheshire is a useful all-purpose cheese to serve on the cheeseboard, as part of a ploughman's lunch, or as a snack with fruit or crudités. It was traditionally served with fruit cake. Cheshire is best eaten fresh and does not store well.

Cooking Cheshire cheese is a versatile cooking cheese. It can be used in most recipes calling for hard cheese; however, its flavour goes particularly well with eggs, in dishes such as cheese omelettes and soufflés.

History The secret of making Cheshire cheese has always lain in the salty quality of the milk produced in the area. There is a story that the Romans hanged a cheese-maker at Chester Cross for refusing to give them the recipe. Cheshire cheese has a well-documented history: it is mentioned in the Doomsday Book, there are records of three hundred tons being sent to the troops in Scotland during the Civil War, and, in 1730, nearly six thousand tons were sent to London. Samuel Johnson and his literary friends used to enjoy the cheese sitting in Ye Olde Cheshire Cheese in Fleet Street, London.

In the past, the cheeses were much larger than today's small cylinders and could weigh anything up to one hundred and forty pounds. There is a tradition that in Peover a farmer would ask his future wife to lift the massive lid of the parish chest in the church: if she could do it with one hand, she would be a valuable addition to the dairy!

Originally, all Cheshire cheese was cream or 'white' in colour. Then the Welsh introduced a cheese similar to Cheshire (but not as good) and coloured it red with carrot juice. People who did not know the area thought that the coloured variety was superior and bought it in preference to Cheshire, so the Cheshire farmers coloured their cheese in self-defence. *See also Blue Cheshire.*

CHESTER

Hard cow's milk cheese. Fat content 45 per cent

This is a French factory produced cheese which has nothing to do with English Cheshire cheese.

Availability Widely available, in France only. Matured for about six months.

Description This cheese is produced in tall cylinders or in oblong blocks. The rind is thin and the paste smooth and even with occasional small cracks. The flavour is not very pronounced, in fact, it is more like a very mild Cheddar than a Cheshire.

Serving Serve as a snack or in sandwiches.

Cooking Can be used in most culinary applications where a very mild flavour is required.

CHÈVRE

Soft goat's milk cheese. Fat content 45 per cent

This is the generic term for French goat's milk cheese and covers many local and creamery versions. By law cheeses described as Chèvre must be made entirely of goat's milk and must contain at least 45 per cent fat.

Availability Widely available.

Description Chèvre may come in all shapes

and sizes, one of the most common is Chèvre Roll or Log. This large log shape, about 6–7.5 cm (2½–3 in) in diameter, is packed in lengths of straw or plastic and has a white rind and a firm texture which becomes progressively more creamy as it matures. The flavour may be fairly mild or more 'goaty'.

Variations Sainte Mauré Laitier is a small log-shaped cheese with a full 'goaty' flavour which is creamery made in Touraine.

Mothe Saint-Héray or Chèvre à la Feuille is a full-flavoured cheese from Poitevin. It is ripened for two weeks between layers of vine or plane tree leaves.

Chevret is a small rare cheese with a nutty flavour and a bluish rind from the farms of the Jura.

Chevrette des Beauges is a pressed cheese from Savoie. It has a thin, glossy, light-coloured rind, a supple texture and is ripened for two to three months in cool cellars.

Chevret is a small cheese from Charentes-Poitou. It is best eaten young.

Serving Serve as part of the cheese course or on its own. Double wrap and store in a cool place for three to four days.

Cooking Use sliced in salads with pine nuts and olive oil, or toast on rounds of French bread. Chèvre can also be melted into sauces for pasta or vegetables. The 'goaty' flavour of this cheese tends to diminish when it is cooked.

CHEVROTIN DES ARAVIS

Semi-hard goat's milk cheese. Fat content 45 per cent

This mild-flavoured pressed cheese from the Haute Savoie is often sold as Tomme de Chèvre.

Availability Specialist cheese shops and ethnic shops. Matured for two months, this cheese is best in the summer and autumn.

Description Produced in 500 g (18 oz) cylinders or discs the cheese has a rough grey rind, a firm paste and a mild, only slightly 'goaty' flavour.

Serving Serve on a cheeseboard or with sliced air-dried sausages and olive oil, as an unusual

first course. Team-up with sliced kiwi fruit and tomatoes on a bed of rocket.

COLBY

Semi-hard cow's milk cheese. Fat content 50 per cent

This American cheese was first made in 1882. It is a popular everyday cheese in the United States.

Availability Widely available, in the United States only.

Description Produced in vacuum-packed blocks of various sizes, Colby is dyed a deep orange-yellow. The paste is fairly open and granular, the flavour quite sweet and mild.

Variations A few cheeses are waxed.

Manufacture Colby is a scalded curd cheese made by a special process in which the whey is drained off and the curds are covered in cold water. Then the Cheddar process follows (see page 68), but without 'cheddaring'!

Serving Serve as a snack or in a ploughman's lunch or use in open or closed sandwiches.

Double wrap and store in the warmest part of the fridge for a week or ten days.

Cooking This cheese can be used in all kinds of cooking, it toasts well and can be used as a topping for creamy vegetable dishes.

COLEFORD BLUE

Hard blue goat's milk cheese. Fat content 55 per cent

This interesting blue goat's milk cheese is made by hand in England in a village near Taunton, Devon.

Availability Specialist cheese shops. The cheese is sold after two to three months' maturation.

Description The cheese is made in 2–2½ kg (4½–5½ lb) truckles with a natural rind. The texture is firm, but creamy, and the flavour a mild blue tang which strengthens as the cheese matures.

Variation A milder version, Coleford Mild, is made without the blueing.

Manufacture The unpressed cheese is made with unpasteurised milk using vegetable rennet. The curd is innoculated with *penicillium Roquefortii*.

Serving Serve as part of the cheese course or on its own. Cut in cubes and serve with aperitifs, or grate and blend into a dip or a stuffing for celery. Mix with grated orange rind and chopped walnuts for savoury cocktail truffles. Keep in cool, moist conditions or in the fridge. Whole cheeses will keep in these conditions for one to two months. Cut cheeses should be used within three weeks.

COMTE

Hard cow's milk cheese. Fat content 45 per cent

Also known as Gruyère de Comte, this is an ancient French cheese which dates back to the thirteenth century. It is protected by the French *Appellation d'Origine* laws. The very best comes from the Verrières-de-Joux.

Availability Widely available, in France only. Matured for three to six months, the best cheeses are available at the end of the summer, autumn and winter.

Description Produced in 38–40 kg (84–88 lb) cylinders, the cheeses have a thin dark yellow rind. The paste is golden in colour and has a scattering of medium-sized holes. The texture is smooth and firm with some elasticity and the flavour rich and fruity, and it compares well with the Swiss cheeses.

Manufacture The cheeses are made in local cooperatives or fruitières. The method is very similar to Swiss Gruyère.

Buying guide Comte is at its best when the holes or eyes are perfectly round and about the size of a large pea or small cherry. They should be just glistening with moisture.

Serving Serve as part of the cheese course, as a snack or on a ploughman's platter with Meaux mustard. Double wrap and store in a cool place or in the fridge for up to two weeks.

Cooking Use as a condiment on soups, pasta and other dishes or use in any dish which calls for Gruyère or Emmenthal. Try it in cheese fritters, gratin dishes, fondue and in grilled or baked canapés.

CORNISH YARG

Semi-hard cow's milk cheese. Fat content 57 per cent

This cheese from Cornwall, England, which is coated in nettles, has gained quite a following. Its name, which sounds very Cornish to the uninitiated, is actually gray spelt backwards – Gray being the name of the cheese-makers who developed the cheese from old recipes found in an attic.

Availability Specialist cheese shops. The cheese leaves the farm after three weeks, but takes another two to three weeks to reach full maturity.

Description The cheese is mould-ripened and coated with nettle leaves. The coating turns black and has the practical advantages of keeping the paste moist and repelling flies. The cheese is produced in 3 kg (7 lb) moulds and 1 kg (2 lb) truckles. The texture is creamy and the flavour fairly mild.

Manufacture Made from pasteurised milk with vegetable rennet.

Serving Serve as part of the cheese course or on its own with biscuits and celery. The mild flavour partners fine wines well.

CORSICA

Semi-soft cow's milk cheese. Fat content 48 per cent

Also known as Niolo, this cheese has been produced on farms in the mountains of Corsica for many years.

Availability Specialist cheese shops and ethnic shops. Ripend for three months or occasionally eaten fresh.

Description Produced in 500 g (18 oz) squares or rounds, the cheese has a dull whitish rind and a yellow paste with scattered holes. The texture is firm and buttery, the flavour sharp, salty and tangy.

Serving Serve as part of the cheese course or as a snack in open sandwiches, garnished with rolls of smoked ham, black olives and sprigs of margoram or oregano. The whole cheese will keep in the fridge for up to two weeks. Once cut the cheese should be eaten within a week.

COTHERSTONE

Semi-soft cow's milk cheese.
Fat content not available

This is a rare cheese, made from unpasteurised milk, which is only found in or around Cotherstone in Teeside. It is usually eaten fairly young after three or four weeks, but can be matured further.

Availability Specialist cheese shops. Traditionally sold spring to first frost, but may be around for most of the year.

Description Produced in 1 kg and 2½ kg (2 lb and 5 lb) millstones, the cheeses have a soft, natural light yellow crust. The paste is also a light buttery yellow in colour. The texture is soft and open with numerous small cracks or broken holes. It has a buttery flavour with quite a sharp finish. There are both white and blue-veined varieties.

Serving Serve as part of the cheese course or honour its rarity and serve it on its own.

Cornish Yarg

COTTAGE CHEESE

Fresh cow's milk cheese. Fat content see below

Today this may either mean the traditional curd cheese made on the farm by souring the milk and draining the curds produced, or it may mean the American-style crumbly cottage cheese.

Availability Widely available. American-style cottage cheese is widely available in supermarkets. Curd cheese of varying fat content is sold in both supermarkets and farm shops.

Description American-style cottage cheese is a low fat soft cheese made from skimmed milk which has a butterfat content of about 4 per cent. It is made up of moist granules of curd and has a very mild flavour.

Curd cheese is also very mild, but it has a smooth, sometimes slightly grainy texture.

Manufacture To make American-style cottage cheese, skimmed milk is pasteurised, cooked and innoculated with a starter culture. Rennet may also be used. The curds are left to stand until they reach the required degree of acidity. This may taked four to five hours or as many as sixteen, depending on the manufacturing procedures used. The curd is then cut and scalded or cooked for two hours. This process firms the curd and kills both the starter bacteria and any spoilage bacteria which may be present. The whey is then drained off and the curd is washed, cooked and packed.

Serving Serve on its own with crisp bread and salad, or mix it with fresh herbs or fruit and include in a selection of cheeses. Eat within a day or two of purchase.

Cooking Cottage cheese is very useful for cooking because its bland taste is unassertive and mixes well with other stronger flavourings. Use it when making cooked cheesecakes and curd tarts, and in savoury cooking for quiches, flans and Italian recipes which call for Ricotta cheese.

COULOMMIERS

Soft cow's milk cheese. Fat content 45–50 per cent

Sometimes known as Brie de Coulommiers or 'Petit Brie', this small Brie-like cheese is usually factory made with pasteurised milk, although some farm produced cheese is still on sale.

Availability Specialist cheese shops or ethnic shops. Matured for one month, the best farmhouse cheese is made in the summer, autumn and winter.

Description Produced in 500 g (18 oz) flat discs, the cheese has a white, lightly bloomy rind. The paste is supple and pale ivory white in colour. The flavour is very delicate and mild; however, it becomes rather more pronounced as it matures.

Serving Serve as part of the cheese course or serve a whole cheese on its own with grapes. Once ripe the cheese will keep, well wrapped, for about three days, so eat as soon after purchase as possible.

Cooking Use as for Brie or Camembert. It makes particularly good croquettes and canapés.

CREAM CHEESE

Fresh cow's milk and cream cheese.
Fat content see below

This is the general term which covers fresh soft cheeses made with single and double cream.

Availability Widely available. Produced both in large creameries and in small scale operations.

Description The cheese has a soft buttery texture and is spreadable. It has a rich, full, often buttery flavour, sometimes with a mild tang to it.

Manufacture Cream cheese is made from cream with a fat content of 20–25 per cent: the finished cheese must contain at least 45 per cent milk fat. Double cream cheese is made from cream with a fat content of 50–55 per cent: the cheese must contain at least 65 per cent milk fat. The desired fat content can be achieved by adding separated milk or cream of a higher fat content.

The cream is usually pasteurised, homogenised and cooled before a starter is added. Rennet may also be added to single cream cheeses. The curd is left to stand before being broken, scalded, drained in linen bags, heated, salted and packed.

Serving Serve as part of a cheeseboard or on biscuits. Eat on the day of purchase or, if necessary, store in the fridge, well covered, for one day.

Cooking Cream cheese can be used to enrich sauces, soups, pâtés, mousses and stuffings. It can also be used on its own, or with flavourings of various kinds on canapés, open sandwiches and salads.

History Cream cheeses may well have been made in the past, but they have become very popular during this century. There has been a triple cream cheese, but it had a tendency to turn to butter!

CROTTINS DE CHAVIGNOL

Semi-hard goat's milk cheese. Fat content 45 per cent

Most of the younger cheeses on sale should be called Chavignol; the name Crottin belongs only to the old dry cheeses which are blackened with age. Today these young French goat's milk cheeses have achieved some fame as an appetizer when toasted on rounds of bread and served on a salad. Genuine Crottins de Chavignol are protected by an *Appellation d'Origine*.

Availability Specialist cheese shops and ethnic shops. The cheese is usually matured for two to three months and longer for the genuine Crottin which is intended for winter use. Young cheeses are eaten after two to three weeks.

Description Produced in small 50 g (2 oz) flattened drums, the cheese has a white rind which darkens through blue-grey to black with maturity. The paste is fairly firm and creamy to start with and hardens with age.

Serving Serve as part of the cheese course or on its own with crusty bread and salad.

Cooking Excellent grilled on toast. An excellent and simple first course just as a salad with mixed leaves and a good dressing.

CROWDIE

*Fresh skimmed cow's milk cheese.
Fat content not available*

This ancient cheese was sometimes known as porridge cheese because it was traditionally eaten for breakfast. It is a simple fresh cheese, curdled with rennet, that used to be made on many Scottish farms.

Availability Widely available. This cheese may be labelled Crowdie or Highland Crowdie.

Description This low fat cheese is crumbly like cottage cheese, but moister. It has a lightly acidic or lemony flavour.

Variations Claymore is Crowdie made by the Scottish Milk Marketing Board at Inverness, and may be plain, with chives or with pineapple. Crowdie and cream is made with one-third cream mixed with two thirds Crowdie. Grunddu is Crowdie and cream rolled in crushed peppercorns and oatmeal. Hramsa is Crowdie mixed with wild garlic leaves and cream.

Manufacture May be made with pasteurised or unpasteurised milk.

Serving Serve with biscuits or oatcakes. Spread on the latter, it used to be known as cruddy butter. The mixture was very popular before a ceilidh, as it was thought to limit the effects of long whisky drinking! Eat it the same day as you buy it.

CUMBERLAND FARMHOUSE

Hard cow's milk cheese. Fat content not available

The English cheeses made at Thornby Moor have a distinctive Cumbrian character.

Availability Available locally. The cheeses are matured for eight to eighteen weeks, depending on the degree of maturity required.

Description This cloth-bound cheese is made in a variety of sizes from 500 g–2.5 kg (1–5 lb) and 4.5–9 kg (10–20 lb) cylinders. The paste has a creamy texture and a smooth mellow flavour.

Variations Smoked or with herbs.

Manufacture Made with unpasteurised milk.

Serving Try it with a selection of medium-bodied cheeses – it will show off your best wine. It's also a great partner for apple pie.

Cooking Use it as you would Cheddar. It's especially nice with potatoes or spinach.

CUSHLEE

Semi-soft cow's milk cheese. Fat content 46 per cent

A new cheese from the Irish Dairy Board with quite a distinctive aroma.

Availability Widely available in Ireland only.

Description Produced in a flat wheel, 1.7 kg (3¾ lb) in weight, Cushlee has a natural rind and a smooth soft paste with a number of small holes. The flavour is fairly full and aromatic.

Serving Serve as part of the cheese course or on its own with grapes. In open sandwiches, try it with mango chutney and watercress.

Manufacture Made in large creameries from pasteurised milk.

DANABLU OR DANISH BLUE

Semi-soft cow's milk blue cheese.
Fat content 50–60 per cent

The Danes invented this blue cheese early this century as an alternative to Roquefort. Though quite unlike Roquefort, the cheese has been a huge commercial success and is sold all over the world. The name Danablu is protected by the Stresa Convention: Danish Blue is not.

Availability Widely available.

Description The cheese may be cylindrical, rectangular or square, but it is always rindless. The paste is milk white in colour with greenish-blue veins and a few irregularly distributed holes. The flavour is often very sharp and salty, though the higher fat content cheeses – sometimes called Mellow Blue or Jutland Blue – are not so strongly flavoured.

Variations Mini sizes are available and the cheese is also layered with cream cheese to produce a loaf-shaped cheese.

Manufacture Like all Danish cheese, Danablu is made from pasteurised milk. The milk is also homogenised to ensure a smooth curd. The blueing is achieved by the addition of strains of *penicillium Roquefortii* and the pressed cheese is mould-ripened and matures very rapidly.

Serving The cheese is surprisingly sliceable – though it may be a little crumbly – for a cheese that is so soft that it can be spread on to bread or biscuits. The Danes often mix it with butter or cream to make a convenient, and milder, sandwich spread.

Wrapped in foil and kept cool, Danablu will keep for eight to ten days.

Cooking Danablu can be used in cooking, but it should be used sparingly and additional salt may not be required. It is quite good in pasta sauces, mixed with cream cheese on celery sticks and in quiches with broccoli or courgettes.

DANBO

Semi-hard cow's milk cheese. Fat content 45 per cent

Danbo is a rather bland member of the Danish Samsoe family

Availability Widely available.

Description A rectangular cheese with a dry yellow rind, it is usually coated with yellow or red cheese wax. The texture is firm with a few holes and is very similar to Samsoe. The flavour is mild.

Variation It is occasionally spiced with caraway seeds.

Manufacture Made from full fat pasteurised cow's milk, in much the same way as Samsoe, it carries the Danish Cascin and Lur marks (see page 147).

Serving It may be served in thin wedges or in slices cut with a hand-held cheese slicer. Wrapped and kept cool, it can be stored for about two weeks.

Cooking This cheese tends to go slightly stringy when cooked. It toasts quite well but, because of its mild flavour, it is probably best used on cheeseboards and in cold dishes.

DEMI-SEL

Fresh soft cow's milk cheese. Fat content 40 per cent

This is a French factory made cheese, now made in all regions of France, but it dates back to 1872 when it was first produced in a creamery in the Pays de Bray in Normandy.

Availability Widely available. The cheese is ready to eat as soon as it is made.

Description Produced in small 60 g (2 oz) blocks, the cheese is white and smooth and has a mild, slightly acid flavour.

Manufacture Made from rennet-coagulated pasteurised milk.

Serving Serve as a snack, with fruit or with salad. It is useful mixed with herbs or other flavourings as a stuffing for raw vegetables or canapé toppings. Eat as soon as possible after purchase.

DERBY

Hard cow's milk cheese. Fat content 48 per cent

Derby was probably the first English cheese to be subjected to factory production because the first cheese factory opened near Derby in 1870. There is now very little from farmhouses. The cheese is probably better known in its green-coloured, sage-flavoured form than in its original version.

Availability Widely available. Derby is mostly sold when it is very immature – at about four to six weeks old. Ripened versions, at around six months old, are occasionally available.

Description In some respects, Derby resembles Cheddar, but it does not usually have the character of this great cheese. It has no rind, the texture is close and rather flaky, the paste is pale yellow in colour and the flavour is mild.

Devon Garland (page 80)

Variations Sage Derby is a mottled green colour and much more strongly flavoured with a very pungent taste of sage.

Celebrity is a Derby cheese flavoured with celery seeds.

Cromwell is layers of Derby with one layer of red Leicester.

Manufacture The production is similar to Cheddar, but the curd is treated very gently because of its softness. The very bright green marbelling of most Sage Derby is achieved by soaking the sage in chlorophyll and adding the juice to the curd.

Serving Serve as part of the cheese course or as part of a ploughman's lunch. It is traditionally eaten with soft bread rolls and sweet pickled onions.

Cooking The distinctive flavour of Sage Derby can be used – with care – to good effect in quiches, vol-au-vent fillings and dips.

History Sage Derby was popular in the past as sage was believed to aid digestion, because of this it was originally made for festive occasions only, presumably with the idea that any over-indulgence would be counteracted by the sage! Harvest Festival and Christmas were traditional times to serve the cheese. Originally the cheese was flavoured with chopped fresh herbs and spinach juice which were added to the curd: this is available again in limited quantities.

DEVON GARLAND

Semi-hard cow's milk cheese.
Fat content 50–55 per cent

Made from unpasteurised Jersey milk on a farm in Devon, this English cheese has a high butter fat content which varies according to the time of the year.

Availability Specialist cheese shops.

Description The cheese, produced in 3½ kg (7 lb) wheels with a thin, natural crust, is deliciously rich and crumbly with a layer of mixed fresh herbs in the middle.

History When cheese-maker Hilary Charnley and her husband moved to Devon, they wanted to produce a Devon cheese, but the area had no tradition of cheese-making. However, on a visit to a local farm sale, Hilary came across an old cheese mould and asked the farmer's wife what she had made on it. The answer was, a soft herb cheese. The farm was called Garland Farm and the idea for the new cheese was born.

Serving Add interest to the cheese course or try just with water biscuits. It makes an interesting ploughman's with soft wholemeal rolls, peach slices and mixed salad leaves.

DOLCELATTE

Soft blue cow's milk cheese. Fat content 50 per cent

This is a factory made cheese invented in 1967 by Egidio Galbani Melzo. Dolcelatte is really a brand name and the cheese is a toned-down version of Gorgonzola. The cheese is still made at the same factory in Pavia near Milan and has quite a following among those who find true Gorgonzola too assertive.

Availability Widely available. Ripened for forty-five days before selling.

Description Produced in 1.75–2 kg (4–4½ lb) rounds or blocks, the cheese develops a natural surface mould and is usually sold packed in foil. The paste is smooth and creamy white with blue-green veins unevenly distributed; the flavour is very good – delicate, mild and sweet.

Serving Serve as part of the cheese course or on its own with water biscuits. It is also good with celery. Wrap in foil and keep in a cool place in the fridge for up to ten days. Please note, it is very important to bring it to room temperature before serving.

Cooking Its creamy quality makes Dolcelatte a good cheese for cooking. Use it to make a creamy sauce for pasta and broccoli or polenta. It also works well in a blue cheese and celery mousse or as an unusual stuffing for chicken breasts.

DOUBLE GLOUCESTER

Hard cow's milk cheese. Fat content 48 per cent

Like Cheddar, Double Gloucester has suffered in the transition from small-scale to factory production. The distinction between Double and Single Gloucester has become blurred and the cheese is only produced, in its traditional form, on a few farms.

Availability Widely available. It is best eaten after four months. Cheeses made from summer milk, which will be on sale in the early winter, are considered to be the best.

Description Traditional cheeses are made in large flattish cylinders with a thick dry rind: some have a cloth bandage, others are waxed. The texture is close and waxy. Creamery cheeses are usually coloured with annatto, but farmhouse cheeses may be a more natural, golden colour. The flavour is deep, smooth and mellow, with an attractive piquancy which is not sharp.

Variations Flavoured versions are available as follows:

Abbeydale: with onions and chives
Cotswold: with chives and onions
County: with Blue Stilton
Huntsman: with bands of Stilton
Peppervale: with finely chopped green and red peppers
Romany: with Caerphilly and onions
Sherwood: with sweet pickles

Manufacture Full fat evening milk is mixed with morning milk. Mostly the milk is pasteurised, but there are one or two farms using unpasteurised milk. The key to the original method was that the renneting took place before the milk lost its natural heat. The main process of cheese-making takes about four hours for Double Gloucester. Traditional cheeses are brined and dipped in lard; they may be bandaged or waxed.

Serving A versatile cheese which slices easily, it shows up as well in the cheese course as it does on a ploughman's platter; or use it in snacks with fruit or raw vegetables. Store it wrapped in foil for two weeks in a cool cupboard or in the salad compartment of the fridge. Bring it to room temperature before serving. It can also be frozen if double wrapped and stored for no more than three months.

Cooking Double Gloucester is very good for all kinds of cooking. It formed the basis of the traditional stewed cheese, when sliced cheese was melted in boiling ale and egg yolks, mustard and seasoning were beaten into the mixture. The thickened mixture was served on toast, rather like Welsh rarebit. Other more modern ideas include English cheese fondue, cheese and egg ramekins and cheese hotpots.

History Gloucester cheese is mentioned by name as early as 1594. The very early full fat cheeses were made from one milking, but in time the full milk from evening and morning milking was used. The use of two full cream milkings may have given the cheese its name, but others believe it was the larger size of the cheese which distinguished it from single Gloucester. The cheese was not coloured except for the London market, where buyers thought that the richer colour indicated a richer cheese.

Gloucestershire cheeses were originally made from the milk of the Gloucestershire cattle, an ancient breed which has since disappeared. During the nineteenth century, Gloucester cheese-making gradually went into decline and, by the end of World War II, there was hardly any Gloucester cheese being made in Gloucestershire. However, the creamery at Sturminster Newton managed to find a cheese-maker who knew how to make the cheese and production has gone on ever since. *See also Single Gloucester (page 136).*

DOUX DE MONTAGNE

Semi-hard cow's milk cheese. Fat content 50 per cent

This is another recently introduced French factory made cheese.

Availability Widely available.

Description Produced in 3 kg (7 lb) slightly flattened balls, this cheese has a dark brown wax coating. The paste is springy, with numerous small holes, and the flavour is mild and buttery, though it becomes a little more fruity as it ages.

Serving Serve as part of the cheese course or in a ploughman's lunch and brighten it with walnut halves, chicory, mandarin segments; or olive bread and olivade. Mature Doux de Montagne goes well with a really fruity tea-bread.

Cooking Slice and melt over pan-fried cooking apples and serve with bacon or black pudding. Also good as a stuffing for home-made burgers, baked ham rolls or jacket potatoes with frank-furters.

DUNLOP

Hard cow's milk cheese. Fat content 48 per cent

Though Dunlop is often described as Scottish Cheddar, it has its own history. It was developed, around 1688, by a woman called Barbara Gilmour who later married a farmer called Dunlop. The couple lived in Dunlop and the cows whose milk was used to make the cheeses were Dunlop cows: this hat trick of possible origins meant the name stuck!

Availability Widely available. The cheese is mostly creamery made in blocks, with a few traditional cheeses made for shows – these are cloth bound, waxed and matured for seven to eight months.

Description Dunlop is similar to block Cheddars, but it is paler in colour, and lighter and moister in texture. It lacks the 'bite' that even block Cheddar usually has.

Variation Some round cheeses are sold under the name Arran. These are basically Dunlop cheeses made on that island and matured for three months.

Serving Try a 'Scottish' ploughman's with oat-based bread and home-made pickles. Good in sandwiches with grated carrot, chopped dates, radishes or sweet and sour gherkins.

Cooking Best in light sauces for fish and seafood.

History Dunlop was the first full cream hard cheese made in Scotland. Prior to that, hard cheeses were made from skimmed milk and were probably very hard indeed. Barbara Gilmour is reputed to have brought the recipe for Dunlop from Ireland where she had travelled to avoid religious persecution. However, the recipe does not resemble any Irish cheeses well known at that time. The new cheese had good keeping properties, travelled well and was much richer and pleasanter to eat than skimmed milk cheeses. Not surprisingly, it was popular and its production spread. However, the nineteenth century saw a lowering of standards and the introduction of factory production so, today, there is hardly a traditional producer left.

DUNSYRE BLUE

Semi-hard blue cow's milk cheese.
Fat content 52 per cent

This Scottish blue cheese is hand made from the unpasteurised milk of Ayrshire cows in Lanark-shire.

Availability Specialist cheese shops. The cheeses are usually sold after three months' maturation, though summer cheeses may be ready a little earlier.

Description This mould-ripened cheese is made in 3 kg (7 lb) cylinders. The rind is grey and thin and the texture is fairly creamy. It has quite a sharp flavour.

Variation A vegetarian-rennet version is also available.

Serving Serve as part of the cheese course or on its own with celery.

EDAM

Semi-hard cow's milk cheese. Fat content 40 per cent

Despite the fact that Edam cheese has a long history on the farms of Holland, the cheese is now only made in large cheese factories. With its red wax coating and round shape, it is probably one of the most easily recognised cheeses in the world. However, it is only the cheeses for export which get the wax coating, cheeses for home use are sold with their natural, thin yellow rind.

Edam cheese has great keeping properties, even in hot climates, and it was exported to the Dutch colonies in large quantities. It also keeps well in cold conditions. A 1956 expedition to the South Pole found a tin of raw-milk Edam cheese left behind by the Scott expedition of 1912 – the cheese was sharp, but not spoiled!

Availability Widely available. A good deal of the Edam production is sold at around six weeks old. Some is sold after three to four months and a few cheeses are aged for up to a year.

Description The cheeses are spherical and, for export, coated in bright red paraffin wax. The paste is smooth, supple and easily sliced. It has a very mild flavour when young. As Edam matures, the texture becomes firmer and drier and the flavour strengthens. Sold in a variety of sizes, including 2 kg (4½ lb) and 900 g (2 lb) balls, Edam is also available in 1.5 kg (3 lb) loaves and 14 kg (31 lb) vaccuum-packed, rindless blocks.

Variations Flavoured versions of Edam are slightly more mature than the red-waxed balls. Herb cheese is coated with green wax; cumin seed cheese with orange wax; black peppercorn cheese with mahogany wax. Mature Edam, sold from seventeen weeks onwards, is available in 2 kg (4½ lb) and 900 g (2 lb) balls and coated in black wax; and Aged Edam (approximately one year old) in 2 kg (4½ lb) balls in yellow and black wax.

Low fat versions of this typical Dutch cheese are also sold. Molbo is the Danish version of Edam.

Manufacture Edam is made from partially skimmed, pasteurised milk in computerised factories. The milk is inoculated with lactic bacteria and rennet is added. The curds are cut into small pieces and then heated. The curd is drained, transferred into moulds and pressed. Edam's spherical shape occurs because the cheese firms very quickly before the interior has had time to settle. The cheeses mature for two weeks at the cheese factory warehouse before being sent to dealers where, in accordance with government regulations, it is stored for a minimum of two more weeks. Edam destined for export is then washed, dried and sprayed or dipped in wax.

Serving In Holland, Edam is often served in thin slices cut with a continental hand-held cheese slicer. It is popular for breakfast, lunch and supper, in sandwiches and with salads. It can also be served on a cheeseboard or on its own with bread, biscuits or crispbreads.

Wrap freshly cut or opened vacuum packs in foil or cling film or put the cheese in a closed container and store in the warmest part of the fridge. Close-wrapping is important to keep the cheese moist.

Young Edam can be double-wrapped and frozen for up to three months. Grated or sliced cheese also freezes well and can be used straight from the freezer.

Cooking Edam has a relatively low fat content and is, therefore, very useful for anyone who wants to keep their calorie intake down, but still cook with cheese. It grates quite easily and can be used in virtually all culinary applications. Try adding small cubes to cocktail kebabs or slice it and use to make cheeseburgers.

History Edam cheese is named after what was once a large and thriving seaport. Today, Edam is a small country town and the cheese is produced all over the Netherlands. It is said that Edam was first exported, probably to the United Kingdom, in the eighth century. The red colour of the cheese is traditional and originated some 600 years ago when the farmers of Northern Holland agreed to distinguish the cheese by rubbing the rind with vermilion-dyed cloth. Exports of cheese continued throughout the centuries to places as far afield as the Dutch East Indies and South America. There is one story that the Uruguayans once defeated the Argentinians in a naval battle by substituting Aged Edam cheese for cannonballs!

EDILPILZKÄSE

Semi-soft blue cow's milk cheese.
Fat content 45 per cent

These blue cheeses are made in Germany and

Austria. They are marketed under various names, such as Pilzkäse or German Blue or under brand names like Bergader Blue.

Availability Specialist cheese shops and ethnic shops. This cheese is matured for about five weeks before sale when it is ready to eat.

Description Produced in either rounds or loaves, the cheeses weigh between 2–5 kg (4–11 lb), and may have thin, natural rinds which develop a white mould. They are usually wrapped in foil. The paste is pale ivory in colour with good blue veining throughout, the flavour is strong and fruity with a fuller, less salty taste than Danish Blue which it resembles.

Variation A lower fat version of Bergader Blue is on sale with a fat content half that of the normal version.

Serving The cheese slices well and can be served as part of the cheese course, with crusty bread and celery, or spread on dark or rye bread. Wrapped in foil, it will keep for two weeks in a cool place or in the fridge. Bring to room temperature well before serving.

Cooking A useful cheese for cooking, but remember the flavour of blue cheese tends to intensify on heating. Use it in salad dressings, soups, quiches and sauces.

History Bergader Blue, the invention of Basil Weixler who decided to use *penicillium Roquefortii* to make a blue cow's milk cheese, was first made in Germany in 1927. It was originally called Bayerisher Gebirgsroquefort. The French cheese-makers objected to the last part of the name, a legal battle was fought through the courts and the French won. The judgment created a generic term for the type Edilpilzkäse and Mr Weixler renamed the cheese Bergader or 'Mountain' Blue.

EMMENTHAL

Hard cow's milk cheese. Fat content 45 per cent

Another cheese with a claim to the title 'the king of cheeses', it is probably the best known Swiss cheese anywhere in the world and it has many imitators, such as Tipperary from Eire and Maasdam from Holland. Commonly known, quite simply, as 'Swiss' cheese, Emmenthal accounts for over half of Swiss cheese production. This cheese seems to grow and grow in popularity and exports of both Swiss and French Emmenthal are on the increase.

The cheese is instantly recognisable by its large round holes and huge size. It takes about 1,000 litres (220 gallons) of unpasteurised milk to make one 80 kg (176 lb) cheese.

Emmenthal, named after the valley of the river Emme in the Canton of Berne, is now made in almost all the German-speaking Cantons.

Availability Widely available. Emmenthal can be eaten after four months, but is more usually sold after five to six months. Mature cheeses are seven to eight months old and may not be exported until they are eleven months old.

Description The cheese is shaped like a huge wheel with bulging sides, measures 80–90 cm (32–36 in) in diameter, is 29 cm (11½ in) thick and has an even, medium-thick yellow rind.

The paste is pale ivory in colour and full of cherry-shaped holes, with a light sheen to them which occur naturally while the cheese is maturing. The texture is very firm, dense and grainy; the flavour fairly mild and nutty. Very young cheeses are very mild indeed, but the flavour develops as they mature.

Variations Allgäu Emmenthal is a German version of Emmenthal that has been made in the Allgäu region of Bavaria for centuries and can be very good indeed. It is sold, usually, after five to seven months' maturation.

More Emmenthal is made in France than in any other country, but it is produced largely for home use. Production was begun in the nineteenth century helped by Swiss cheese-makers, but it is now almost all factory produced in the Comte and Savoie. It is often not aged as long as the Swiss and German types.

Emmenthal look-alikes are also made in Australia and sold simply as 'Swiss'.

Manufacture Emmenthal is made with unpasteurised milk. The morning milk is mixed with the milk from the previous evening and heated. Lactic acid, proprionic (hole inducing) bacteria, and rennet are added to the milk and it coagulates within half an hour. The curds are cut in a criss-cross pattern with a cheese-harp (an instrument made of tightly strung wires) then stirred until they are the size of a grain of wheat. The process continues by heating the curds and whey and cutting and stirring until the cheese grains become harder and drier. They are removed from the vat in a large muslin bag and transferred to the cheese-press.

The next day, the cheese is salted and brined and placed on wooden boards. It remains in the cool salting cellar for ten to fourteen days. It then moves to warmer fermentation cellars where the holes start to form in the cheese. Gas collects at various points and causes the holes. The more evenly this process takes place, the more uniformly they will grow. The final ripening takes place in the cool curing cellars, where the cheese remains until it is about three months old. Then it is transferred to the wholesalers' cellars where it stays until it reaches full maturity. During the whole of the ripening process the cheeses have to be turned regularly. In the past, this had to be done by hand and the strong muscles of the cheese makers were much feared in the wrestling ring! Nowadays, machinery does the job.

Because there are so many critical factors in its manufacture, Emmenthal is considered one of the most difficult cheeses to make.

Serving Serve, as the Swiss do, thinly sliced with a hand-held continental cheese slicer at breakfast or as part of a selection of cheeses at lunch or supper time. Serve chunks with crusty bread or use in sandwiches.

Cooking Mature Emmenthal melts better and has a better flavour than the young cheese and is, therefore, the best choice for cooking. The texture also grows crisper and finer and makes it easier to grate.

Ripe Emmenthal is particularly suited to use in fondues, sauces and gratin toppings. It is used in the classic Obwalden cheese tart.

Emmenthal is extremely versatile and can be used in almost all culinary applications: try it in cheese mousses, omelettes and Croque Monsieur.

ÉPOISSES

Soft cow's milk cheese. Fat content 45 per cent

This small cheese is certainly another candidate for the top ten smelliest French cheeses. It is made in Burgundy and is sometimes macerated in burgundy marc to become the even stronger Fromage Fort. It was the favourite cheese of the character Porthos in *The Three Musketeers*.

Availability Specialist cheese shops and ethnic shops. Matured for one to three months.

Description Produced in small 500 g (1 lb) discs, the cheese has a pale brick-coloured washed rind which deepens in colour as it ripens. The paste is soft to supple, the aroma pungent and the flavour very spicy.

Variations The cheese is sometimes flavoured with black pepper, fennel or cloves.

Manufacture The cheeses are matured in humid cellars and the rind is washed with white wine or eau de vie. The best cheese is soaked in eau de vie for a further month.

Serving Serve as part of the cheese course, if you have an especially robust wine and guests who enjoy strong cheeses. Eat as soon as it is cut, it does not store well even in the fridge.

ESROM

Semi-soft cow's milk cheese.
Fat content 60 per cent and 45 per cent

Invented in Denmark in the 1930s, Esrom was said to resemble Port Salut and was for a time named Danish Port Salut. In fact, it does not really taste like Port Salut being stronger than that cheese. When many of the Danish cheeses were renamed in the fifties, the Danish authorities chose the name of a cheese traditionally made by the monks of Esrom but long since forgotten.

Availability Widely available.

Description A flattish rectangular cheese, about 1.3 kg (3 lb) in weight, with a thin, moist rind which may be coated with yellow cheese wax or wrapped in foil. The texture is supple

Époisses (page 85)

with irregularly shaped holes. The paste is creamy in colour and easy to slice. The flavour is quite rich and aromatic and seems to grow on the palate. It gains an even more spicy flavour on ageing and, for this reason, often tastes better in countries other than Denmark because it is more mature.

Variations Some cheeses are flavoured with onion, garlic, peppers or herbs. There are also larger and smaller versions.

Manufacture Made from pasteurised full fat cow's milk, the manufacture of Esrom is similar to Samsoe. However, the random holes in the cheese are achieved by pouring the curds into perforated moulds without previous pressing and before the last of the whey is drained out of the cheese vat. The cheeses are not pressed mechanically; the weight of the cheese grains themselves cause enough pressing to take place and the whey to drain off.

The cheese carries the Danish Casein and Lur marks (see page 148).

Serving An excellent breakfast cheese when cut into slices with a knife or with a continental or hand–held cheese slicer, or serve as part of the cheese course. Some Esrom enthusiasts suggest that the rind should be eaten with the cheese. This, of course, does not apply to any wax coating which may be present!

When well wrapped and kept in a cool place, the cheese will keep for up to two weeks.

Cooking The cheese goes slightly stringy on cooking, but gives a good flavour to the dish. It is very good cut into batons and used in salads.

ETORKI

Semi-hard ewe's milk cheese. Fat content 50 per cent

This French cheese is made from pure ewe's milk in the foothills of the Pyrénées.

Availability Widely available. Matured for six months before it goes on sale, the cheese is

creamery made and available all the year round.
Description Produced in small wheels, the cheese has a reddish-brown rind and a yellow paste which is firm but supple with eyes scattered throughout the paste. The flavour is fairly mild.
Serving This is nice as a mild-flavoured component of a selection, or with granary bread, tomatoes and chutney. Try in canapés with stuffed olives and grapes.
Cooking Etorki grates well and so can be used in many cooked dishes – without the 'farmyardy' flavour of some non-cow's-milk cheeses. Mix with Roquefort for a milder flavour in sauces, quiches or soups.

EVORA

*Semi-hard ewe's milk and goat's milk cheese.
Fat content 45 per cent*

This strongly flavoured cheese comes from the town of the same name in the Alentejo area of Portugal. It may be made with ewe's milk only or with a mixture of ewe's and goat's milk.
Availability Locally available in Portugal only. Matured for six to twelve months before being sold.
Description Produced in small 80–120 g (3–4 oz) discs, this cheese has a hard, dark yellow crust and a pale crumbly paste which gets harder as it gets older. The flavour is very salty and pungent.
Serving Serve on its own with wholemeal or rye bread and salad.

EXPLORATEUR

Soft cow's milk cheese. Fat content 75 per cent

This deliciously rich triple cream cheese was invented in 1958 at the time when the space rocket, *Explorer*, was in the news. The French dairy which produced it decided on a topical name.

Availability Specialist cheese shops and French delicatessens. Ripened for three weeks.
Description Produced in 275 g (9 oz) discs, the cheese has a light, downy white rind, a soft texture, an extremely creamy paste and a mild, rich flavour.
Serving Serve as part of the cheese course or with a platter of fresh fruit with a dessert wine. A whole cheese will keep for a week in a cool place, but it should be consumed as soon as it is cut, so buy a portion of the cheese on the day you want to serve it.
Cooking Use in Chicken Kiev in place of garlic butter, or for a rich sauce for guinea-fowl or poussin.

FETA

*Semi-hard sheep's or cow's milk cheese.
Fat content 40–50 per cent*

Feta cheese is so popular in Greece that the Greeks import large quantities from places like Denmark as well as manufacturing a good deal of their own. In Greece, and in Bulgaria where it is also popular, Feta cheese is made from ewe's milk or sometimes a mixture of ewe's milk and goat's milk but, in the many other countries where it is now made, pasteurised cow's milk is used. These include Denmark, Australia, Germany, Italy and the United States.
Availability Widely available. Feta cheese is usually sold while it is still quite fresh and soft, that is after fifteen to thirty days. If it is kept in brine for up to two to three months it becomes rather harder in texture.
Description Feta cheese is sold in large blocks or slices which are called *fetes* – hence the name – which vary in weight from 900 g–2 kg (2–4½ lb). The cheese has no rind and the paste is very white, quite dense but crumbles easily. There are small holes and cracks scattered throughout the paste. The flavour is very sharp and salty.
Manufacture The milk is curdled by lactic fermentation and the curds and whey are heated together. The curds are scooped into cloths or

ladelled into moulds to drain. They are then lightly pressed and turned at regular intervals. When they are firm enough, they are cut into blocks and soaked in brine for varying amounts of time.

Buying guide Outside Greece, Feta cheese is usually sold vacuum packed but it is still important to make sure that the cheese does not look too dried out. In Greece it is sold from a brine bath and this keeps the cheese moist.

Serving In Greece, Feta is eaten at all times of the day and night. It might form a healthy breakfast with plenty of crusty bread or be served at lunchtime with tomatoes and olives or crumbled over a mixed salad. It turns up at the evening meal crumbled over casseroles or used to fill filo pastry parcels or it might just be nibbled as a snack. In addition to all these applications, Feta cheese can be successfully deep fried in breadcrumbs, served on cocktail canapés or crumbled over stir-fry vegetables.

Cooking Feta is usually used as an addition after the dish has been cooked. However, Feta can be cooked in pastry or stuffings. Take care with added salt as the cheese itself is very salty. This can be tempered by soaking the cheese in a little milk or lukewarm water for a while before using.

FONTINA

Semi-hard cow's milk cheese. Fat content 45 per cent

Made from unpasteurised milk, genuine Fontina is only made in the Valle d'Aosta, in the Italian Alps near to the border with France and Switzerland.

Availability Specialist cheese shops and Italian delicatessens. Matured for around two months, the best cheeses are made in the mountain chalets between May and September. These will be on sale from July onwards.

Description Produced in various size wheels from 8–18 kg (18–40 lb), Fontina has a creamy brown rind which is thin and oily and imprinted with the seal of the local cooperative.

The paste is smooth and buttery when young,

is a pale straw colour and has a few small holes fairly evenly distributed throughout. The texture is supple and almost spreadable, but as the cheese matures the paste becomes drier. The flavour of the young cheese is nutty but delicate, and it becomes more piquant as it ages.

Variations Fontal is a Fontina-type cheese which is factory produced from pasteurised milk throughout Piedmont and Lombardy. It has fewer eyes, a slightly darker rind and the flavour is not as buttery or as interesting.

Fontina-style cheeses are produced in different countries such as Switzerland and Sweden and the United States. The latter country produces a cheese called Midget Fontina.

Manufacture Genuine Fontina is made in the chalets of the Alpine valleys during the summer and down in the small cooperative cheese factories in the winter. The cheese has to be made within two hours of milking. The curds are coagulated with rennet; after forty minutes or so the curd is turned and cut with a cheese-harp until the cheese grains are the size of wheat grains. The curds are then cooked, stirred and lifted out in cheese muslin and placed in moulds for pressing. Next the cheeses are brined and matured in underground caves or in carefully controlled cheese cellars. The cheeses are continually wiped with brine-soaked or damp cloths until they are ripe.

Serving Serve as part of the cheese course or slice or spread on to biscuits and serve with celery or grapes. Use in sandwiches.

Cooking Fontina is the traditional cheese used in the Piedmontese version of fondue, Fondula. White truffles are also included in the mix. Use it in any recipe which calls for melted cheese, and in toasted sandwiches.

FOURME D'AMBERT

Blue semi-soft cow's milk cheese.
Fat content 45 per cent

'Fourme' refers to the shape of the cheese and this one is a particularly deep drum shape. Covered by the French *Appellation d'Origine*, the cheese is made in the Auvergne on farms and in dairies from unpasteurised milk.

Availability Specialist cheese shops and French delicatessens. Ripened for about four to five months, it is best bought in the autumn and winter.

Description Produced in 2 kg (4 lb) elongated drums, the cheese has a dark brownish-grey rind with dull yellow and red moulds and is usually wrapped in foil. The texture is smooth and fairly moist with regular blue veining in the creamy white paste. The flavour is very pronounced and slightly bitter.

Variations Fourme de Forez and Fourme de Montbrison are both very similar to Fourme d'Ambert.

Manufacture The cheese is unpressed so that the blue veining can develop naturally. It is matured in extremely damp conditions.

Serving Serve on a cheeseboard or in a ploughman's lunch with celery or apples. Cut horizontally like Stilton. Fourme d'Ambert keeps well and, provided it is well wrapped, it is so moist it will not dry out. Store for up to two weeks in the warmest section of the fridge.

Cooking This cheese can be used with care in cooking. Try it with eggs baked en cocotte or in a blue cheese and broccoli flan or in a celeriac and blue cheese soup.

FRIESIAN CLOVE

Semi-hard cow's milk cheese.
Fat content 20–40 per cent

This is a very hard Dutch cheese, sometimes called Friesian Nagelkaas or 'nail cheese'; it is made from whole milk, but is sometimes mixed with skimmed milk.

Availability Locally available, in Holland only. Matured for four to thirteen weeks and sometimes longer.

Description Produced in 7–9 kg (15–20 lb) wheels, this cheese is very hard indeed. The cheeses are coated in red or yellow wax. The paste is greyish white and dry. The flavour is extremely spicy and strong, particularly in the

mature cheese. The cheese may be plain or flavoured with cloves and cumin seeds.

Serving Serve with grapes on black bread, or add, grated, to canapés.

FROMAGE FRAIS

Fresh soft cow's milk cheese. Fat content 0–60 per cent

This is the generic name given to a range of types and brands of fresh soft French cheese. Some are smooth with a texture like thick cream, others are more like cream cheese.

Availability Widely available. Soft creamy textured versions of Fromage Frais are sold in tubs and may vary in their fat content from 0–60 per cent. Other firmer, fattier types, such as Demi-Sel and Petit Suisse, are also available.

Description Fromage Frais in tubs is white in colour and very soft and smooth. The fattier products are also very white and smooth, but the texture is thicker and firmer.

Variations Fromage Blanc made from skimmed milk and used a great deal in modern French cooking.

Manufacture Fromage Frais may be made with a starter culture alone or with a starter culture and rennet. The milk is pasteurised and coagulated in the usual way.

Serving Serve on its own or mixed with herbs or other flavourings as part of the cheese course. Serve the fattier varieties with fruit. Eat as soon as possible after purchase.

Cooking Despite its creamy, almost runny texture, Fromage Frais behaves like cheese and not like cream in cooking. This means that it will melt into a sauce or soup but, if it is heated beyond a certain level, it will seize up and separate the milk proteins from the fat.

Fromage Frais is very versatile and can be used in all kinds of sweet and savoury cooking. Use in soups, dips, canapés, baked egg dishes and pasta sauces. Add to pie and flan fillings, stuffings and sauces, or to salad dressings, sweet flans, cheesecakes, cake fillings and fruit salads.

Gjetost (page 92)

FYNBO

Semi-hard cow's milk cheese. Fat content 45 per cent

Fynbo, a smaller member of the Danish Samsoe family, was first produced on the Island of Fyn, the home of Hans Andersen. The name Fynbo has limited protection and it may not be used, for a cheese from a country other than Denmark, unless it is qualified by the name of the producing nation.

Availability Widely available.

Description A flat cylindrical cheese with rounded corners and a dry, yellowish rind, it is usually coated with a yellow or red cheese wax. The texture is similar to Samsoe but with fewer, smaller holes. The flavour is mild.

Variations Mini-Fynbo which is normally 1 kg (2 lb) in size and tropical Fynbo which is drier and saltier. These cheeses have been treated for export to the tropics and are stamped 'T'.

Manufacture It is made from full fat pasteurised milk in much the same way as Samsoe. The cheeses all carry the Danish Casein and Lur marks (see page 148).

Serving It may be served in thin wedges or in slices cut with a hand-held slicer. Wrapped and kept cool, it will keep for about two weeks.

Cooking This cheese tends to go slightly stringy on cooking and toasts quite well but, because of the mild flavour, is probably best used on cheeseboards and in cold cookery.

GAMMELÖST

Semi-hard blue cow's milk cheese.
Fat content 5 per cent

Unique to Norway, this very strongly flavoured cheese is ripened by both internal and external moulds. It looks as if it has been maturing for years but in fact it is ready quite quickly. However, it does have long keeping qualities and the Vikings are said to have made it in summer for use on winter voyages.

Availability Specialist cheese shops. Matured for one month.

Description Produced in small 3 kg (7 lb) drums, the cheese has a thick, greenish-brown crust which is soft when young but hardens with keeping. It has a slightly sticky sheen to it. The paste is soft and brownish yellow in colour with blue veins. The flavour is very potent, aromatic and quite unique.

Manufacture Gammelöst is made from skimmed milk which is coagulated with lactic acid bacteria.

Serving Best served in thin slices with rye bread or pumpernickel. Mix it with soft cheese for tasty canapés or use to stuff celery sticks. Wrap it in foil and store in a cool place or in the fridge for a month or so.

GAPERON

Semi-soft cow's milk cheese. Fat content 35 per cent

This French cheese, moulded in a small pudding basin shape, used to be hung from the kitchen rafters or at the kitchen windows to ripen and, it was said, a farmer's wealth could be gauged by counting them. They were also considered to be a good guide to the size of dowry a man might expect if he married the daughter of the house.

Availability Specialist cheese shops. Usually ripened for two months, the cheese could be eaten fresh at three to four weeks.

Description Produced in a 300–500 g (10–18 oz) shape like a ball which has been flattened on one side, the cheese has a greyish-white rind and an ivory-coloured paste which is soft and supple. The cheeses are flavoured with garlic, and occasionally with peppercorns, and the taste is quite strong.

Serving Serve on a cheeseboard or as a snack with sliced onions, celery and chunky-cut bread. The whole cheese can be stored in a cool place for up to a month. The cut cheese should be double wrapped in foil and eaten fairly quickly.

Cooking Gaperon gives instant flavour to dips, canapés and savoury biscuits. Dice mixed with walnuts as a good salad topping. Slice and melt over burgers, chops or steaks.

Gaperon

GJETOST

Semi-hard cow's and goat's milk whey cheese.
Fat content not available

This distinctively flavoured deep-orange coloured cheese is not, strictly speaking, a cheese at all. It is made from the whey left after the production of a normal cheese. Very popular in Scandinavia, it is now finding its way to other countries as well. The curiously sweet, fudge-like flavour is an acquired taste.

Availability Widely available. This cheese is ready to eat as soon as it is produced.

Description Produced in squares or brick-shaped blocks, the cheese has no rind. It is a rich orange or pale tan colour and has a texture that can be hard or soft, depending on the moisture content. The flavour is sweetish and quite unmistakable.

Variations Made just from goat's milk, Ekte Gjetost has a sharper taste than that made from the mixture of milks.

Manufacture The whey is reduced and thickened by boiling and the milk sugar or lactose caramelises. This can take up to twelve hours. The whey is then drained off and, sometimes, a little cream or extra goat's milk is added before the mixture is poured into moulds. The cheese is not ripened, but sold at once.

Serving In Norway, Gjetost is eaten for breakfast; shaved into very thin slices with a continental cheese slicer and served on rye bread, crispbread or biscuits. At Christmastime, it is served with a special spiced fruit cake. It also makes a good topping for open sandwiches with grapefruit segments or can be eaten with fruit. Wrap well in foil and store in the fridge for two or three weeks.

Cooking Gjetost melts well and can be toasted or melted into sauces. Its sweetish flavour makes it possible to experiment with unusual desserts, such as sweet fondue with cubes of fruit and grapes as dippers or in a hot ice cream sundae sauce. More traditionally, it can be grated into salads or used on cocktail kebabs with pineapple or kiwi fruit.

History Gjetost was first made over a hundred years ago in the small summer farms of the Gudbrandsdalen Valley. In those days, the cheese was probably made only from goat's milk as the cow's milk was used for butter making.

GORGONZOLA

Blue semi-soft cow's milk cheese.
Fat content 48 per cent

One of Italy's oldest cheeses, Gorgonzola is made in Lombardy. Farmhouse Gorgonzola has largely been overtaken by factory made cheese, but the standard is still very high. It was originally a *stracchino* cheese – one made from the winter milk – now it is produced all the year round.

Availability Widely available. The cheeses are matured for fifty to sixty days and then wrapped in foil and sold. However, it can be kept for a further three to six months. The best cheese is usually sold between November and March.

Description The drum-shaped cheeses vary in size from 6–13 kg (13–29 lb) and have a thick, coarse, reddish-grey crust which has some powdery patches. The paste is white to straw-yellow with a good spread of greenish-blue veins. The texture is quite creamy; moister than Stilton and more buttery than Roquefort. The flavour is lightly piquant and spicy. The aroma is probably stronger than the flavour which is tempered by the delicacy of the creamy paste base.

Variations Dolcelatte.

Gorgonzola Bianco or Pannerone is a rare unveined version of the cheese. It is ripened at a higher temperature and produced slightly differently.

Torta San Gaudenzio is one of several trade names for a Gorgonzola and Mascarpone layered cheese gâteau. The mixture is a traditional one from the Trieste area where is may be flavoured with anchovy and caraway seeds. This version is named for the patron saint of Novara in Piedmont where it was first made. The cockerel, which is the crest of Novara, is also used as the symbol for the cheese (it has nothing to do with the Chianti Classico cockerel!).

Gondola is the Danish version of Gorgonzola.
Manufacture Pasteurised milk from both the evening and morning milkings is inoculated with *penicillium glaucum,* a different variety of *penicillium* to that used in Roquefort and Stilton. At one time the two sets of curds were coagulated separately, cut into pieces (about the size of walnuts) and packed into boxes with the warm morning curds in the centre and the cool evening curds on the outside.

Today the factory process is more likely to mix the two lots of milk at the beginning of the cheese-making process. The cheeses are brined and turned and matured for about two to three months which is considerably less time that the old 'two paste' method required. The cheeses are pierced with needles to help the veining process.
Buying guide Contrary to popular belief, Gorgonzola should not be very pungent and smelly, so avoid cheeses which have a sour, strong and bitter smell or which are brownish or hard. The cheese should have a sharp, clean smell.
Serving Serve as part of the cheese course or on its own with bread or biscuits. It makes an excellent ploughman's lunch with radicchio and black olives. Wrap whole cheeses or large pieces in a damp cloth and keep in a cool cellar. Failing that, store well wrapped in foil and an enclosing polythene bag in the door of the fridge for up to three weeks.
Cooking In Milan, Gorgonzola is used to stuff pears or to make a sauce for pasta flavoured with sage and garlic. Try it in soups, potato casseroles, vegetable sauces and stuffings. Mixed with spinach it makes an unusual filling for pancakes or use the mixture in mousses or soufflés.
History Though it is no longer made there, Gorgonzola probably originated in the town of Gorgonzola in Lombardy over a thousand years ago. However, there are numerous well embroidered and overlapping stories surrounding its history. One such story relates that back in the eighth or ninth century, during the trek back to the villages of the Po Valley from the Alpine meadows, a herdsman found that he had

forgotten to bring along the usual equipment for making cheese. So he left the milk to curdle in a container. The next day he still didn't have the correct equipment and so left the morning milk to curdle, too. He then layered the two curds and the double cheese paste was born.

Another story suggests that our herdsman made his cheese in the usual way and decided to pay his innkeeper's bill with one of his cheeses. The innkeeper accepted, but didn't have much call for cheese and so left it in his cellar. Here it matured and gained its natural mould formation. The innkeeper got rid of it by selling portions to his customers and they so enjoyed it that they demanded more and more!

During the twentieth century, production of Gorgonzola transferred to the factories and its fame began to spread. It is now made by a consortium of producers who mark their cheeses with the letters CG.

GOUDA

Semi-hard cow's milk cheese. Fat content 48 per cent

This is Holland's most important cheese and, as such, it has many imitators. It is protected by a law which states that any cheese produced outside Holland and given its name must carry the stamp of its country of origin, such as German Gouda. Other similar cheeses simply have another name: Redesdale, Langskaill, Broodkaas are respectively English, Scottish and Belgian versions of the cheese.

Today, Holland is one of the world's largest exporters of cheese, sending out more than 400,000 tons every year – much of it Gouda.

Most of the cheese is factory produced from pasteurised milk, but there are still quite a large number of farms in Zuid-Holland and Utrecht which make the cheese from unpasteurised milk in the traditional way.
Availability Widely available. Young Gouda is sold between four and eight weeks old. Other cheeses are sold at twelve weeks and mature Gouda is matured for a minimum of seventeen weeks. Also available are one-year-old Gouda

and aged Gouda. The latter has matured for at least eighteen months to two years.

Farmhouse cheeses are stamped with the word *Boeren*.

Description Produced in traditional flat wheels, either 1 kg (2 lb) or 4 kg (9 lb) in weight, the cheeses have a thin yellow rind and a coating of yellow paraffin wax. There are also vacuum-packed blocks.

The young cheese has a firm straw-coloured paste, scattered with small irregular holes or a few larger holes. The flavour is mild and creamy. As the cheese matures, the paste becomes drier, more crumbly and darkens in colour. The flavour matures to give a much more robust taste and a spicy aroma.

Variations Flavoured versions of the young cheese are available as follows:

Herb-flavoured cheeses with a green wax coating
Black peppercorn-flavoured cheese with a mahogany wax coating
Roasted cumin-seed-flavoured cheese with an orange or yellow wax coating
Gouda with garlic pieces
Gouda with dill and cream

Mature and aged Goudas are available in black or black and yellow wax.

Manufacture Traditional cheeses are made from unpasteurised whole milk. It takes 12.5 litres (17 pints) of milk to make 1 kg (2 lb) of cheese. The milk is warmed and coagulated with rennet. The curds are left to stand for some time before they are cut to separate them from the whey.

After the whey has been drained off, warm water is added and the mass cut and heated quite gently. The curds are transferred to moulds which are lined with muslin so that the cheese can be turned during pressing – this takes six hours. The cheese is then ready to go into a brine bath for several days. The cheeses are dried out on wooden shelves and matured.

Serving Serve as the Dutch do, cut into thin slices with a hand-held continental cheese slicer, for breakfast, lunch or supper or as part of the cheese course. Gouda is also very good served in the traditional way with brown bread and potatoes.

Wrap well and store in the warmest part of the fridge, or double-wrap and freeze for up to three months. Gouda can also be frozen either sliced or grated for easy use.

Cooking Gouda is a very versatile cheese for cooking. It melts well when it is young, and grates well when it is older. Try using the cumin-flavoured cheese to make cheese straws or cocktail biscuits and mature Gouda in cheese truffles, sauces, Dutch cheese soup and Dutch fondue or *kaasdoop*.

GRANA PADANO

Extra hard cow's milk cheese. Fat content 32 per cent

Grana is the generic name for all Italian finely grained, extra hard cheeses made from partly skimmed milk. They originated in the Po Valley and Parmigianio Reggiano or Parmesan is probably the best known. About one quarter of all Italy's cow's milk production goes into making Grana cheeses.

Grana Padano is made throughout the Po Valley and, in fact, twenty-seven provinces have the right to make it. It is almost interchangeable with Parmesan in the kitchen, but it is not as widely exported as Parmesan.

Availability Specialist cheese shops and Italian delicatessens. Grana is ripened for at least a year before it is sold and many cheeses are matured for longer. They may be sold when between one and two years old.

Description Produced in 24-40 kg (53-88 lb) drums, the cheese has a thin, shiny old gold or black rind. The paste has a granular texture with tiny holes evenly scattered through it. The grain of the cheese is radial, the texture hard and crumbly – though younger cheeses can be sliced – and the colour is a mellow yellow which darkens with age. The flavour is excellent, mellow and intense, strengthening as it ages.

Variations Bagozzo is made in the Cattaro where the locals claim it has aphrodisiac qualities and refer to it as the 'cheese of love'.

Grana Lodigiano, produced in and around Milan, is a little more crumbly than some of the other Grana cheeses and, when cut, the paste takes on a slightly greenish colour. It may be matured for up to five years and is very expensive.

Emiliano is similar and produced in Emilia Romagna. It has a dark almost black rind.

Manufacture The evening milk is mixed with the morning milk and some of the cream is skimmed off. Starter cultures and rennet are added and the production proceeds in a manner basically similar to that for Parmesan . However Grana Padano is made all the year round. The cheese is cooked, pressed and ripened. The cheese is marked with the words Grana Padana and numbers which identify the cheese-maker. The same words are also imprinted on the rind of the cheese with a hot branding iron.

Buying guide Buy in chunks rather than ready grated to enjoy the full flavour.

Serving Young cheese is very good sliced and served with wholemeal bread, biscuits or simply on its own.

Do not store in the fridge unless you have to. It is best stored covered with a cloth or greaseproof paper in a cool cupboard or cellar. If you do have to use the fridge, double wrap the cheese. Small chunks can be stored in the freezer but the cheese will loose a little of its flavour.

Cooking Grana cheeses are traditionally grated and used as a condiment. In Italy there is hardly a first course that does not have cheese sprinkled over it.

For soups, pasta, polenta and oven-baked dishes it is a must. These cheeses do not form elastic threads when they are cooked, they just melt. It can be used in toppings and stuffings.

Unusual ideas include the use of grated Grana in breadcrumb coatings for deep fried food, cheese-flavoured pastry, crèpes or scones.

Grana Padano

GRAVIERA

Hard cow's milk cheese. Fat content 50 per cent

After Feta cheese this is Greece's most popular cheese.

Availability widely available, in Greece only.

Description Produced in cylinders varying in weight from 20–40 kg (44–88 lb), the cheese has a thin, pale orange rind. The paste is pale yellow and full of small holes. The flavour is creamy and mild.

Variation There is a Cretan version made with ewe's milk which is said to be particularly good.

Serving In Greece Graviera is served as an hors d'oeuvre, at the end of the meal and as a side dish to the main course. Slice it with a hand-held cheese slicer and use it in open and closed sandwiches and cut in cubes for cocktail kebabs.

GRUYÈRE

Hard cow's milk cheese. Fat content 45 per cent

There is no doubt that Gruyère originated in Switzerland, but its use is so widespread in France that the French might be forgiven for thinking it is their own. Indeed, a great deal of it is produced in France but genuine Swiss Gruyère has the word Switzerland stamped all over the rind.

Swiss Gruyère is made from the milk of Fribourg and Simmenthal cows which graze the Alpine pastures. This gives the cheese a quality and fragrance which is often missing from the many imitations. It takes more than 400 litres (88 gallons) of milk to produce one cheese.

Availability Widely available. Gruyère is ready to eat after three months, but much of it is matured for four to six months and it may be matured for up to ten months.

Description Gruyère is produced in huge 25 kg (55 lb) wheels with slightly bulging sides. The rind is fairly thick and reddish brown in colour. The paste is firm, but slightly softer than Emmenthal and feels smoother on the tongue.

The paste has a small number of tiny holes scattered through it. The flavour is rich and creamy with a definite and distinctive flavour of its own – stronger than Emmenthal and sweeter. Gruyère also has an unmistakable nutty aroma. See also: Beaufort and Comte.

Manufacture Gruyère is made in much the same way as Emmenthal, but the curds are less finely cut and are scalded at a higher temperature. The cheeses are pressed harder and longer and ripened at a lower temperature.

Unlike Emmenthal, Gruyère is kept damp with salt water. This leads to the formation of a grease layer which intensifies the maturing process and has an effect on the flavour.

Buying guide The very best cheeses have a slight dampness in the eyes or holes and fine slits just beneath the rind.

Serving Though Gruyère is not often served on its own or even with the cheese course, except in Switzerland and perhaps in France, it does have much to offer on its own. Serve it with figs and grapes. It is also good in sandwiches, on its own or with tomato or watercress. Toasted sandwiches made with Gruyère are excellent.

Store in a cool place, wrapped in a cloth dampened with salt water or double wrap in foil and store in the fridge.

Cooking Gruyère is a particularly good cheese for cooking. It hardly draws any threads and melts easily. It gives an excellent flavour to the dishes in which it is used. When used as a topping, it gives a beautiful, even, not too dry crust and when used with breadcrumbs makes a moist crunchy topping.

Classic dishes using Gruyère include French sauce mornay and Swiss and Belgian fondue, Swiss sale, chicken and veal Cordon Bleu and spinach gratin. Try also in cheese biscuits, gougères, cheese soufflés, soups, potato dishes and seafood gratins. Uncooked cubes or sticks of Gruyère make good cocktail kebabs or a chef's salad ingredient.

History Dating back to the twelfth century, Gruyère was once made only around the village of Gruyère in Fribourg. It is still made in this area in small village dairies and in the adjacent French-speaking part of Switzerland. The cheeses were exported to France very early in their history.

GUBBEEN

Semi-soft cow's milk cheese. Fat content not available

This is an Irish washed-rind cheese of the Port Salut type first produced in 1980. It is made and named after a farm in west Cork. The name means 'little gob'!

Availability Specialist cheese shops. Cured on the farm for three weeks by daily washing and turning, the cheese may be further matured by the cheese-monger. The cheeses vary somewhat with the season: in the spring the cheese has a soft, creamy texture, in winter the paste is firmer.

Description Produced in flat rounds 500 g and 1.5 kg (1 lb and 3 lb) in weight, the cheese has a pinkish-orange washed rind and a pale yellow, almost spongy, semi-soft paste. The flavour is quite definite, but clean and smooth.

Variations Gubbeen Oak is smoked over oak wood and matured for several months. It is a semi-hard cheese with a wax coating.

Serving Serve a whole cheese on its own or in a selection of cheeses. Young cheeses complement a good claret; mature ones a Châteauneuf du Pâpe.

Cooking Slice and serve on a bed of leaves with a good olive oil dressing made with fresh herbs and wholegrain mustard, or, best of all, grated orange rind. Gubbeen is excellent deep-fried in breadcrumbs or as a stuffing for veal Cordon Bleu.

HALOUMI

Semi-hard ewe's, goat's or cow's milk cheese. Fat content 40 per cent

Originating in Cyprus, this cheese is now copied in a number of countries. It was originally made from ewe's or goat's milk but the copies, like the Danish version, are made with pasteurised cow's milk.

Availability Widely available. Some Haloumi is designated for immediate consumption and some is matured for up to a month. The cow's milk version needs to be eaten before that time as it has a tendency to become very hard indeed.

Description Like Feta, this cheese is produced in block form and stored in whey brine. Cow's milk versions are usually vacuum packed. The cheese has no rind and a fairly springy texture which cannot be crumbled but slices well. The texture hardens as it matures. The flavour is less salty than Feta.

Manufacture Haloumi cheese is made in a similar way to Feta cheese . In Cyprus, the cheese is dipped in hot water, kneaded together with chopped mint, rolled out and cut into bars.

Serving Serve sliced with crusty bread and salads or with a good Greek olive oil and fresh herbs. In Cyprus it is dipped into hot water and pulled out in strips to eat as a snack.

Cooking Haloumi is used a good deal in Cypriot cooking. It may be grated on top of moussaka, sliced into salads or used in stuffings. Very often it is sliced and fried in oil. This dish may be served for breakfast with fried eggs and tomatoes or as part of a meze of appetisers. The texture of Haloumi cheese is such that it does not melt on frying, rather the protein seizes up and becomes hard. Care should be taken not to overcook it or it will be very tough. This characteristic means that sticks of cheese can be tossed into stir-fry vegetables – a useful addition for meat eaters and vegetarians. It can also be grilled and served with olive oil.

HAVARTI

Semi-soft cow's milk cheese. Fat content 50 per cent

This widely exported Danish cheese is named after the farm owned by Hanne Nielsen, an intrepid nineteenth century cheese-maker who, despite her lack of languages, travelled widely to increase her knowledge of cheese-making.

Havarti was her greatest success and it is now factory made.

Availability Widely available. Sold after three months or longer.

Description This large loaf-shaped or cylindrical cheese with a thin, moist rind may be coated with yellow cheese wax. It is a supple creamy cheese with numerous small irregular holes in the paste. It is pale yellow in colour and sliceable. The flavour is fairly full after three months and becomes much stronger and more pungent with age.

Variations Higher fat versions (60 per cent) are available. Some of the cheeses are flavoured with caraway seeds or with herbs.

Manufacture Made from pasteurised full fat cow's milk, the manufacture of Havarti is similar to that of Samsoe, but the random holes are achieved by pouring the curds into erforated moulds without previous pressing and before the last of the whey is drained out of the cheese vat. The cheeses are not pressed mechanically, but the weight of the cheese grains themselves causes mild pressing and the whey to drain off. These cheeses carry the Danish Casein and Lur marks (see page 148).

Serving Makes a good dessert and breakfast cheese thinly sliced with a hand-held cheese slicer. Wrapped and kept in a cool place it will keep for ten to twelve days.

Cooking This cheese tends to go slightly stringy on cooking. As such, it can replace Mozzarella on pizzas or toasted sandwiches.

HERRGÄRDSOST

Hard cow's milk cheese. Fat content 30-45 per cent

The name means manor or home cheese in Swedish. It was once produced on small farms in west Gotland but is now factory made all over Sweden.

Availability Specialist cheese shops and ethnic shops. The cheese is matured for four to seven months.

Description The cheese, made in 12–18 kg (26½–40 lb) cylinders, has a thin rind which is usually covered in yellow paraffin wax. The texture is rather like, but slightly softer than, Gruyère and the paste has a scattering of smaller holes. The flavour is mild and nutty. If the cheese is left to mature to its full term the eyes become moist and the flavour strengthens a little.

Variations There are lower fat versions which have an even milder flavour.

Manufacture The cheese is basically made like the Swiss cheeses and is cooked, and pressed.

Serving This is a popular breakfast cheese in Sweden and is served cut into thin slices with a hand-held cheese slicer. It can also be used on open and closed sandwiches and in salads.

Cooking This cheese melts well and can be used in most recipes calling for cheese.

HERVÉ

Soft cow's milk cheese. Fat content 45 per cent

This is the generic name for a group of cheeses originating in the small town of Hervé in east Belgium. It is often produced on farms and transferred to the dairies to mature.

Availability Specialist cheese shops. Two to three months' maturation.

Description Produced in bar or cube shapes, Hervé has a washed rind and matures from the outside. The rind is reddish gold in colour and the paste is soft, smooth and creamy. The flavour varies from sweet to spicy, depending on its age and the aroma can be quite strong.

Variations See Remoudou and Romadur.

Serving Serve on its own with coffee or port or as part of the cheese course. With well flavoured salad leaves, it's good with a caraway vinaigrette.

History Cheese-making in Hervé dates back several hundred years and documents as early as 1230 refer to it. The smell of the cheeses must have been considerable since an English writer, visiting Hervé after the Battle of Waterloo, described the air of Hervé as 'oppressive with the scent of cheese'.

HUSHÄLLSOST

Semi-hard cow's milk cheese.
Fat content 30-45 per cent

One of Sweden's everyday foods (the name means household cheese), it is one of Sweden's oldest types of cheese. It is now factory made and sold under a variety of brand names.

Availability widely available, in Sweden only. Sold after one to three months.

Description Produced in 3 kg (7 lb) drums, the cheese is usually covered in paraffin wax or vacuum packed. The paste is straw coloured and may have scattered or regular holes. The flavour is very mild.

Variations Spiced with cumin and cloves.

Serving Served in Sweden for breakfast, but it could be used in sandwiches and salads or in open sandwiches in curls with gravadlax.

IDIAZABAL

Hard ewe's milk cheese. Fat content 53 per cent

Produced in the Basque area of northern Spain, the cheese has a number of different names, including Entzia, Urbia, Gorbea and Orduna. It is covered by the Spanish denomination of origin laws.

Availability widely available in Spain. Matured for not less than two months.

Description Produced in flattish drums or cylinders varying in weight from 500 g to 3 kg (1–7 lb), Idiazabal has a hard, pale yellow rind if unsmoked and a dark brown rind if smoked. The paste is creamy white and fairly compact, with irregular, small holes scattered through it. The flavour is delicately smoky.

Manufacture Smoked cheeses are smoked in natural wood smoke from beech or hawthorn trees.

Serving Serve as part of the cheese course or on its own with biscuits and celery.

ILHA

Hard cow's milk cheese. Fat content 45 per cent

This cheese is made in the Portuguese Azores and is known as Island cheese. It is a little like strong farmhouse Cheddar and was almost certainly introduced to the islands by English immigrants.

Availability Widely available, in Portugal only. This cheese is ripened for one to three months and may be kept for a further three months.

Description Produced in 5–10 kg (11–22 lb) drums, the cheese has a hard natural crust. The paste is firm and pale yellow in colour. The flavour varies from mild to mellow and nutty depending on its age.

Manufacture Both pasteurised and unpasteurised versions are available.

Serving Serve as part of the cheese course, a ploughman's lunch or on open or closed sandwiches. Double wrap in foil and store in a cool place or in the fridge for up to ten days.

Cooking This cheese can be used for almost any culinary application.

IRATY BREBIS PYRÉNÉES

Semi-hard ewe's milk cheese.
Fat content 45–50 per cent

This is an original Basque cheese produced for many hundreds of years in the Pyrénées mountains near to the French border with Spain. It is now widely imitated, but the farm-produced and small dairy cheeses made in the area are protected by the French *Appellation d'Origine* laws.

Availability Specialist cheese shops and french delicatessens. Matured for three months, the best cheese is on sale in the late summer and autumn.

Description Produced in 4–5 kg (9–11 lb) cylinders, the cheese has a smooth orange-yellow to brown rind and a supple texture. The paste is golden in colour and has small holes and openings scattered irregularly through it. The flavour is very definitive, but mellow.

Serving Serve as part of the cheese course or on its own with water biscuits and celery. As a snack, try it with poppyseed rolls, orange slices and watercress.

Cooking Grate, mix with mild chutney and grill.

JARLSBERG

Semi-hard cow's milk cheese. Fat content 45 per cent

Based on an old Norwegian cheese, Jarlsberg was reintroduced in the 1950s and has proved to be exceedingly popular both in Norway and elsewhere. Quite a large proportion of the total production is exported to the United States. It is difficult to decide whether this is a hard or a semi-hard cheese, but is has an elastic texture which is rather more like Gouda than Emmenthal, which it also resembles.

Availability Widely available. Sold after six months' maturation.

Description Produced in large round wheels weighing 10 kg (22 lb), the cheese has a natural yellow rind. The paste is golden yellow, smooth and elastic with quite a large number of eyes or holes of various shapes and sizes. The flavour is mellow and slightly sweet and nutty with a more buttery taste than Emmenthal.

Variation The cheese is also made in large vacuum-packed blocks with no rind.

Manufacture Made from pasteurised milk, Jarlsberg is factory made in large dairies.

Serving Serve sliced with a mixture of other sliced cheeses or use in sandwiches. Cut into cubes and serve on sticks with grapes, or simply serve on its own with celery and biscuits. Closely wrap in foil and store in a cool place or in the fridge for three weeks. Double-wrap and freeze for a month or so. Alternatively, slice or grate and freeze it. Siced cheese can be stored between double layers of baking parchment or freezer film for easy use.

Cooking Jarlsberg melts well and is very useful in cooking. It can be used in most of the recipes which call for Emmenthal, Gruyère or even Cheddar. Try it in golden toppings for fish pies, flans and lasagnes or melt into soups and sauces. Thinly sliced it can be rolled round leeks, asparagus or ham for unusual canapés.

KASERI

Hard ewe's milk cheese. Fat content 40 per cent

This is a spun curd or *pasta filata* cheese similar to Provolone. It was developed in Greece to use up unsuccessful cheeses before the advent of scientific cheese making. The curds are baked at high temperatures, kneaded, then shaped or moulded into large cheeses.

Availability widely available, in Greece only.

Description Produced in 9 kg (20 lb) cylinders, the cheese has a soft white crust, a firm texture with a scattering of very small holes and quite a sharp and distinct flavour.

Serving Serve with crusty bread, or biscuits, as part of a cheeseboard or on a ploughman's platter. It can also be used for sandwiches and snacks.

Cooking Kaseri goes quite stringy on cooking; the Greeks prefer it to Mozzarella on their pizzas and it certainly has more flavour. I have also seen it dipped in flour and fried in olive oil.

KEFALOTIRI

Hard ewe's milk cheese. Fat content 40 per cent

This is a strongly flavoured Greek cheese. Much of the Kefalotiri sold outside Greece is actually a toned-down version, which is something like a cross between Kefalotiri and Graviera with the emphasis on the latter. This version is more properly called Kefalograviera: it is made from cow's milk.

Availability Widely available. Kefalotiri is matured for two to three months before being sold.

Description Produced in 6–8 kg (13–17½ lb)

drums, the cheese has a thin, hard crust which varies in colour from white to yellow. The paste, too, varies in colour in much the same way. It is very hard and has numerous small holes and irregular splitting. The flavour is salty and strongly sharp.

Serving Kefalotiri is hard to slice and is more usually grated for cooking. However curls can be served as appetisers with aperitifs. This cheese lasts well. Wrap and store it in a cool place or in the fridge. Grate, and freeze for two to three months and use straight from the freezer.

Cooking This cheese gives a good flavour to pasta dishes and is widely used in this way in Greece. It can also be used on moussaka or in stuffed vegetable toppings.

History The cheese is called 'head cheese' in Greek because its shape is supposed to resemble a Greek hat!

KERNHEM

Soft cow's milk cheese. Fat content 60 per cent

Kernhem is a relative newcomer to the Dutch dairy scene. The story goes that during wet winters, before the days of improved storage conditions, some Edam cheeses collapsed in the warehouses. The result was a strong-smelling flat disc with an orange-coloured rind flora of bacteria. The farmers found that they liked eating this accidental cheese and so the Dutch Dairy Institute experimented to produce a similar cheese which would be more stable.

Availability Specialist cheese shops. Ripe after four weeks.

Description Produced in flat 1.6 kg (3½ lb) discs, the cheese is creamy-white to yellow in colour and sticks to the knife on cutting; in fact, it is almost spreadable. The flavour is mild.

Manufacture Made from pasteurised milk with added cream, the cheese is lightly pressed and stored in a cool, damp cellar for thirty days.

Serving Serve as part of the cheese course or on its own with biscuits and grapes. For a light lunch try it with crusty bread, potato salad, sliced tomatoes and apples.

KOPANISTI

Soft blue ewe's or cow's milk cheese. Fat content not available

This is a blue-veined cheese from the Aegean islands; the best is said to come from the island of Mykonos.

Availability Locally available, in Greece only. Kopanisti is ripened for one to two months before being sold.

Description The cheeses are ripened in pots until they are soft and creamy, but still firm. The greenish-blue veining spreads throughout the paste. The flavour is quite strong and sharp.

Manufacture The cheeses may be made from either ewe's or cow's milk. The curds are cut into large pieces and drained in cloths. They are then moulded by hand into balls which are left to dry. After a time the surface of the cheese grows a mould; this mould is worked back into the cheese with a little salt. The cheese is left to mature for a further period.

Serving Serve as part of the cheese course, or take on a picnic with Greek bread, olives and tomatoes.

KRYDDOST

Semi-hard cow's milk cheese. Fat content 45 per cent

This is the best of a group of Swedish cheeses called Sveciaost. These are factory produced to suit all tastes, from very mild to very strong. Kryddost falls into the second category.

Availability Specialist cheese shops. Matured for up to a year.

Description Produced in 12–16 kg (26½–35 lb) squat drum or tall cylinder shapes the cheese has a smooth surface. The paste, full of small holes, is flavoured with cumin seeds and cloves to give a strong spicy aroma and flavour.

Serving Kryddost was traditionally served with crayfish at special parties given in the late summer and early August. It can be served in the cheese course, also cut into small chunks and served with aperitifs.

LABNA

Fresh ewe's, goat's or cow's milk cheese.
Fat content varies

This fresh, soft, acid-curd cheese made originally in the Lebanon, is quite easy to make at home by hanging set yoghurt in a muslin bag to drain.

Availability Widely available. Labna is ready to eat as soon as it is made.

Description Sold in tubs or pots, Labna is white and creamy rather like very thick cream although it may be quite low in fat. The fat content will depend upon the milk from which it is made. Labna has quite a sharply acidic flavour.

Serving In the Lebanon, Labna is served as a dip for pitta-style bread and crudités with a little olive oil poured over it and a garnish of parsley.

LAGUIOLE

Semi-hard cow's milk cheese.
Fat content 45–50 per cent

Produced in mountain *burons* or chalets in the Aubrac Mountains of Aquitaine or in small creameries, this French cheese is also known as Fourme de Laguiole or Laguiole Aubrac. It is protected by the French *Appellation d'Origine* laws and is much sought after by connoisseurs.

Availability Locally available, in France only. Most cheeses are ripened for three months, but a few of the best cheeses are kept for up to six months.

Description Produced in 50 kg (110 lb) drums, the cheese has a fairly delicate, grey rind which darkens and cracks as it matures beyond three months. The paste is a light straw colour, the texture firm but supple and the aroma penetrating. The flavour is full, fruity and tangy.

Serving Serve as part of the cheese course or on its own with crusty bread, or in sandwiches.

Cooking The cheese is grated and used in local dishes, like Aligiot. This is made by stirring the cheese together with garlic, butter, cream and puréed potatoes.

LANARK BLUE

Semi-soft blue ewe's milk cheese.
Fat content 52 per cent

This Scottish blue milk cheese is handmade from unpasteurised ewe's milk in Lanarkshire.

Availability Specialist cheese shops. The cheeses are usually sold after three months' maturation, though summer cheeses may be ready a little earlier.

Description This mould-ripened cheese, made in 3 kg (7 lb) cylinders, has a soft, white, creamy, almost spreadable paste with blue veins running through it and the flavour is excellent with a smoky or peaty after-taste.

Serving Serve as part of the cheese course or show it off by serving on its own with biscuits and celery, or a sweet wine like Sauternes. It can also be used to make interesting snacks with wholemeal rolls, fresh apricots and dandelion leaves.

LANCASHIRE

Semi-hard cow's milk cheese. Fat content 48 per cent

Sadly, the real tangy taste of Lancashire cheese – as I remember it from farmhouse cheese bought on Ashton market – has been submerged by the mild creamery type on sale in most supermarkets. In those days, it was sold both when it was quite young, after a couple of months or so, and when it had been matured to a deeper, richer flavour.

Availability Widely available. Mainly creamery cheese with a handful of traditional producers in the Preston area. The creamery cheese has been labelled 'New Lancashire' because it has so few of the characteristics of the traditional cheese. It is also called 'single acid' Lancashire. Traditional cheeses are sold after three months, but some are kept for up to six months.

Description Real farmhouse Lancashire cheese is made in an 18 kg (40 lb) cylindrical shape, with rounded edges, which may be cloth-bound or, more usually, waxed. The texture is very soft, creamy and quite difficult to slice because it is so crumbly. The paste is very white in colour, and the taste is slightly salty with a rich tang that matures to a strong, mellow, flavour.

Variation Smaller sizes are available particularly at festive seasons. Sage Lancashire has chopped sage added to the curd. This results in a very strongly flavoured cheese.

Manufacture Unpasteurised milk is used for traditional farmhouse Lancashire. The curd made on one day is drained, milled and salted and mixed with half the next day's curd. Both curds are milled again, placed in moulds and pressed for twenty-four hours. They are then bandaged, waxed and ripened for two to three months or more.

Serving Serve as part of the cheese course or in a ploughman's lunch. It is so soft that it can almost be spread straight on to bread or biscuits.

Wrapped in foil, the cheese will keep for a week in a cool place. Lancashire housewives used to place it under a large bowl in a larder.

Cooking Lancashire is one of the very best cheeses for melting and Lancastrians will argue that theirs was the original toasted cheese. For this reason it used to be known as 'the Leigh toaster' after a small Lancashire town near Manchester where the cheese was made.

Grated Lancashire cheese mixes very well with grated carrot and chopped pickles, to make a Lancashire cheese log. Alternatively, try it in cheese and onion pie; cheese soup; cheese, date and walnut spread and in cauliflower au gratin.

History Lancashire cheese was first made by farmers in the Fylde, between the rivers Ribble and Lune. They only had a little milk to spare each day and, as a result, developed a technique for making a large cheese out of more than one day's milking. The curds were often kept for as long as a week or two to encourage the required degree of acidity. This gave the cheese its really white colour. Made in farmhouse kitchens, it was ripened on shelves near the kitchen range.

Farmhouse Lancashire continued to be made in large quantities up to World War II. Today, there are only a handful of farmhouse producers left.

LANGRES

Soft cow's milk cheese. Fat content 45 per cent

A small French cheese from the Champagne area which, at its best, can match any of the classic cheeses of France and is one of my favourites. It has a pungent aroma and is one of France's smelly cheeses.

Availability Specialist cheese shops and French delicatessens. Matured for three months before sale.

Description Produced in tiny 200 g (7 oz) drums, the cheese has a sunken top and a yellow-orange washed rind. The paste is supple with a strong smell and a tangy flavour.

Serving Serve as part of the cheese course or on its own with a red Burgundy or Beaujolais Cru, such as Côte de Beaune or Moulin à Vent.

LEICESTER

Hard cow's milk cheese. Fat content 48 per cent

This cheese is sometimes known as Red Leicester because of its colour, but there is only one type.

Availability Widely available. Leicester is a quick-maturing cheese and may be sold between ten and twelve weeks, but it can also be matured for six months for a more mature flavour.

Description Traditionally made like a flat cartwheel, the cheese has a thin, dry rind. The cheese is close-textured, but more like Cheshire than Cheddar, being more flaky, and the colour is a rich red due to the addition of annatto. The flavour is fairly mild, but with a piquant lemony quality which distinguishes it from other English country cheeses.

Variations Beauchamp, with herbs and garlic. Cromwell, which is one layer of Leicester with two of Derby. Walgrove, with walnuts.

Manufacture Made from whole milk, the evening milk is mixed with the morning milk in the same way as Cheddar. The curds are finely cut and double milled before salting, then packed into moulds and pressed

Serving Another versatile cheese, equally at

home on the cheeseboard or in a ploughman's lunch, it goes very well with watercress and spring onions.

Cooking Red Leicester is really good melting cheese which makes it useful for cheese on toast, Welsh rarebit and cheese sauces. It gives a good colour, too, to all these dishes. In its native Leicestershire, the cheese is sprinkled over milk-soaked bread and baked in the oven with mustard.

History Leicester was first made by farmers to use up surplus milk left over from the production of Stilton. It came mainly from the Hinckley, Lutterworth and Market Bosworth areas around the city of Leicester.

The cheese has always been brightly coloured. The farmers used to use carrot or beetroot juice, but have now switched to the flavourless annatto. Its bright colour made the cheese very popular in Victorian times. Then, with the change to factory production, Leicester nearly died out, but there has been a revival in recent years and there are a number of farmhouses making traditional cheeses.

LEIDEN

Hard cow's milk cheese.
Fat content 20 to 30/40 per cent

This strong-tasting Dutch cheese, flavoured with cumin seeds, is quite a difficult cheese to make. Some is made on farms in the area of Leiden and some in the various cheese factories.

Availability Specialist cheese shops. Matured for at least three months, farmhouse cheeses are marked by a pair of crossed keys – the arms of the city of Leiden – carry the words *Boeren Leidse* and must have a fat content of 30 per cent, but it is usually more like 34–35 per cent. Factory cheese must have a fat content of 40 per cent or, more rarely, 20 per cent (a special low-fat version).

Description Produced in flat wheels weighing about 16 kg (35 lb), factory-made Lciden cheese has a natural yellow rind. Farmhouse cheeses

have their rinds rubbed with annatto to give a deep orange-red colour.

The texture of the paste is fairly crumbly, though factory-made cheeses are rather less dry than farmhouse cheeses. The paste is greyish-yellow in colour and full of cumin seeds. The flavour is quite strong and salty and gets even stronger as it matures and absorbs more of the flavour of the seeds.

Variations It is sometimes made with caraway seeds or with cloves. Nokkelöst is the Norwegian version of Leiden – *nokkel* means keys. There may be some connection, but it is not known for certain.

Manufacture In the past, the fresh whole milk was set to cool in vats standing in cold water so that the cream rose to the surface. Now, it is cooled in cheese-making tubs. After twelve or twenty-four hours the cream is skimmed off. Some of the skimmed milk is heated and used to curdle the remainder. Then buttermilk and rennet are added. The curd is stirred and cut and the whey is drawn off. Part of the curd is mixed with cumin and kneaded. The spiced curd is set between two layers of plain curd and pressed twice. Ripening takes place in damp, cool cellars.

Serving Serve as part of the cheese course or cut in small chunks and serve with aperitifs.

Cooking Leiden can be used in cooking and it goes particularly well with cabbage.

History The traditional method of kneading the cumin seeds into the curds has been abandoned in the light of modern ideas on hygiene. The cheese-maker used to wash his feet in the whey and then tread the seeds into the curd. Today, feet have been replaced by machines.

The old method of rubbing vegetable dye and beestings into the rind of the cheese has also been dropped and annatto is used instead. The beestings are thick with protein and soon develop unpleasant smells. It is said that naughty children were punished on Dutch farms by being required to sit by the beestings bucket.

LIEDERKRANZ

Soft cow's milk cheese. Fat content 50 per cent

This American cheese was invented by a German immigrant to the United States in 1892. The cheese is rather like a milder and less pungent form of Limburg. It is now made by the Borden Cheese Company in Ohio, from pasteurised milk.

Availability Widely available, in the United States only.

Description Produced in 110 g (4 oz) blocks, the cheese has a soft, pale-brown washed rind and a golden yellow paste which is quite rich and velvety. The flavour is good, tangy but not too strong.

Variation Old Heidelberg is a very similar cheese produced in Lena, Illinois.

Serving Serve as part of the cheese board or as a snack with fruit or salad. Slice and serve in open or closed sandwiches. Double-wrap in foil and store in a cool place or in the fridge for three or four days.

Cooking Liederkranz can be melted into soups and sauces or used in cheese croquettes, flans or soufflés.

History Invented by Emil Frey in Monroe, New York, the cheese was an attempt to duplicate a popular cheese called Bismarck Schlosskäse which was being imported into the United States at the time. The new cheese turned out to be a mild form of Limburg. Emil Frey decided to name it 'wreath of song' after a singing group to which he belonged.

LIMBURG

Soft cow's milk cheese. Fat content 20–50 per cent

Originally made in the monasteries near Limburg in Belgium, this cheese was adopted and indeed largely taken over by the German cheese-makers of Allgau in the nineteenth century. To all intents and purposes, it is now regarded as a German cheese.

Availability Widely available. The cheese is ripened for two to three months before it is ready to eat.

Description Produced in small loaves or squares, varying from 200 g–1 kg (7 oz–2 lb), the cheese has a washed rind and is surface-ripened. The skin is reddish brown in colour and slightly moist, the paste a rich and creamy yellow.

Limburg's outstanding characteristic is its strong aroma which appeals to some tastes, but not to others. However, its smell is very much stronger than its flavour.

Variations Frühstückskäse or 'breakfast cheese' is a smaller version of Limburg which is eaten, as the name suggests, at breakfast. It is made from whole or partly skimmed milk and eaten either fresh, or after a short ripening period, as it just begins to develop a coating of coryne bacteria.

Hauskäse and Klosterkäse are both small cheeses similar to Limburg.

Limburg is available in various grades according to its fat content. The lower the fat content the firmer and less creamy the cheese.

The cheese is made in many countries other than Germany, including Austria, France, Israel, Switzerland and the United States and each one has its own characteristics – and smell!

Manufacture Made from pasteurised milk, injected with starter bacteria and coagulated with rennet, Limburg is made in much the same way as other soft cheeses of this type. After moulding and draining, the cheeses are salted in brine and then washed at intervals with coryne bacteria. After a month or so, the yellow rind starts to develop on the surface, becoming darker and firmer as ripening proceeds. The surface is also rubbed with salt to bring out the distinctive pungent flavour.

Buying guide Avoid cheeses which have a runny paste or where the rind is slimy. These cheeses are well past their best.

Serving Serve at the cheese course or on its own with an interesting bread and a robust red wine like a Rioja Reserva or a Portugese Garrafeira. Eat as soon as possible after purchase. Once Limburg has reached its peak, it falls off quickly.

Limburg (page 105)

LIPTAUER

Soft ewe's milk cheese. Fat content 50 per cent

This is the German or Austrian name for Hungarian Liptoi cheese. The cheese was first made at Liptov in the Tatra mountains but is now made all over Hungary.

Availability Widely available, in Hungary and Austria. The cheese is ready to eat almost as soon as it is prepared. It is exported to Austria and, in small quantities, to Germany, but not much finds its way further than this.

Description The cheese is sold in small blocks as a soft creamy spread, usually mixed with ingredients such as salt, paprika, caraway seeds, onion or mustard. The flavour is quite strong.

Serving Serve on its own with bread or biscuits, or use as a canapé topping or as a stuffing for raw vegetables. Similar cheese spreads can be made at home by mixing fresh soft cheese, such as a dryish curd cheese with paprika and other flavourings.

LIVAROT

Soft cow's milk cheese. Fat content 40–45 per cent

Jokingly called the 'Livarot-colonel' or 'five-striper' in reference to the strips of sedge running round the sides, this cheese is one of France's finest. It comes from the Pays d'Auge in Normandy and is protected by the French *Appellation d'Origine* laws.

Availability Specialist cheese shops and French delicatessens. Matured for three months.

Description Produced in small 300–500 g (10 oz) discs, the cheese has a glossy, oily, brown, washed rind with a soft but springy golden paste. The smell is extremely pungent and the flavour strong and tangy.

Manufacture Livarot used to be a farmhouse cheese, but increasingly creameries are taking over its production. The cheese is made from a mixture of unpasteurised, skimmed, evening milk mixed with the full-cream morning milk. The curds are roughly chopped, gathered in muslin and set in wooden moulds. The cheeses are ripened in a warm, humid cheese store. During this time the cheeses are washed regularly with brine. Some cheese stores are specially built with hay mixed into the mortar to encourage humidity and the bacteria which ripen the cheese.

The cheeses tend to dip in the centre and to prevent this they are bound round the outside with fine narrow strips of sedge, cattail leaf or paper.

Buying guide Genuine Livarot cheese will carry the name Pays d'Auge on the label. Avoid cheeses which are very dry, very sticky or sunk in the centre. They should smell strong but not unpleasant.

Serving Serve at the end of the meal. In Normandy, Calvados is drunk with it. It is best to buy and eat this cheese at once. It will keep in the fridge for a day or two but, even well wrapped, is likely to remind you it is there!

LLANBOIDY

Hard cow's milk cheese. Fat content not available

This traditional hand made and pressed Welsh cheese is made on a farm in Whitland, Dyfed, from the unpasteurised milk of Red Poll cows. Vegetable rennet is used.

Availability Specialist cheese shops. Sold after eight to ten weeks' maturation.

Description Produced in 4.5 kg (10 lb) wheels, this cheese has a natural rind. The cheeses are well matured and have a good flavour.

Variation Flavoured with Welsh laverbread.

Serving Serve on a cheese board or alone with Welsh *bara brith*. Good with crusty rolls, sweetcorn relish and cucumber.

Cooking It grates well for most cheese dishes. Try it on leeks *au gratin* or jacket potatoes.

LLANGLOFFAN

Hard cow's milk cheese. Fat content 60 per cent

A Welsh cheese made in Pembrokeshire from the unpasteurised milk of Jersey cows.

Availability Available in one or two supermarkets and specialist cheese shops. Sold after four to five weeks, the cheese may be matured for a little longer if desired.

Description Produced in various sizes from 2–13.5 kg (4–30 lb), the cheese has a natural rind. The texture is firm and fairly creamy, the flavour is mild.

Variation Red with chives and garlic.

Serving Serve as part of the cheese course or on its own with biscuits and celery or a crisp apple. For canapés, dip cubes in mild paprika, celery salt or ground cumin, dusting off any excess.

LYMESWOLD

Soft cow's milk cheese with added cream. Fat content 70 per cent

This is a brand name invented in 1982 for an English soft blue cheese with a white mould rind. It is made in Cheshire in a fully automated factory. The brand name Lymeswold is now also used to market an English Brie and a very mild, soft, white cheese.

Availability Widely available. The cheeses are sold after twelve to fourteen days' ripening.

Description Made in 1.2 kg (2½ lb) wheels, the cheese has a soft white mould rind. The paste is creamy white with blue veining which increases somewhat with maturity. It is firm with a mild, delicate flavour when young; as it ripens, the texture softens and a slightly fuller flavour develops.

Variations English Country Brie is a clean, mild-flavoured Brie-style cheese which develops a slightly maturer flavour with age. Creamy White is a very mild almost tasteless cheese, with a firmish not very creamy paste, and a white mould.

Manufacture Blue Lymeswold is made from full-fat pasteurised milk with added cream. It is made in a continuous automatic coagulator. A starter culture and a strain of *penicillium Roquefortii* are added to the milk. Rennet is added as the curds reach the correct acidity levels. The curd takes about three hours to move from one end of the coagulator to the other – 27 metres (30 yards). During this time, it is cut and drained. The curd is filled into block moulds which continue along the conveyor belt to the cheese room for an overnight stay and then into the brining room. Before entering the cheese room, the cheeses are automatically turned in their block moulds to remove all the whey. The next two weeks are spent in the ripening room. After two days here, the cheeses are pierced with ninety-two holes to help promote blueing.

Serving Serve on a cheeseboard or as part of a ploughman's lunch with French bread. Young cheeses are good diced and threaded with prawns and red pepper onto cocktail sticks.

Cooking The mild flavour and creamy texture of Lymeswold blends well into sauces for vegetables like broccoli or for pasta. It can also be used very successfully in soups, quiches and flans. Mature cheeses are good deep-fried in breadcrumbs.

Cheese made from unpasteurised milk is not sold until it has matured for at least two months.

Description Produced in small, slightly bulging, irregular-to-squarish cylinders, weighing between 1–4 kg (2–9 lb), the cheese has a compact, slightly greasy rind which is pale yellow with a white bloom. The rind deepens and darkens in colour as the cheese ages. The paste is ivory-yellow and slightly chalky, it hardens and deepens in colour as it ages and has small irregular holes throughout. The flavour and smell are distinctive with an almost fruity touch.

Manufacture The best Mahón cheeses are made by hand with untreated milk. The curds are gathered in linen or cotton cloth. The cloth is shaped by a peg holding together the four corners and placed on a table where each cheese is individually pressed by hand. It is then transferred to a press for ten to fourteen hours. A design called a *mamella* is etched in the upper surface of the cheese by the folds of the cloth. The cheese is then brined and coated in olive oil.

Serving Serve as part of the cheese course or sliced with other cheeses or on its own in open and closed sandwiches, or cubed with aperitifs or sherry. In Minorca, I have seen it sliced and eaten sprinkled with olive oil, pepper and tarragon.

MAHÓN

Semi-hard cow's milk cheese.
Fat content 38–45 per cent

This is a traditional cheese from the island of Minorca in the Balearic Islands. It is made from the milk of Friesian cattle and ewe's milk can be added to a maximum of 5 per cent. However, this traditional practice is slowly dying out. The cheese is protected by the Spanish Denomination of Origin laws.

Availability Specialist cheese shops and Spanish delicatessens. Mahón cheese, made from pasteurised milk, is ready to eat within ten days, but may be ripened for two, five or ten months.

MALAGA

Soft goat's milk cheese. Fat content 58 per cent

Made in and around Malaga in southern Spain, this cheese is typical of several goat's cheeses made in Andalucia and Extremadura.

Availability Available locally, in Spain only. Matured for five days before sale.

Description Produced in a 2 kg (4½ lb) cylinder, this cheese has a pale rind, which usually shows an impression of the mould, and a thick white paste with a mild, creamy, slightly goaty flavour.

Serving Eat at once and serve on its own with bread or as part of the cheese course.

MANCHEGO

Hard ewe's milk cheese. Fat content 50 per cent

This is probably Spain's best-known cheese. It is named after the province where it is made – La Mancha, home of Don Quixote. It is covered by the Spanish Denomination of Origin laws.

Availability Specialist cheese shops and Spanish delicatessens. Most cheeses are matured for a minimum of two months when they are sold as *curado*. Cheeses matured for three months are *viejo* and those which are matured in olive oil for at least a year are called *en aceite*.

Description Produced in squat drums about 2–5 kg (4½–11 lb) in weight, the cheese has a hard, pale yellow rind which retains the elaborate patterns of the cheese press. During the ripening period the surface becomes covered with a greenish-black mould which is sometimes rubbed off before the cheese is sold and the surface is then rubbed with olive oil.

The paste is firm and compact and varies from ivory to pale gold in colour, dotted with small eyes. The flavour is excellent, strong and slightly tangy.

Variations Copies of this cheese are made in Belgium and Italy.

Manufacture Most Manchego is made from pasteurised milk in creameries these days, but there are a few farms still making the cheese in the traditional way. The milk is coagulated with rennet and left to stand for an hour or so. The curd is cut a number of times to form tiny grains. It is then stirred and heated before being placed in cylindrical moulds. These moulds have a distinctive plaited pattern on the sides and a floral pattern on the top and bottom and these patterns are transferred to the cheese when it is pressed. The cheese is then salted or brined, or both, and left to mature. The best cheeses are said to be made in the region of Ciudad Réal.

Serving Serve as part of the cheese course, sliced in sandwiches or in a ploughman's lunch. The Spanish sometimes serve it as a dessert with quince preserves.

Cooking The mature cheese grates well and can be used in cooked dishes. The Spanish sometimes cube it and fry it in olive oil. They also use it in tiny fish and cheese croquettes served as *tapas*. Try it in olive oil with shallots and in vegetable timbales.

MARIBO

Semi-hard cow's milk cheese. Fat content 45 per cent

This Danish cheese is named after the town on the island of Lolland.

Availability Widely available, in Denmark only. Sold after about four months' ripening.

Description A cylindrical cheese with a dry yellow rind normally coated in yellow cheese wax. The texture is firm with numerous irregular small holes – a little firmer and drier than Samsoe – and slices easily. The paste is yellowish white in colour. The flavour is slightly acid and fairly full.

Variation A large rectangular rindless cheese matured in vacuum plastic packaging.

Manufacture Made from full-fat pasteurised cow's milk. The manufacture of Maribo is similar to that of Samsoe, but the random holes on this cheese are achieved by pouring the curds into perforated moulds without previous pressing and before the last of the whey is drained out of the cheese vat. The cheeses are not pressed mechanically, but the weight of the cheese grains themselves causes mild pressing to take place and the whey to drain off. The cheeses carry the Danish Casein and Lur marks (see page 148).

Serving Makes a good dessert or breakfast cheese thinly sliced with a hand-held cheese slicer. Wrapped and kept in a cool place it will keep for about ten days.

MAROILLES

Soft cow's milk cheese. Fat content 45–50 per cent

This ancient French cheese was invented in the tenth century at the Abbey of Maroilles in Flanders. In those days it was known as

Maroilles (page 109)

Craquegnon. It is well flavoured and pungent and is one of France's smellier cheeses. Today it is known as *vieux paunt* or 'old stinker'! The cheese is protected by the French *Appellation d'Origine* laws.

Availability Specialist cheese shops and French delicatessens. Maroilles is matured for four months and the best cheeses are on sale in the autumn and winter months.

Description Produced in 200–800 g (7–28 oz) squares, the cheese has a reddish moist rind and a pale yellow paste. The texture is smooth and supple, the smell strong and the flavour tangy but subtle.

Variations Dauphin is similar to Maroilles but is flavoured with tarragon and pepper or, sometimes, with cloves and parsley. It is matured for two to three months according to its size. Gris de Lille is a type of Maroilles which is ripened for much longer and is really very pungent indeed. It may also be called Vieux Lille, Maroilles Gris or Paunt Macere.

Manufacture The method for making Maroilles seems quite simple, but a good deal of skill goes into producing a first class cheese. The unpasteurised milk is set with rennet and left to coagulate for about four hours. The curd is then drained in perforated boxes. The cheeses are turned and salted and cured in humid cellars.

Serving Serve as part of the cheese course or on its own with biscuits or fruit. Once ripe Maroilles should be eaten within two or three days. Store in a cool place during that time.

MASCARPONE

Fresh cow's cream cheese. Fat content 90 per cent

In some ways Mascarpone is more like clotted cream than cheese, it is extremely rich and, before the days of refrigeration, could only be made during the winter months. Now, of course, it is sold all the year round.

Availability Widely available. Mascarpone is ready to eat as soon as it is made.

Description Sold in small tubs or in muslin bags, Mascarpone is soft, thick and very creamy indeed. It has a delicate, sweet flavour.

Manufacture Mascarpone is made from cream, skimmed or centrifuged from whole milk. It is heated over water and stirred. Citric or tartaric acid is added to stimulate mild lactic fermentation. Small lumps of curd grow and are drained in muslin for twenty-four hours. The Mascarpone is then whipped or beaten.

Serving In Italy, Mascarpone is served in much the same way as whipped double cream: with fruit, in cakes or whipped with brandy. Speciality tarts or gâteaux are made by layering Mascarpone with fresh basil or nuts, or it may be flavoured with chocolate, liqueurs or cinnamon. Savoury tarts are made by layering it with Provolone or Gorgonzola. Mix with prawns or other ingredients for salads or stuff inside ham or prosciutto or use in tomatoes or avocados.

Mascarpone is quite perishable and should be eaten as soon after purchase as possible.

Cooking Mascarpone can also be used in savoury cooking. Try using it as a base for pasta sauces or layer it between sliced potatoes and bake. Try it in quiche recipes instead of cream.

MENDIP

Semi-hard goat's milk cheese.
Fat content not available

This unusual English goat's cheese has quite a soft, almost spongy texture and the paste has a number of small holes.

Availability Specialist cheese shops. Best during the summer and early autumn because the cheeses are made from spring milk. The cheese takes five or six months to mature fully, but may be sold after two or three months.

Description The cheeses are made in plastic colanders which give the cheese a squat oval shape and the rind a kind of basket-shape pattern, rather resembling Pecorino. The cheeses weigh around 2–2.5 kg (4–6 lb) and have a natural, brownish-yellow rind. The paste is pale primrose yellow in colour and is quite creamy when young. The flavour is fairly mild.

Variation Small, very fresh goat's cheeses are also sold under this name.

Milleens

Serving Serve on a cheese board with other goat's cheese and a fairly robust red wine such as Fitou or Côte du Rhône. Slice and serve as a snack with cold meat, smoked ham or salami.

Cooking Melt into soups and sauces or cut into strips and use in salads, with cucumber, chicory, hard-boiled eggs and mayonnaise.

Buying guide Avoid cheeses which are cracked or those with wrinkled rinds – both indicate poor storage.

MESOST

Semi-hard cow's milk whey cheese.
Fat content 10–20 per cent

This is a whey cheese which is extremely popular in Sweden.

Availability Mesost is ready for sale immediately.

Description Sold in foil-wrapped blocks or boxes, Mesost is a pale tan colour. It has a dense paste and a distinctively bitter-sweet flavour.

Variation Some Mesost is mixed with cream and sold in a spreadable version.

Manufacture The whey is now usually mixed with a little whole milk, cream or buttermilk and heated to precipitate the proteins. The mixture is boiled until the liquid reduces and the solids condense to a sticky brown mass produced by the caramelisation of the milk sugar, or lactose. This substance is then pressed into moulds and cooled before cutting and packing.

Serving Serve sliced with other Scandinavian cheeses or use on open sandwiches or canapés with fruit, olives or salad ingredients.

Cooking Mesost melts easily and can be used in sauces for both sweet and savoury foods.

MILLEENS

Soft cow's milk cheese. Fat content not available

This is a washed-rind, surface-ripening cheese made in the west of Ireland, near Cork. It has been a success since its first appearance in 1980.

Availability Specialist cheese shops. Now available all the year round, Milleens is matured on the farm for ten days. Some shops sell it straight away, others mature the cheese for another two or three weeks.

Description Produced in small 228 g (8 oz) or larger 1.5 kg (3 lb) sizes, Milleens is a round, flat cheese with a pale yellow, washed rind and a soft paste. The flavour is very good and strengthens with maturity. The cheese is packed into a strong wooden box to enable it to travel both by post and by refrigerated transport.

Manufacture Made from unpasteurised milk.

Serving Serve the young cheese with a good Beaujolais or the mature cheese with a Hermitage. Slice and serve on open sandwiches with peach slices and mustard and cress or serve an Irish 'ploughman's' with soda bread, whole-grain mustard pickle and crunchy apples, all washed down with Guinness.

Cooking Slice and serve on a salad with asparagus spears and a little rolled Parma ham. Coat in egg and breadcrumbs and deep-fry or melt into a cornflour roux to make a Belgian fondue.

MONSIEUR FROMAGE

Soft cow's milk cheese. Fat content 50 per cent

This is a small French double cream cheese made by small local dairies in Normandy. The name is not a brand name as you might suppose, but is actually the rather appropriate name of the man who invented the cheese.

Availability Specialist cheese shops and French delicatessens. Matured for six weeks the best cheeses are on sale in the summer and autumn.

Description Produced in small 150 g (5 oz) rounds, the cheese has a thick bloomy rind which becomes spotted with red as it matures. The paste is firm but velvety, the smell quite definite and the flavour very fruity.

Serving Serve at the cheese course or on its own with grapes or other fruit, and a good white Burgundy. As a snack, have it with toasted cashew nuts, Cos lettuce and cherry tomatoes.

MONTENEBRO

Soft goat's milk cheese. Fat content not available

This Spanish cheese is also known as Valle de Tietar.
Availability Widely available, in Spain only. Matured for one to fifteen days.
Description Shaped like a long cylinder, Montenebro has a thin rind with a greyish-white bloom. The paste is firm, with occasional small holes, compact and white in colour. The flavour is quite strongly 'goaty'.
Serving Serve as part of the cheese course or on its own with biscuits.

MONTEREY JACK

Semi-hard cow's milk cheese. Fat content 50 per cent

This cheeese was first made in Monterey, California, in the 1840s. It is distantly related to Cheddar but is now quite distinct. There are two varieties: High Moisture Jack and Dry Jack.
Availability Widely available, in the United States only. High Moisture Jack is matured for three to four weeks. Dry Jack is matured for six to nine weeks.
Description High Moisture Jack is produced in various shapes and sizes and may be vacuum-packed or waxed. The texture is firm and easy to slice, the flavour pleasantly buttery but rather bland.

Dry Jack is usually lower in fat and hard. It is made in a variety of shapes and sizes and is often oiled black. The flavour is much more tangy than High Moisture Jack.
Serving Serve as part of the cheese course or in sandwiches and snacks. Use Dry Jack in cooking.

MOORLANDS

Soft goat's milk cheese. Fat content not available

Moorlands is both the name of a soft goat's milk

cheese and a brand name. The company is one of the largest manufacturers of goat's milk cheese and operates from a creamery in north Stafford-shire. All the milk is pasteurised.
Availability Specialist cheese shops. Plain cheeses are sold fresh; Blackwood (see below) after two weeks' maturation.
Description Mild cheeses weighing 100 g (4 oz) or 1 kg (2 lb) are available plain or with the addition of garlic, mixed herbs or chives.
Variation Blackwood is a blue mould-ripened cheese with a creamy white paste produced in 1 kg (2 lb) wheels.
Serving Serve as part of a selection or with salads.

MORBIER

Semi-hard cow's milk cheese. Fat content 45 per cent

At first glance this French cheese from the Jura looks as if it has a band of mould running through the middle but, in fact, it is ash or charcoal. These cheeses are made in mountain chalets on lower slopes during the winter months.
Availability Specialist cheese shops. Matured for two to three months, the best cheeses are on sale in the spring.
Description Produced in 6–8 kg (13–18 lb) flattish cylinders, the cheese has a greyish-brown rind. The paste, with tiny holes scattered throughout, is pale ivory and has a blue band of ash running through the centre. The texture is firm, but with some degree of suppleness; the flavour is quite mellow and a little like Gruyère.
Manufacture The cheese was originally made partly from the morning milk and partly from the evening milk which were coagulated separately. The curds from the morning milk were covered with a protective layer of charcoal or ash until the evening curds were ready. Nowadays the cheese is made in one and after an initial pre-pressing the cheese is cut in two and the charcoal dust is added. The two halves are rejoined and pressed. It is matured in humid cellars where it is constantly washed with brine.

Morbier (page 113)

Serving Serve as part of the cheese course or slice and serve for breakfast as they do in the Jura. It is also good with crusty bread or on sandwiches.

MOZZARELLA

Semi-soft cow's or buffalo's milk cheese.
Fat content 45 per cent

Traditionally made in southern Italy with buffalo milk, this cheese is now made all over the world from pasteurised cow's milk. The result is, I feel, an extremely boring cheese which is used to give an expected stringiness to the ubiquitous pizza.

Availability Widely available. Real buffalo milk Mozzarella is still made in small quantities but it is difficult to find. It is made mainly in the winter and spring when the buffalo milk is more plentiful. A version of cow's milk Mozzarella is available almost everywhere. Mozzarella ripens after only a few days and is ready to sell very soon after manufacture.

Description Italian Mozzarella is produced in small, almost oval-shaped, balls and it is stored in bowls or bags of whey. Most non-Italian Mozzarella is produced in small rectangular blocks for retail sale and large blocks for catering.

Mozzarella is white in colour with a very thin shiny skin. The texture of the very young cheese is quite elastic and supple but, as it ripens more, it becomes rather softer. Buffalo milk Mozzarella is softer and less rubbery than the cow's milk version and has a more definite aroma and flavour.

Variations Mozzarella Affumicata is a smoked version. *Fior di Latte* is the official designation for Mozzarella made with cow's milk. It means 'the cream of the milk' though no cream is added. Many countries such as the United Kingdom, United States, Denmark and Australia make their own version.

Manufacture Mozzarella is a spun-curd or *pasta filata* cheese. It is traditionally made from the milk of water buffalos and now may be mixed with cow's milk. In factory made

Mozzarella

Mozzarella, cow's milk alone is used. A starter and rennet are added to coagulate the milk and the curds are cut into fairly small pieces and allowed to settle. The curd is then lifted out of the whey and kneaded in hot water until it forms a smooth shiny mass. Small pieces are cut off and shaped into individual cheeses. It is this process that gives the cheese its name as the Italian word for the cutting up process is *mozzare*. The cheeses are then brined and sold.

Buying guide Look out for genuine buffalo milk Mozzarella but, failing that, stick to Italian Mozzarella. If you are buying the cheese in little bags make sure that there is still some whey in the bag with the cheese.

Serving Mozzarella is not suitable for serving with the cheese course nor is it usually worth serving on its own. In Italy the uncooked cheese is sliced and eaten with olive oil and fresh herbs or in a tricolore salad with avocado and tomatoes. Other salad ideas include sliced oranges and olives, sliced kiwi fruit and mint or sliced sharon fruit and hazelnut oil.

Ideally it should be used as soon after purchase as possible, but it can be stored in its bag in the fridge. If you have bought a loose one from an Italian grocer, moisten it with fresh milk before placing it in the fridge.

Cooking On cooking Mozzarella becomes extremely stringy and it is *the* cheese to use with pizza. It is also classic as Mozzarella in carrozza. Here the cheese is placed in a sandwich, dipped in egg and milk and fried. Supplì, or rice balls stuffed with cheese, and Italian Mozzarella bread also use this cheese.

MUNAJUUSTO

Soft cow's milk cheese. Fat content 40 per cent

The name means 'egg cheese' in Finnish and eggs are used in its rather unusual manufacture. The cheeses are made both on farms in the south and west of Finland and in factories. The latter are sold under various brand names like Ilves.

Availability Widely available, in Finland only. Sold when it is still very young.

Description Produced in 1 kg (2 lb) cylinders, the egg gives the paste a deep golden colour. The texture is firm, but soft.

Manufacture One or two eggs are added to about six litres (10 pints) of milk and the mixture is then coagulated by heating. The whey is drained off and the curds are pressed into wicker baskets.

Serving Serve with salads and rye bread. Eat as soon as possible after purchase. The fresh cheese can be toasted in front of an open fire or under a grill. It will then keep for a few days longer.

MYCELLA

Semi-soft cow's milk blue cheese.
Fat content 50 per cent

A Danish cheese, Mycella takes its name from the mould, *mycelium,* which produces its blue-green veins. This mould is also used for Gorgonzola, and Mycella was once known as Danish Gorgonzola.

Availability Widely available.

Description A deep cylindrical cheese with a thin, pale yellowish-brown rind. The paste, with some irregularly distributed holes, is yellowish white with greenish-blue veins. The flavour is aromatic, but fairly mild.

Manufacture Unlike Danablu, Mycella uses the mould *mycelium.*

Serving Serve as part of the cheese course or as part of a ploughman's lunch. The cheese will slice quite well or can be spread straight on to biscuits.

Cooking Mycella can be used in much the same way as Danablu. Its milder flavour probably makes it a more acceptable ingredient in milk-based sauces for poultry or fish.

NEPICAR

Hard ewe's milk cheese. Fat content 53 per cent

Claimed to be the first pasteurised ewe's milk

cheese in the United Kingdom, Nepicar is made in Kent. It is named after the farm at which it, and the similar Carolina, are made.

Availability Specialist cheese shops. The cheese is sold after maturing for three months and it improves with keeping.

Description Made in 500 g (1–1½ lb) and 2 kg (4½ lb) drums, the cheese has a natural rind. Mildly ewe's-milk in flavour, with a hard texture that becomes creamier on maturing. A very pale yellow coloured cheese.

Serving Serve on its own with pears or apples or as part of the cheese course.

Cooking Grate into soups and sauces or crumble over salads or into stir-fry vegetables.

NEUFCHÂTEL

Soft cow's milk cheese. Fat content 45 per cent

This rich and creamy French cheese is made in the Pays de Bray in Normandy. It is sometimes known as Bondon Neufchâtel. There is still some farmhouse Neufchâtel about but mostly the cheese is factory made.

Availability Specialist cheese shops, a few supermarkets and French delicatessens. Matured for three weeks.

Description Neufchâtel comes in a variety of shapes including *coeur* or heart-shaped, *briquette, bondon* or bung-shaped or square. The fresh cheese has a soft white rind which becomes slightly reddish on keeping. The paste is white and smooth with a velvety texture. The flavour is slightly sour and salty.

Serving Serve at the cheese course or on its own with grapes or celery.

ORKNEY

Hard cow's milk cheese. Fat content 52.5 per cent

This Scottish cheese is now a modified Dunlop cheese which is made either in the creamery at Kirkwall or by traditional methods on the farms on Shapinsay.

Availability Widely available.
Description The creamery cheeses are produced as 500 g (1 lb) vacuum-packed round cheeses and 19.5 kg (40 lb) blocks. The traditional cheeses, which are difficult to find, are softer and made in slightly larger sizes. The cheese may be plain, coloured with annatto, or smoked. The texture is quite close and the flavour tangy.
Manufacture Made from pasteurised milk, Orkney is a dry-stirred curd cheese. After the whey is drained off, the curd is stirred into a granular form, salted and filled into moulds.
Serving Serve as part of the cheese course or on its own as a ploughman's lunch. The smoked cheese is good with green apples.

Orkney cheese keeps quite well. Wrap in foil, place it in a cool storecupboard or the fridge door and it will keep for two to three weeks.

OXFORD

Hard cow's milk cheese. Fat content 53 per cent

Introduced in 1983, this traditional hard cheese produced in a top-hat shape is based on an eighteenth-century recipe.
Availability Specialist cheese shops.
Description Produced in 4 kg (9 lb) and 8 kg (17½ lb) 'top hats', 4 kg (9 lb) rings and in blocks. The top hats are coated in red wax. The paste is firm and creamy in colour, and the flavour medium mellow.
Variation A smoked version is available.
Serving Serve as part of the cheese course or in a ploughman's lunch.
Cooking The cheese melts well and is quite useful in cooking. Try it in cheese sauces, cheese on toast and cheese soufflés.

PANT-YS-GAWN

Fresh goat's milk cheese. Fat content 54 per cent

This soft goat's milk cheese is made on a sixteenth-century hill farm in the Brecon Beacons National Park.

Availability Available in one or two supermarkets and specialist cheese shops.
Description Pant-ys-Gawn is soft, white and easily spreadable. It has a mild, 'ungoaty' flavour. It is sold in loaf-shaped logs or sliced.
Variations Flavoured with herbs, black cherry and brandy, or honey and spices, or coated with black peppers, herbs or green and red sweet peppers.
Manufacture Made from pasteurised goat's milk with vegetable rennet.
Serving Serve on its own with wholemeal rolls and salad, or as part of a cheese board, after a heavy main course, such as game. Eat as soon as possible after purchase, or wrap in foil or cling film and store in the fridge for a day or two. It can also be frozen for up to three months.
Cooking Use to top jacket potatoes or coat with eggs and breadcrumbs and deep-fry.

PARMESAN

Extra-hard cow's milk cheese. Fat content 32 per cent

This Italian cheese is one of the world's best-known. Its full Italian name is Parmigiano Reggiano and it is produced in certain provinces of the Po Valley. It is made only from unpasteurised milk between 1st April and 11th November.

Parmesan is another of the Grana family of hard Italian cheeses (see Grana Padano page 90); around two million cheeses are produced every year and a large proportion is consumed in Italy.
Availability Widely available. Because Parmesan is matured for so long it is on sale all the year round. It is matured for anything from one to four years. It is sold at one of four stages as follows:
giovane young, after a year,
vecchio old, after eighteen months to two years,
stravecchio mature, after two to three years,
stravecchione extra mature, after three to four years.
Description Produced in 30 kg (66 lb) squat drums which look a little like tiny beer barrels,

the cheese has a shiny golden-brown rind with its name stamped all over the sides. The paste is a good straw-yellow colour with a grainy, flaky and brittle texture which hardens even more as the cheese matures. The cheese has a radial grain and can be split open using a special tool. Pieces can also be broken off along the grain.

The flavour is both full and delicate. It has an unmistakable aroma and flavour which is fruity and not at all bitter.

Manufacture Made only from unpasteurised milk, one kilogram represents sixteen kilos of milk. Parmesan cheese is still made in relatively small dairies in the proscribed regions. The previous evening's milk is mixed with partially skimmed morning milk, a starter is added and the milk is heated. When the lactic acid reaches the required level, rennet is added. Coagulation occurs quickly and the curd is then turned and broken up by a special sharp-edged tool, known as a *spino* or thornbrush, into pieces the size of wheat grains ready for cooking. The curds are heated, after which they fall to the bottom of the cheese kettle to form a solid mass. The curds are removed in muslin, placed in the moulds and lightly pressed. The cheeses are printed with the name Parmigiano Reggiano and then brined and stored for ripening.

Testing At a much later stage and after at least one year of maturation the cheeses are tested and graded. The tester works with a percussion hammer, a screw needle and a sampling dowel. With his hammer the expert knocks the cheese at various points while listening carefully to the way the crust takes the blows; this tells him what is going on inside. The reverberations tell the expert whether the cheese has reached any of five levels of quality. His diagnosis is confirmed by the use of a screw needle which gives an indication of the degree of resistance in the cheese and a small sample to smell and taste. The sampling dowel is used only as a last resort.

Buying guide Genuine Parmesan cheeses are not only stamped with the name of the cheese but also with the year the cheese was made. Export cheeses also carry an export mark.

Many people buy only ready-grated Parmesan in cardboard tubs and this bears no relationship to the whole cheese. Parmesan should always be bought in a piece off a whole cheese and be used as needed.

Parmesan is at its peak when it is *congocciola:* this means that when the cheese is split open you can just see tiny tears of moisture glistening on the surface.

Serving Parmesan is not just a cheese for sprinkling over food or using in cooked dishes. When it is young it makes a very good dessert cheese and is well worth including on a cheese-board. It is delicious, too, on its own with fruit or celery. The Italians eat it with pears or figs. It can also be broken into small pieces and served with aperitifs. In the right conditions Parmesan will keep for a long time. Wrap in foil and store in the fridge for up to two months. Freeze for up to three months. Parmesan can be grated straight from the freezer if you use a little force.

Cooking Like all Grana cheeses, Parmesan melts perfectly without any hint of stringiness. It is used as a condiment on all kinds of foods from soups and pasta to baked casseroles and rice dishes. It is the classic ingredient in numerous Italian dishes, such as aubergine parmigiana, zuppa alla pavese and pesto sauce for pasta as well as dishes like lobster thermidor and fish mornay. Indeed it can be used in almost any dish that calls for cheese and is often used with other cheeses to add flavour. Try mixing it with cheddar in cauliflower cheese, devilled crab or cheese soufflé.

History Parmesan has been famous for more than seven hundred years, but the Grana family of cheeses to which it belongs dates back even further. They were well known in Roman times and some experts believe that their history goes back even beyond the Romans.

The most noteworthy early reference to Parmesan is found in Boccaccio's *Decameron.* One character tells the other about the 'whole mountain of Parmigiano cheese, all finely grated, on top of which stood people who were doing nothing but making macaroni and ravioli'. He adds that all these delicacies were being 'rolled into the cheese after cooking, the better to season them'.

A recipe book dated around 1545 describes a

dinner party where the dessert course included as an accompaniment to a great basket of fruit, 'Six platefuls of Parmigiano cheese'.

Molière was also supposed to be a fan of Parmesan. Many biographers state that the great playwright lived mainly on Parmesan cheese during his declining years. The cheese was considered to be particularly easy on the digestion and was often recommended for infants and the elderly.

PASSENDALE

Semi-soft cow's milk cheese. Fat content 50 per cent

Shaped like a loaf of soda bread, this is a relatively new cheese from Belgium.

Availability Specialist cheese shops. Sold after six weeks' maturation, it may continue to be ripened for a further six weeks. Best from mid-May to mid-December.

Description Produced in a round loaf shape, the cheese has a greyish rind with a white bloom. The paste is quite soft and supple with tiny cracks or holes in it and is straw-yellow in colour. The flavour is positive and reminiscent of mature Gouda.

Serving Serve sliced with a continental hand-held cheese slicer at any meal. The Belgians are particularly fond of it for breakfast.

Double-wrap and store in a cool place for up to ten days.

Cooking Use in the same way as Tilsit or Gouda.

PASTORELLO

Semi-soft cow's milk cheese. Fat content not available

One of Australia's few original cheeses, it was invented in Sydney by an Italian named Daniele Lostia and is reminiscent of Fontina cheese.

Availability Widely available, in Australia only.

Description This soft mild cheese has a high moisture content, is almost spreadable and has a good aroma and flavour.

Variation Creamy blue-veined version ripened in foil and similar to Gorgonzola.

Manufacture Drained in wicker baskets to give a patterned effect on the rind.

Serving Serve at the cheese course, or slice and serve with black olives and crusty bread, washed down with Chianti.

PECORINO

Hard ewe's milk cheese.
Fat content (Romano) 35 per cent

Any Italian cheese made exclusively from ewe's milk belongs to the Pecorino family. They are generally hard, compact cheeses used mainly, but not always for grating. These cheeses come usually from central and south Italy and there are several regions which add their name to Pecorino (see Variations, below). Pecorino Romano is the best known of these cheeses.

Availability Specialist cheese shops. Usually matured for six to nine months. Pecorino Romano must be matured for at least eight months. Pecorino Toscana may be sold earlier.

Description Pecorino Romano is produced in 6–22 kg (13–48 lb) drum shapes and has a dark brown or black, very hard rind which is rubbed with oil and coloured with wood ash, yellow clay or wax.

The paste is greyish white, close textured and slightly oily. The flavour is quite salty and piquant with a typical ewe's milk after taste. Young cheeses are softer and milder.

Variations Pecorino Sardo from Sardinia is almost identical to Romano though experts can taste the difference. Pecorino Toscana or Toscanella is the Tuscan version: it is often eaten while it is still quite young and creamy. Pecorino Senese is a special Pecorino which is sometimes rubbed with tomato paste instead of oil and wood ash. Pecorino Siciliano is made between October and June on the island of Sicily. The cheese has a rough, yellowish, oiled rind and a typically sharp flavour. It is often given an additional bite by scattering peppercorns throughout the paste. The Siciliano version of Pecorino is often called Canestrato after the wicker baskets used to form the cheese (see page 61).

Manufacture Pecorino may be made with whole or skimmed, unpasteurised milk. The milk is usually coagulated with sheep's rennet. After cutting and stirring the curds are moulded and pressed. Some (like Pecorino Romano) are cooked, some are not, the exact recipe varies from region to region.

Serving Pecorino may be served as a dessert cheese with fruit – I have seen the Tuscans eat theirs with raw broad beans – or with coarse bread. Young cheeses complement a Valpolicella; mature ones suit a Chianti Reserva.

Cooking Mature Pecorino of all kinds is grated and used in cooking. It is an essential part of many of the regional dishes. When hot it has a very characteristic acrid smell but this does not carry through to the flavour. Try it in herb and potato flans, in stuffed tomatoes or mushrooms or in stir-fried vegetables. It is also very good mixed with olive oil and walnuts and used in salads or as a canapé topping.

PÈRE JOSEPH

Semi-hard cow's milk cheese. Fat content 50 per cent

This is one of the many semi-hard and semi-soft factory-made 'trappist' cheeses, inspired by Port Salut and other monastery cheeses. It is produced at the Passendale dairy in Belgium.

Availability Specialist cheese shops. Matured for five weeks.

Description Produced in a flat disc about 20 cm (8 in) in diameter, the cheese has a natural mould rind, a black wax coating and a yellow paste scattered with holes. The flavour is fairly full with a nutty aroma.

Variations Echte Loo has a washed rind and a brown wax coating.

Serving Serve sliced at any meal. Try it with rye or caraway bread, pickles or cranberry relish and smoked turkey.

PETIT SUISSE

Fresh soft cow's milk cheese.
Fat content 60 and 75 per cent

This fresh double cream cheese was invented in a cheese factory in Paris in the mid-nineteenth century. It is not Swiss but French, the name came from the nationality of a worker in the factory who suggested some changes in the manufacture of fresh cheeses and who used to transport the cheeses to the Paris markets.

Availability Widely available. Petit Suisse is ready to eat as soon as it is produced.

Description Produced and packed into 30–60 g (1–2 oz) tubs, the cheese is quite runny. It is unsalted and very bland in flavour. There is also a triple-cream version.

Serving Serve with fruit or other desserts. Eat the day it is bought.

PHILADELPHIA

Fresh soft cow's milk cheese. Fat content 70 per cent

This is the brand name of America's best-known cream cheese. It was invented by an enterprising farmer in New York State in 1872. In 1880 another cheese-maker contracted to distribute the cheese under the Philadelphia brand name. At that time Philadelphia was famous for its superb dairy products.

Availability Widely available. Philadelphia is ready to eat as soon as it is produced.

Description Produced in small 100 g (3½ oz) or 225 g (8 oz) blocks, the cheese is white in colour and has a soft, spreadable texture.

Variations Lower fat (48%) and flavoured versions are also available.

Serving Serve at the cheese course, on its own with fruit or salad, or in sandwiches. In America Philadelphia and jelly or jam sandwiches are a national favourite.

Cooking Use in cheesecakes, soups, sauces and any dish which calls for cream cheese.

PICADON

Soft goat's milk cheese. Fat content 45 per cent

These are a variety of soft goat's milk cheeses produced on French farms in the Rhône Valley and its environs. They include Picadon de Dieulefit from the Montélimar region, Picadon de Saint Agrève from Vivarais and the Cevennes mountains and Picadon de Valréas from Valréas near Avignon. Picadon is covered by the French *Appéllation d'Origine* laws.

Availability Locally available, in France only. Matured for one to four weeks, the cheeses are best in the summer and autumn.

Description They are small 100 g (3½ oz) disc-shaped cheeses, usually with a soft, thin, natural rind. The paste is white and fairly firm without being at all hard. The flavour is nutty or moderately sharp.

Serving Serve as part of the cheese course with a good Rhône wine.

PIORA

Hard cow's and goat's milk cheese.
Fat content 45 per cent

Made from a mixture of both cow's and goat's milk in the Ticino area of Switzerland, this cheese has a rich but delicate flavour.

Availability Locally available, in Switzerland only. The cheeses are matured for at least three to four months and often for as much as six months.

Description Shaped like a squat cylinder, the cheeses weigh 7–12 kg (15½–26½ lb), and the paste is pale yellow in colour with numerous small holes.

Serving Serve at the cheese course; or try in sandwiches, washed down with a continental lager.

PIPO CREM'

Semi-soft blue cow's milk cheese.
Fat content 50 per cent

This cheese was invented in 1961 after the success of Bleu de Bresse in an attempt to produce a similar, but larger, cheese. It is creamery produced from pasteurised milk.

Availability Widely available.

Description Produced in 28×11 cm (11×4¼in) cylinders, the cheese has a soft, washed rind which is creamy in colour. The paste is whiter with light blue veining in the centre, and the flavour is mild and milky with an unaggressive tanginess.

Serving Serve at the cheese course or on its own with celery.

Double-wrap in foil and store in the fridge for ten to fourteen days. Allow it to come to room temperature before you eat it.

Cooking Pipo Crem' melts easily into sauces and is very good mixed with single cream as a pasta topping with walnuts, broccoli or celeriac. Its mild flavour partners sauces for fish and veal well.

PONT L'ÉVÊQUE

Soft cow's milk cheese. Fat content 40–50 per cent

A French cheese still made mostly on farms from unpasteurised milk, Pont L'Évêque is probably one of the oldest cheeses in Normandy. It is protected by the French *Appellation d'Origine* laws.

Availability Widely available. Matured for six weeks before going on sale.

Description The cheese, produced in 350 g (12 oz) squares, has a yellow to light tan rind which may be washed or brushed. The cheese has a fairly pungent smell, the paste is supple with a few small holes and the flavour is rich and tangy.

Variations Pavé d'Auge or Pavé de Moyeaux is a larger, stronger version of Pont l'Évêque. It

Pont l'Evêque (page 121)

is ripened for anything from two-and-a-half to four months. The paste is firm and full of small elliptical holes, the flavour can be rather bitter. Calvador, produced in a flat disc, is a milder, rather watered down, creamery-made version of Pont l'Évêque.

Manufacture The milk is coagulated as soon after milking as possible and traditionally the morning and evening milk are coagulated separately to produce two batches of cheese a day. The curds are divided into large blocks rather than cut into small pieces or grains and one block makes up one cheese. They are drained and placed in square moulds. After dry-salting, the cheeses are ripened in humid cellars where they may be washed with brine or brushed.

Serving Serve as part of the cheese course or on its own with grapes and water biscuits and a robust red wine, such as Câhors or Côte de Provence.

Double wrap, with a flat board against any cut surfaces, and store in a cool place for two or three days.

Cooking The flavour of Pont l'Évêque goes very well with potatoes. Remove the rind and layer in a casserole with onions and sliced potatoes or serve on jacket baked potatoes.

PORT SALUT

Semi-soft cow's milk cheese. Fat content 45 per cent

This cheese was originally made at the French abbey of Entrammes. It is also known as Port du Salut. However after World War II the name was sold to a commercial enterprise. The monks continued to make their cheese which they now sell under the name of Entrammes.

Availability Specialist cheese shops and French delicatessens.

Description Produced in 1–2 kg (2–4½ lb) flat discs, the cheese has a tawny, washed rind and a smooth, springy, semi-soft paste which is fairly mild in flavour.

Serving Serve as part of the cheese course and as Saint-Paulin.

History This was a typical monastery rind-washed cheese. It started life around 1815 when a group of Trappist monks returned from exile in Switzerland and took over the abbey at Entrammes. They renamed the abbey L'Abbaye de Notre Dame de Port du Salut. The cheese they made became very popular and was widely copied. The monks took steps to protect their cheese and, in 1938, the name Port Salut was legally defined as the trade mark of Port du Salut cheeses.

POULIGNY-SAINT-PIERRE

Soft goat's milk cheese. Fat content 45 per cent

This small pyramid-shaped cheese is made in the region of Berry. It is protected by the French *Appellation d'Origine* laws.

Availability Locally available, in France only. Matured for four to five weeks, the cheese is best bought in summer and autumn.

Description Produced in 200 g (7 oz) pyramids, the cheese has a natural blueish-grey rind and a tangy flavour.

Serving Serve as part of the cheese course.

PRÄSTOST

Semi-hard cow's milk cheese. Fat content 50 per cent

Known in Swedish as 'priest's' or 'parsonage' cheese, it is now nearly all factory made.

Availability Widely available, in Sweden only. Sold after a month or so.

Description Produced in 12–15 kg (26½–33 lb) cylinders, the cheese has a paraffin wax coating or is vacuum-packed and rindless. The paste is full of numerous small holes and the flavour is very mild.

Serving Serve sliced with other cheeses.

PROVOLONE

Hard cow's milk cheese. Fat content 44 per cent

A spun curd or *pasta filata* cheese originally from southern Italy, it is now made in both the United States and Latin America. It is also mass-produced in Italy iself and here the tendency has been to produce milder, younger cheese with a less piquant flavour. They are sold in all sizes and under all kinds of names.

Availability Specialist cheese shops and Italian delicatessens. Young mild Provolone is sold after two to three months, but it may be matured for six months or even as long as two years though this is rare.

Description The cheeses come in all shapes and sizes since the plastic curd lends itself to improvisation. Some of the cheeses are hung up in rafia and these tend to be pear shaped. The rind, often given a coating of wax, is smooth and shiny and yellow-golden in colour. Older cheeses have a tougher and harder rind.

The paste is pale yellow in colour and without holes, however, older cheeses develop small cracks and the colour darkens. The flavour is almost 'farmyardy' with a sharp aftertaste and the cheese takes on a stronger, spicier flavour as it ages.

Variations Provole may be an unripened Provolone rolled into small balls; but it may also be a Mozzarella which has been ripened for longer. Burrini are sometimes sold under this name. A variety of other diminutive names are also used, but they are all small versions of Provolone. Some cheeses are smoked.

Manufacture Traditional manufacture uses raw milk and fermented whey left from the previous day as a starter. Factory-made cheese uses pasteurised milk and a starter culture. The curds are coagulated with calf's rennet to make mild Provolone Dolce, or kid's rennet to make the stronger Provolone Piccante.

The curds are cut to the size of hazelnuts and stirred before being allowed to fall to the bottom of the vat. Some of the whey is drawn off and the remaining curds and whey are cooked. After standing, more whey is drawn off and the curds are washed to reduce the calcium content of the cheese and then cut into thick slices and piled on to drainage tables. When the lactic acid content of the curd rises to the correct level, the curds are kneaded and spun. They take on a stretchy elasticity which makes them look a little like pasta – hence the Italian name for the process. The kneaded curd goes back into hot water and is then shaped, brined and ripened.

Serving Serve young Provolone in slices with other cheeses, or use in open or closed sandwiches. It can also be cut into chunks and used on cocktail kebabs with olives or pineapple.

Cooking Older cheese grates easily and can be used in all kinds of cooking. Try it in cheese gnocchi, potato salad or cheese fritters.

PULTOST

Soft cow's milk cheese. Fat content not available

Made all over Norway, there are numerous local variations of this cheese which may also be called Knaost or Ramost.

Availability Widely available, in Norway only. Available after about three weeks' ripening.

Description Produced in various shapes and sizes, the cheese has no rind. The cheese is pale and varies from mild to quite acidic or spiced.

Variation Spiced with caraway seeds.

Manufacture Pultost may be made from low- or full-fat milk and it may have buttermilk or cream added to it. It is made only by the action of lactic-acid-producing bacteria. The curd is heated to release the whey and the curd is salted, moulded and ripened for around three weeks.

Serving Serve on its own with rye bread, crispbread and fruit or salad stuffs. Mix with fresh herbs and serve with the cheese course or use to fill celery sticks for canapés.

PYRÉNÉES

*Semi-hard cow's milk cheese.
Fat content not available*

This is a French, factory produced cheese.

Availability Widely available.

Description Produced in rounds or discs with a shiny black rind, this cheese has a firm but supple yellow paste with lots of small holes scattered through it; the flavour is very mild and bland.

There is also a French ewe's milk cheese which may be sold by the same name in France.

Serving Use to make a fruity 'ploughman's' with tangerines, grapes and pickled pears. Cut into cubes, dip in paprika, celery salt or ground cumin seed and serve with cocktails.

Cooking Pyrénées can be grated into any dish calling for Edam. It gives a very mild flavour to fish pies, scallops mornay and *gratin* dishes.

QUARK

Fresh cow's milk cheese. Fat content 0–60 per cent

Quark is quite simply the German word for curds and it is Germany's most popular cheese. The per capita consumption is currently running at around 5 kg (11 lb) a year, or about half the total consumption of cheese. Quark may be made from skimmed milk, whole milk, buttermilk or a mixture of milk and cream: this means that there is a wide choice of different fat contents.

Availability Widely available.

Description Quark is smooth and thick with a texture somewhere between that of yogurt and cream cheese. It is white in colour and has a clean, mild flavour, sometimes with just a hint of acidity.

Manufacture Quark can be prepared in a variety of ways, but generally large-scale factory methods are used. The basic principles involve the pasteurisation of the milk, coagulation with a starter culture and a small amount of rennet, and separation of the whey. The latter process is now carried out in a centrifuge. Some plants subject the curds and whey to a second heat treatment after coagulation. This retains the whey proteins in the curd and gives a higher yield and a more nutritious product. Other methods require the milk to be homogenised to produce a pasty rather than a firm, grainy texture.

Serving Serve mixed with fresh herbs or spices as part of the cheese course, or use as a substitute for cream with fresh fruit.

Eat within a day or two of purchase.

Cooking Though sometimes more like thick cream than curd cheese, Quark behaves like cheese on cooking which means it seizes up rather than melts with excess heat. It blends well if the temperature is not too high.

Quark is extremely versatile. It can be used in savoury dishes, in cold dressings and sauces, dips and soups, canapé fillings and stuffings, as well as in dumplings, salads and pies. In sweet applications, it works well in cheesecakes, puddings, cake and flan fillings and in sundaes.

RACLETTE

Semi-hard cow's milk cheese. Fat content 50 per cent

Raclette means 'scraper' and this is the name given to a family of Swiss cheeses made originally in the Canton of Valais. It is a very popular cheese in Switzerland and, as a result, it is manufactured in more and more dairies throughout the country. Cheeses from the original area are often marked with the name 'Valais'.

Availability Specialist cheese shops. Usually sold at four to five months, some connoisseurs prefer the stronger flavour of seven month-old cheese.

Description Produced in 6–7 kg (13–15 lb) wheels, the cheese has a rough brown rind and a yellow paste with a few small holes scattered through it. The flavour is full and somewhat similar to Gruyère.

Variations There are quite a number of other Swiss cheeses which could be included under the umbrella of Raclette. They include Walliser, Gomser and Simplon among others. French versions of the cheese include: Raclette Livaradoux and Raclette de Busseau.

Manufacture Made with unpasteurised milk.

Serving Raclette cheeses are not usually served uncooked, though there is no reason why they should not be.

Cooking Raclette melts to a lovely velvety, buttery mass and it is nearly always served in the dish which has the same name as the cheese. To make Raclette, cut a whole cheese in half. Place the cut surface before an open flame. As the cheese melts, scrape it on to a dish and eat it with potatoes boiled in their skins, and pickles.

RAMBOL

Semi-soft cow's milk cheese.
Fat content 55–58 per cent

This is the brand name of a French creamery produced cheese which features walnuts.

Availability Widely available.

Description Produced in various sizes. the cheese may either be coated with walnuts – Rambolux Noix – or be layered with walnuts – Rambol Fourre aux Noix.

Serving Serve as part of the cheese course. It's good with an old-style white Rioja. For a snack, try it with crisp apples and raisin bread.

REBLOCHON

Semi-soft cow's milk cheese. Fat content 50 per cent

Another ancient French cheese, this time from the mountains of the Haute Savoie. Protected by the French *Appellation d'Origine* laws, the cheese may be made on farms or in commercial dairies from either unpasteurised or pasteurised milk.

Availability Specialist cheese shops or French delicatessens. Matured for four to five weeks, the best cheese is on sale in the summer and autumn months.

Description Produced in 240–500 g (8–18 oz) discs, the cheese has a pale pinkish-white, washed rind. The paste is very supple with a number of small holes and the mild, fruity and creamy flavour is excellent.

Serving Serve at the cheese course or serve a whole cheese on its own with celery or radishes and a fine claret.

Double wrap and keep in a cool place for up to a week. Eat as soon as possible after cutting.

Cooking Slice and serve as a salad starter, with artichoke hearts, mixed leaves and toasted pine nuts. Deep-fry in breadcrumbs and serve with home-made chutney.

History Reblochon is a cheese with a long history, but for many years no one outside the area where it was made knew about it. This was because it was made from milk which was withheld (*lait de rebloche*) when the stewards came to inspect the yields. The farmers did not milk the cows dry then, after the stewards had gone, the farmers finished the milking and used the rich milk to make cheese for their own use.

REMOUDOU

Soft cow's milk cheese. Fat content 45 per cent

This, Belgium's most smelly cheese, is a particularly strong type of Hervé deriving from the town of that name. A similar cheese, called Romadur, is produced in Germany.

Availability Specialist cheese shops. Ripened for at least three months before it goes on sale.

Description Produced in 200 g (7 oz) loaves, it has a dark brownish-orange washed rind and a rich paste. The smelliness derives from the rind, and the paste is not nearly so pungent.

Variations German Romadur has a slightly lighter yellowish-brown skin and a rich golden paste with irregular small holes. In some ways, it is similar to Limburg, but it is not so strong.

Serving Serve at the cheese course or on its own with biscuits and celery.

History Remoudou originated in the sixteenth century. The name refers to the Walloon word for the specially rich milk which is provided by the cow towards the end of the lactation period.

REQUEIJAO

Fresh soft ewe's milk whey cheese.
Fat content not available

This is a popular cheese throughout Portugal and is sold on market stalls and at grocers everywhere. It is rather similar to Ricotta.

Availability Widely available, in Portugal only. Requeijao is a fresh cheese which is ready to eat as soon as it is made.

Description Moulded into rounds weighing around 100 g (3½ oz) to 200 g (7 oz), the cheese has a close texture and is quite mild.

Manufacture This cheese is a by-product of the ewe's milk cheese-making industry. Then whey is boiled to precipitate the proteins which are skimmed off and drained in baskets.

Serving The Portuguese eat Requeijao for breakfast, on its own or with fruit. It is also eaten before meals with herbs and spices or for dessert with sugar, jam or honey and possibly a sprinkling of cinnamon.

Eat fairly soon after purchase. However, really fresh Requeijao can be kept for three or four days in the fridge.

RIBCHESTER

Hard goat's milk cheese. Fat content not available

This is a relatively new, hard-pressed English goat's milk cheese produced in Lancashire and named after the local town.

Availability Specialist cheese shops.

Description Produced in 2 kg (4½ lb) wheels the cheese is coated in yellow wax and the paste is firm and white with a mild creamy flavour.

Variations A smoked version is available. The smoking process over oak chippings gives a natural glossy finish to the cheese.

Manufacture Based on a traditional regional recipe, Ribchester is made from full-fat pasteurised goat's milk with vegetable rennet. The cheese is pressed.

Serving Serve with well-flavoured accompaniments like watercress or kiwi fruit.

Cooking This is a useful cheese for cooking. Simply grate into sauces and stuffing mixtures.

RICOTTA

Fresh soft cow's or ewe's milk whey cheese.
Fat content not available

Made with whey, so this is not a cheese in the strict sense of the word. Mostly made after cheese-making with cow's milk, but there are many different versions of this cheese. It may be made in the traditional way with ewe's milk whey, or have whole milk or cream added to the mix to make a much richer cheese. Ricotta from Piedmont uses cow's milk, but that from Tuscany, Romano, Sardinia and Sicily will usually be made from ewe's milk whey from the production of Pecorino.

Availability Specialist cheese shops and Italian

food shops. Ricotta is usually ready to eat as soon as it is made.

Description Ricotta is usually sold as a fresh cheese. It is white, has a granular consistency and is usually shaped like an upturned basin with basketwork marks on the outside. It may also be salted and dried or pressed and matured for grating. The latter may be known as Canestrata. The flavour is mild when young, though ewe's milk Ricotta is not as bland as the cow's milk version. The matured grating cheese is stronger in flavour.

Manufacture The whey is heated and treated with citric or tartaric acid to help the whey proteins to coagulate. Flakes of milk albumen rise to the top and are skimmed off and placed in moulds to drain.

Serving Serve at the cheese course sprinkled with salt and pepper or fresh herbs or use in a ploughman's lunch, in open sandwiches or in salad in much the same way as cottage cheese.

Eat as soon as possible after purchase.

Cooking Ricotta is used widely in Italian cooking, in savoury dishes like crespelle (little stuffed pancakes), gnocchi and tortelloni, or in sweet dishes like cheesecake. It is also eaten as a dessert with fruit or sprinkled with powdered coffee, chocolate or chopped nuts.

RIDDER

Semi-hard cow's milk cheese. Fat content 60 per cent

This very new cheese from Norway, which is rather similar to Saint-Paulin, is also produced in Sweden.

Availability Available in one or two super-markets and in specialist cheese shops. The cheese is surface-ripened for five to six weeks before sale.

Description The cheese is produced in 2 kg (4½ lb) flat wheels with an orange, washed rind. The paste is deep yellow in colour, the texture very buttery and the flavour slightly nutty.

Serving Serve at the cheese course or on its own with fruit like fresh strawberries, grapes and pears.

Cooking Use this rich cheese in rolls and spear on to cocktail sticks with cubes of melon and sprigs of mint, or roll up in small curls with smoked ham, anchovies or pickled onions and serve on black bread. Ridder also melts well and can be used in soufflé toppings for toast or soufflé omelettes. It can also be used to make unusual toasted sandwiches with smoked chicken, chopped Frankfurter sausages or simply tomatoes and spring onions.

RIGOTTE

Soft cow's and/or goat's milk cheese.
Fat content 40–50 per cent

There are a number of different variations of this French cheese, depending on the area in which it is made. Some are cured in white wine or oil and some are coloured artificially to brighten up the rind.

Availability Specialist cheese shops and French delicatessens. Ripened for about two weeks.

Description The cheeses, produced in tiny 70 g (2½ oz) drum shapes, have a pale greyish-white or bright orange rind. The paste is white and fairly firm, the flavour mild. However, if the orange rind is coated in paprika this flavour dominates the cheese.

Serving Serve at the cheese course or as a snack with crusty bread. It is also good sliced and served with salad and a vinaigrette dressing.

Double-wrap and keep cool and the cheese will last for two weeks provided it is not cut. Avoid the fridge. Best eaten all in one go.

ROLLOT

Soft cow's milk cheese. Fat content 45 per cent

The name of this Maroilles-type cheese derives from the French market town of Rollot, in the Somme, where it was originally made.

Availability Specialist cheese shops and

French delicatessens. Matured for two months before going on sale.

Description Produced in 200 g (7 oz) rounds or heart-shapes (also known as Guerbigny), the cheese has a moist orange-coloured, washed rind and a supple yellow paste scattered with holes. The flavour is quite spicy.

Serving Serve at the cheese course or on its own with celery and water biscuits. Whole cheeses may be kept in a cool place for six to seven days. Once cut it should be double-wrapped and eaten within a day or two.

History Louis XIV is said to have been offered Rollot for lunch on May Day 1678. The king was so impressed with the cheese that he appointed his host *maître fromager* and gave him a pension for life.

RONCAL

Hard ewe's milk cheese. Fat content 60 per cent

The production of this cheese from Navarre in northern Spain is restricted to seven towns which make up the Valle de Roncál. It is covered by the Spanish Denomination of Origin laws.

Availability Widely available, in Spain only. Roncal is made only during the months of July and December. It is matured for four months and so is on sale between December and May.

Description Produced in squat, cylindrical drums weighing around 2 kg (4½ lb), Roncal has a thick hard rind which is light brown in colour and slightly greasy to the touch. The paste is yellowish-white in colour, the texture hard and fairly open and the flavour is fairly pungent.

Manufacture The milk is coagulated with rennet and the curds cut into small grains. The whey is drained off and the curds moulded and pressed. The cheese may be dry-salted or brined.

Serving Serve at the cheese course or on its own with biscuits and black olives.

Cooking Roncal grates well and can be used in a variety of cooked dishes requiring a good flavour. Try it in cheese soufflés, sauces for cauliflower or broccoli, or in soup.

ROQUEFORT

Soft ewe's milk cheese. Fat content 45 per cent

Roquefort has been made in the Les Causses area of Aquitaine for thousands of years and the name has been protected for longer than any other cheese. Some cheeses, made from Corsican milk, are brought to Combalou to be ripened in the same caves as the local cheeses and this means that Roquefort is available almost all the year round. Cheeses must be matured in the caves at Combalou to qualify as Roquefort under the French *Appellation d'Origine* laws.

Availability Widely available. Matured for three months.

Description Produced in 2.5 kg (5½ lb) drums, the cheese has virtually no rind. It is closely wrapped in foil. The paste is very white in colour with a uniform greenish-blue marbling throughout. The texture is firm, smooth and almost spreadable. There is a faint smell of mould and ewe's milk, and the flavour is delicate and subtle with a tangy finish. Some export cheeses may be rather salty.

Matured Roquefort are classified as Surchoix, first, second and third grade and rebuks, and the quality of each cheese is shown by the colour of its foil wrapping.

Manufacture The main production season lasts from February to July. Unpasteurised Larzac ewe's milk, from the morning and the evening milkings, is mixed and curdled with rennet. The curds form in two hours. It is then cut and placed in hoops with perforated sides. The mould, which used to grow naturally, is now sprinkled in powdered form on to the curds as they are ladelled into the hoops. (The mould, *penicillium Roquefortii*, is produced from rye and wheat flour loaves which are left to go mouldy, then dried, crushed and sifted ready to use.) The cheeses are pierced with steel needles during the three months' ripening period.

The special qualities of Roquefort derive in some part from its ripening in the natural grottos or *cabanes* of Combalou, a collapsed mountain in the Cévennes. The cracks and fissures ensure a steady vertical and horizontal movement of air at an almost constant temperature. The humidity of the air is high because of the presence of a huge underground lake.

An annual total of 16,000 tons of Roquefort is produced and the cheeses are made in farms over a wide area, though they are all transported to Combalou for curing.

Buying guide The best cheeses are made for the French market; they are not usually as heavily salted as those which are for export.

Avoid cheese with a crumbling edge or which does not have a great deal of blue veining. Excessively sharp cheese should also be avoided.

Serving Serve with the cheese course or on its own with pears or grapes. It is also very good in open and closed sandwiches, with fruit, chopped nuts or salad ingredients.

Keep well wrapped in foil in the salad compartment of the fridge. Always bring up to room temperature before eating it or you will lose some of its unique flavour. Roquefort can also be frozen for use in cooking.

Cooking Roquefort is an excellent cheese to use in any recipe which calls for blue cheese. Try it in salad dressings, tartlet fillings, canapé toppings, stuffed vegetables, soups and sauces for steak or veal. Unusual applications are as a stuffing for stoned dates or in blue cheese and banana truffles.

History Roquefort is probably one of the ancient cheeses of Gaul mentioned by Pliny the Elder in his *Historia Naturalis* written in the first century AD. Six centuries later Charlemagne is said to have had two mule loads of it sent to his palace every Christmas and New Year. Other historical figures to have sung the praises of Roquefort include Rabelais and Casanova. The latter ate it with ham and a bottle of Chambertin 'to restore love'!

In 1411 a royal charter of Charles VI gave the people of Roquefort the monopoly of curing the cheese in the local caves at Combalou. A succession of French kings renewed this charter. In 1951 it was one of the four cheeses given complete international protection by the Stresa Convention. This means that no one can produce a cheese and call it Roquefort unless it comes from the defined area of that *appellation*.

There is no such thing, for example, as Italian Roquefort.

ROULÉ

Fresh soft cow's milk cheese. Fat content not available

Sometimes known as Roulette, this fresh cheese is formed in the shape of a log and is flavoured in various ways. It usually comes from French creameries.

Availability Widely available. Ready to eat as soon as it is made.

Description Produced in 1 kg (2 lb) logs, the fresh white paste is in concentric rings with layers of flavourings such as garlic, herbs and peppercorns.

Serving Serve as part of the cheese course or on its own with crusty bread or biscuits. It can also be used in a salad or as a topping for canapés. Thin with milk or yogurt to make an interesting dip.

RYGEOST

Smoked cow's milk cheese. Fat content not available

Made on the Danish island of Fyn, home of Hans Andersen, this cheese is something of a local speciality. Sadly, cheese smoking is a dying art and the number of smoked cheese producers is falling all the time.

Availability Available locally, in Denmark only.

Description This is an acid-curd cheese smoked over fires of dried grass and straw.

Serving Some reports suggest that this is a cheese for summer eatings sitting around midsummer bonfires, others make it a Twelfth Night speciality.

SAINT AGUR

Semi-soft blue cow's milk cheese.
Fat content 60 per cent

This is a relatively new factory produced cheese made from pasteurised milk.

Availability Widely available.

Description Produced in octagonal shapes, the cheese has little or no rind and is wrapped in foil. The creamy coloured paste has well-distributed blue veins and resembles Danish Blue, though the flavour is milder and rather less salty.

Serving Serve as part of the cheese course or on its own with celery and a light, sweet wine, such as Vouvray or a German spätlese. Cube and serve with cocktails or aperitifs.

Cooking This cheese melts into liquids well and can be used in much the same way as Pipo Crem'. Use to make a mild blue salad dressing for avocados or spinach and bacon salad.

SAINT ALBRAY

Semi-soft cow's milk cheese. Fat content 50 per cent

This is a French creamery cheese produced from pasteurised milk. It is manufactured in Béarn in the foothills of the Pyrénées.

Availability Widely available.

Description Produced in a 1.8 kg (4 lb) flower shape, the cheese has a pale-orange bloomy rind. The paste is pale yellow with a number of small holes scattered through it, the flavour mellow and delicate.

Serving Serve as part of the cheese course or slice and serve with other cheeses or in open or closed sandwiches. Cube and serve on cocktail canapés with pickles or in a diced salad.

Wrap in foil and keep in the salad compartment of the fridge for two weeks or more.

SAINT BERNARD-WATOU

Semi-hard cow's milk cheese. Fat content 50 per cent

This Belgian cheese is rather similar to Gouda, but with a higher fat content.

Availability Widely available, in Belgium only. Matured for six weeks.

Description Produced in 4 kg (9 lb) wheels with a very thick, tough black rind and a straw-yellow coloured smooth paste.

Manufacture The cheese is processed from creamy milk and is salted only with sea salt. The tough rind is achieved by using a charcoal fire to keep the acidity level stable.

Serving Serve as part of the cheese course or in a ploughman's lunch with a glass of lager.

History This cheese is said to be made according to a recipe originating from Trappist monks who took refuge from persecution in the valley of the river Leie.

SAINT-FLORENTIN

Soft cow's milk cheese. Fat content 45 per cent

Rather similar to Époisses, this French cheese is produced in Burgundy.

Availability Specialist cheese shops and French delicatessens. Matured for two months before going on sale.

Description Produced in 500 g (18 oz) rounds, the cheese has a smooth shiny mid-brown rind with a yellow springy paste, a strong smell and a tangy flavour. Nowadays a much younger creamery made version of the cheese is sold about a week after it is made, it has no rind and is rather like a fresh cheese.

Serving Serve either version as part of the cheese course or use the younger version on canapés, or in cooking in place of curd.

SAINT-MARCELLIN

Soft cow's milk cheese. Fat content 50 per cent

This small French cheese used to be made with goat's milk in an area just south of Lyon. It is now mainly creamery made, with pasteurised milk.

Availability Specialist cheese shops and French delicatessens. Matured for two weeks before being sold.

Description Produced in small 90 g (3 oz) rounds, the rind is very thin and may be covered in light blue mould but this gives way to a pale orange tint as the cheese matures. The cheese is firm but spreadable and a pale creamy colour. The flavour is mild and slightly sour.

Variations Some cheeses are wrapped in chestnut leaves. Others are macerated in dry white wine from Savoy; these are known as Fromage Vin Blanc.

Serving Serve as part of the cheese course or eat on its own as a snack. Eat as soon as it is purchased.

History The first mention of Saint-Marcellin is in 1461, in the account books of Louis IX.

SAINTE-MAURÉ

Soft goat's milk cheese. Fat content 45 per cent

There are both farm and creamery versions of this French goat's milk cheese. It is produced in Poitou and Touraine.

Availability Specialist cheese shops. Matured for two weeks or a month, both farm and creamery versions are at their best between April and September.

Description Produced in 300 g (10 oz) logs, Sainte-Mauré usually has a length of straw running through the centre of the cheese. However, some creameries are beginning to

Sainte Mauré

leave out the straw. The cheese has a white downy rind and the texture is firm but spreadable. The flavour is full and 'goaty', but not unpleasantly so.

Variations Sainte-Mauré Cendré is rolled in ash.

Serving Serve as part of a cheeseboard or on its own with crusty bread and tomatoes. Sainte Mauré tends to a blue surface mould, so eat as soon after purchase as possible.

Cooking Use in soups and sauces for an unusual but good flavour. Try mixing it with cream and fresh herbs and serve with poached fish fillets or with veal. Dilute with water and a little lemon juice to make a tangy salad dressing for well-flavoured leaves like rocket or watercress or for tomatoes and avocados.

SAINT-NECTAIRE

Semi-hard cow's milk cheese. Fat content 45 per cent

This ancient French cheese from the Auvergne is made twice a day from morning and evening milk separately. It is protected by the French *Appéllation d'Origine* laws.

Availability Specialist cheese shops and French delicatessens. Matured for eight weeks before being sold.

Description Produced in 800 g–1.5 kg (28 oz–3 lb) flat discs the cheese has a greyish crust which may have light yellow or reddish moulds. The paste is pale gold in colour, has small holes scattered throughout and is supple and slices well. The cheese has a slightly mouldy smell and a mild, delicate flavour.

Serving Serve as part of the cheese course or slice and serve in open and closed sandwiches or on a platter of mixed sliced cheeses.

Double-wrap and keep in a cool place or in the fridge for ten days or so.

Cooking Saint-Nectaire toasts well and can be used on baked croûtes and as a topping for gratin dishes. In the Auvergne it is served in a bread soup at Christmastime. Try slicing and using it to stuff baked trout or in a stuffing for a rolled meat loaf.

SAINT-PAULIN

*Semi-soft cow's milk cheese.
Fat content 45–50 per cent*

This is a factory made version of Port du Salut which may be made anywhere in France and, indeed, in a number of other cheese-producing countries as well.

Availability Widely available. Matured for two months before being sold.

Description Produced in 1.5–2 kg (3–4½ lb) flat discs, Saint-Paulin has a bright orange rind and a pale gold paste. The texture is supple and the flavour mild.

Serving Serve as part of the cheese course or in a ploughman's lunch with sweet pickles, or slice and use in sandwiches.

Double-wrap and store in the fridge for a week or ten days.

Cooking Saint-Paulin melts well into soups and sauces and can be used in cheese pastries, scones, stuffings and gougères.

SAMSOE

Semi-hard cow's milk cheese. Fat content 45 per cent

Sometimes known as the 'father of Danish cheese', Samsoe started off life as a Danish version of Swiss Emmenthal cheese, but today it has developed a character all its own. Once a farmhouse cheese, Samsoe and its descendants are now factory produced.

Availability Widely available. Sold after eight to ten weeks or after several months' ageing.

Description A flat round, cartwheel-shaped cheese with a golden-yellow dry rind usually coated with yellow cheese wax. The texture is firm but not hard and the cheese is easily sliceable – more like Cheddar than Emmenthal. The paste is pale yellow in colour with a limited number of shiny holes or eyes about the size of cherries.

The flavour is quite mild and nutty in the young cheese, but this strengthens and takes on a more pungent quality as the cheese matures.

Variations Large rindless rectangular cheeses matured in vacuum plastic packaging and mini-cheeses in red wax coating. Other Samsoe-style cheeses are Danbo; Fynbo; Elbo, a rectangular red wax-coated cheese with small holes and a mild flavour; and, Tybo, a rectangular red wax-coated cheese very similar to Elbo, but with slightly smaller holes in the paste.

Manufacture Made from pasteurised milk, as are all Danish cow's milk cheeses. There are provisions within the Danish food laws which allow for the production of cheese from the milk of other animals, but this special permission has never been granted. Thus there are no Danish goat's or ewe's milk cheeses.

The milk spends around half an hour in the cheese vat with the starter culture, rennet and hole-forming bacteria. After this time the curds are cut into small squares. The curd is then stirred and heated. The regular holes are achieved by pressing the curds underneath the whey at the bottom of the cheese vat by means of a cheese press. This helps to avoid air traps forming. The whey is drained off and the curd cut into suitable blocks to fit into the cheese moulds. The cheeses are pressed again in the moulds. The regular holes develop during the storage or ripening period which lasts for at least four weeks. Cheeses for export are usually stored for longer periods.

Serving May be served in wedges or, as they do in Scandinavia, in thin slices – a hand-held cheese slicer is useful for this. Wrapped and kept cool, it will keep for about two weeks.

Cooking Very versatile, this cheese can be used for most culinary applications. It tends to go slightly stringy on cooking and has a fairly mild flavour in the dish. It toasts quite well. Useful cut into batons for chef's salads and diced for canapé kebabs.

History Tradition has it that around 1800 an estate owner named Constantin Brunn invited Swiss cheese-makers to make Emmenthal from the entire milk yield of his dairy cows. Production was very successful but, as time went on, the cheese made on the estate gradually developed its own Scandinavian character. Earlier this century the authorities decided to rename the cheese in order to emphasise its Danish origin. Thus Danish Emmenthal was re-named Samsoe after the island of that name.

Denmark has a history of experimenting with cheese styles from other countries and some of these have, in recent years, developed a larger international market than the originals.

SATTERLEIGH

Semi-soft goat's milk cheese. Fat content not available

A surprisingly creamy English cheese made from the milk of Anglo-Nubian goats.

Availability Specialist cheese shops. Almost all the year round.

Description Smooth, firm, almost spreadable cheese, made in 2.5 kg (5 lb) drums, with a thin, natural pale yellow crust. The flavour is fairly full.

Serving Serve as part of your cheese course or on its own with grapes and plums.

Cooking This is an easy cheese to melt into soups and sauces or to mash into canapé toppings or raw vegetable stuffings.

SBRINZ

Extra-hard cow's milk cheese. Fat content 45 per cent

The oldest of all the Swiss cheeses with a history that goes back to Roman times, it takes its name from the village of Brienz in the Bernese Oberland. It is made now, though, in central Switzerland in Lucerne, Unterwalden, Schwyz and Zug.

The time taken to mature this extra-hard cheese is almost twice as long as for Emmenthal or Gruyère.

Availability Specialist cheese shops. Immature Sbrinz is sold in Switzerland and Italy when it is easy to slice but elsewhere only the fully matured cheese is on sale. These cheeses will be at least eighteen months or even two years old.

Description Produced in flattish wheels weighing between 25–40 kg (55–85 lb), Sbrinz has a hard thick, golden-brown rind and an extremely hard, grainy pale yellow paste. The flavour is very tangy and piquant.

Manufacture The manufacture of Sbrinz starts off in a similar fashion to Emmenthal, but the all-important ripening process is rather different. After the salt bath, Sbrinz is taken to a heated room where it exudes fat and water. The Sbrinz storage cellars are not climatised and are less humid than other maturing cellars. The rind is regularly rubbed with a dry cloth.

After one year, the Sbrinz cheeses are placed on edge in special racks, so that the air may reach them evenly on all sides. This long period of dry ·storing gives Sbrinz its special flavour and hard, brittle texture.

Serving This cheese is so hard that it is rarely served on its own when it is fully mature.

However, it is sometimes served as an appetiser shaved into paper-thin curly slices. Try breaking the cheese into small pieces and serve it on cocktail sticks with aperitifs.

Cooking Sbrinz is usually grated and used in cooked dishes as it melts well and gives a lovely piquant taste to any dish. It can be used in most dishes that use Parmesan.

Sbrinz is thought to be very good for the digestion and people with weak stomachs used to be given a small piece of the cheese to chew every night before going to bed.

History Some experts think that Sbrinz is the cheese which Pliny knew as *caseus helveticus*. The trade between Switzerland and Italy continued after the Romans left, and the cheeses were transported on mule back over the St Gotthard Pass and traded for rice, chestnuts and wine.

Shropshire Blue (page 136)

SCHABZIEGER (SAPSAGO)

Hard cow's milk cheese. Fat content 3 per cent

This is a very hard, pale green cheese, made from skimmed milk or whey. It is flavoured with herbs and pressed into the shape of a small truncated cone. It has many names, but may just be called 'Green Cheese'. It is found in Switzerland and in the United States.

Availability Widely available in Switzerland and the United States only. May be available whole, wrapped in foil, or ready grated or powdered in cartons.

Description These small cheeses, shaped like truncated cones, weigh between 110–200 g (3½–7 oz). They are pale green in colour, very hard and the flavour is very distinctive.

Manufacture The skimmed milk or whey may be mixed with buttermilk. It is mixed with lactic acid and heated to precipitate the protein solids. These are fermented for three to five weeks and then heavily pressed, ground up and mixed with a special herb called blue melilot. The mixture is pressed again, this time into specially shaped moulds called *stöckli*

Serving This cheese is only served grated. It is used as a condiment and sprinkled on bread or over ready-prepared dishes. The powdered form may be mixed with butter and used as a sandwich spread.

History The cheese is supposed to have been introduced by Irish monks over five hundred years ago. In Ireland, the monks were used to adding clover to their cheeses; once in Switzerland they found melilot to be an agreeable substitute – it, too, is a kind of clover. The plant was brought back from Asia Minor by the Crusaders and is still only found in the area where the cheese is made.

SELLES SUR CHER

Semi-soft goat's milk cheese. Fat content 45 per cent

A small French goat's milk cheese from Orléans,

it is protected by the French *Appellation d'Origine* laws.

Availability Locally available, in France only. Matured for three weeks, the cheese is only available during the summer and autumn months.

Description Produced in tiny 100 g (3½ oz) discs, the cheese has a soft blue rind which is tinted with ash. The paste is white and has a mild nutty flavour.

Serving Serve as part of the cheese course or on its own as a snack with bread and salad and a good red or white Loire wine.

SELVA

Cow's milk cheese. Fat content not available

There are two types of Spanish cheese which carry this name: one is consumed young, the other when more mature.

Availability Widely available, in Spain only. Matured from one to six weeks.

Description The cheese is made in cylinders weighing about 2 kg (4½ lb). The young cheese is soft, white and compact with a grainy texture. The older cheese is yellowish in colour with a more densely textured, creamy paste. They are both slightly salty.

Serving Eat both styles of cheeses as soon as possible after purchase. Try with olives or oranges; mature Selva complements a red Penedes wine, such as Coronas.

SERRA

Soft ewe's milk cheese. Fat content 45 per cent

This is the best known and indeed the best of all Portuguese cheeses. Portugal is not really a cheese-producing country and cheese is not used a lot in the traditional cuisine.

Availability On sale for most of the year, the young cheese is ripened for about four to six weeks. Some cheeses are aged for five to six months. The young cheese is best bought between December and April.

Description Produced in 1.5–2 kg (3–4½ lb) cylinders, the cheese has a soft golden, smooth rind. In the young cheese the paste is very creamy, pale yellow in colour and scattered at intervals with small holes. The texture is almost buttery and the flavour is fresh and mildly lactic. The mature cheese can be sliced, but it retains its creamy texture and characteristic flavour.

Variations Serra Velho is the matured version. Tipo Serra is the factory produced cheese. Serpa is a variety of Serra made at Serpa. It has a sharper, more peppery flavour and the matured version is very hard and pungent.

Manufacture Serra was traditionally a farm produced cheese from the Serra da Estrela in the Beira region. Today it is just as likely to be factory produced.

Serving Serve as part of the cheese course or on its own with crusty bread.

SHARPHAM

Soft cow's milk cheese. Fat content 55–60 per cent

Made from unpasteurised Jersey milk, with vegetarian rennet. Some experts believe that this English cheese is as good as the best of the now rare Brie de Montereau.

Availability Specialist cheese shops.

Description Made in 1 kg (2 lb) wheels, this cheese has a white surface mould and a full, mellow flavour.

Manufacture The cheese is made rather like Coulommiers and is aged for three weeks.

Serving Serve on its own with biscuits, celery and a good red wine or include in a selection of English cheese. As a snack, have it with crusty rolls, crispy apples, nuts and dry cider.

SHROPSHIRE BLUE

Hard blue cow's milk cheese.
Fat content 48–54 per cent

Despite the name, this cheese has nothing to do with Shropshire: it was invented and produced in Scotland in the early 1980s. Production then moved to Leicestershire where it is now made at the Long Clawson Dairy.

Availability Widely available. The cheese is sold after about twelve weeks' ripening.

Description This cheese has a thick, hard, dry crust and is made in medium-sized drums. The paste is bright orange in colour with random blue veining spreading out from the centre and the texture is creamy, but firm. It resembles Blue Cheshire, but is rather richer.

Manufacture Shropshire Blue is made from pasteurised milk in a manner similar to other English blue cheeses. *Penicillium Roquefortii* is added to produce the veins and annatto to give the colour. The cheeses are turned daily while in store and pierced with needles after a period of ripening to promote the blueing process.

Serving Serve as part of the cheese course or on its own with biscuits and celery.

Wrapped in foil and stored in a cool place, it will keep for up to two weeks.

SINGLE GLOUCESTER

Hard cow's milk cheese.
Fat content not available

After a long period of neglect, Single Gloucester cheese is becoming more widely available.

Availability Available in one or two supermarkets and specialist cheese shops. Single Gloucester is sold after only two months of ripening.

Description The cheese is made in a disc shape – half the depth of the traditional drum-shaped Double Gloucester – and has a thin yellow rind.

The colour is pale yellow, the texture softer than Double Gloucester, and the flavour is milder but still quite tangy.

Variations Flavoured with herbs or with nettles.

Manufacture The cheese is made at lower temperatures and lower acidity levels than those used for Double Gloucester. The curds are cut more finely and there is a much shorter ripening time.

Serving Serve in the same way as Double Gloucester as part of the cheese course or in a ploughman's lunch. Try cubes with pieces of air-dried ham wrapped around celery sticks, and speared on cocktail sticks.

Cooking Use in cooking when a milder flavour is required.

History The cheese was traditionally made from skimmed evening milk, ripened overnight and mixed with the full-cream early-morning milk. It was an early season cheese and, because of this, was sometimes known as haymaking cheese.

SPENWOOD

Hard ewe's milk cheese. Fat content not available

Made by a microbiologist-turned-cheese-maker, Ann Wigmore, the first step in producing the cheese was a two-month study tour in Corsica. This was followed by a year's experimentation and the final product was named after Mrs Wigmore's home – Spencer's Wood.

Availability Specialist cheese shops. Like most ewe's milk cheeses, Spenwood is best when made from spring milk. So, with two to three months' maturation, the best cheeses are on sale during the summer.

Description Produced in 2.5 kg (5 lb) wheels, the cheese has a greyish-brown natural rind or a waxed finish. The paste is a deepish-yellow colour, smooth and firm, with a slightly grainy texture. The flavour is fairly mild and reminiscent of barley.

Manufacture Made from unpasteurised ewe's milk with vegetable rennet.

Buying guide The unwaxed version is slightly milder than the waxed version which can tend towards sharpness. This is because moisture retained inside the wax affects the acidity of the cheese. In natural-rind versions, avoid any cheese with grey lines extending from the rind into the paste, as these indicate a dry cheese.

Serving Seve as part of an English cheeseboard or with thick-cut bread and pickles. It makes interesting sandwiches, with dates, peanut butter or mashed bananas.

ST KILLIAN

Semi-soft cow's milk cheese. Fat content 50 per cent

At present this cheese is made from unpasteurised milk in County Wexford, Republic of Ireland.

Availability Specialist cheese shops.

Description These surface-ripened cheeses are either 250 g (8 oz) hexagonal or 1.3 kg (2 lb) octagonal shapes and fairly flat. The cheese has a white mould rind and a creamy white paste. It can be eaten young, when it is quite firm, or when it is ripe and soft. The flavour is mild, but fills out a little with maturity.

Serving Serve as part of the cheese course or spread the ripe cheese directly on to pumpernickel, celery sticks or cheese biscuits.

Cooking Remove the rind and melt the cheese into sauces and soups.

STILTON

Semi-soft blue cow's milk cheese.
Fat content 48 per cent

Known in Britain as the 'king of cheeses', Stilton is the only English cheese to be protected by a copyright invested in the Stilton Cheese-makers Association. The cheese must be made within the counties of Leicestershire (now including Rutland), Derbyshire and Nottinghamshire.

Stilton takes its name from a small village on the Great North Road near Melton Mowbray, but it has never been made there. However, in 1727 Daniel Defoe mentions Stilton as 'a town famous for its cheese' and the Bell Inn constantly sold first class cheese to coach travellers throughout the eighteenth century.

Nowadays, Stilton is made by five companies scattered across the authorised area. These dairies between them produced eight thousand tonnes of cheese in 1987. The cheese is exported to all parts of the world, including Japan and the United States. Sales in the home market are on the increase as more and more people are prepared to experiment with blue cheese.

Availability Blue Stilton is sold after at least twelve weeks' maturation and some are sold when they are more mature. The best Stilton, made from the summer milk, is in the shops from September up to Christmas. The age at which Stilton should be eaten is very much a matter of personal preference. Much of the Stilton sold in supermarkets is fairly immature because the mass market retailers have to consider the shelf life of their products. Specialist shops are more likely to be able to supply a mature cheese.

Description Blue Stilton is a drum-shaped cheese with a thick, hard, uncracked crust which is usually greyish-brown in colour, slightly wrinkled with whitish powdery patches. The crust is not a rind, but a naturally grown surface of yeast moulds in a particular balance. The crust should be pliable enough to be springy and alive to the touch, it has a flavour of its own and though not often eaten is perfectly edible.

The texture of the cheese varies from crumbly to smooth and from firm to soft. The cheese softens as it matures. The paste is a creamy yellow colour with well-spread blue veins growing from the centre outwards and these increase in area and turn a bright blue green with maturity. Stilton has a distinctive flavour which strengthens as the cheese matures.

Variations Blue Stilton is made in small sizes, including a baby cheese at 2.25 kg (5 lb) and in presentation jars and pots. A white version is also available. Admiral is a combination of Stilton with Cheddar cheese and port. County is Stilton in alternate layers with Double Gloucester. Huntsman is two layers of Stilton curd sandwiched between three layers of Double Gloucester. 'Walton' is Stilton mixed with Cheddar and finely chopped walnuts, and coated with nibbled walnuts.

Manufacture It takes 77 litres (17 gallons) of milk to make one 8 kg (18 lb) cheese. Stilton is a temperamental product and it needs to be nursed through the different stages of cheese-making by highly skilled and dedicated cheese-makers. Not for Stilton the high-tech automated factories which churn out some other well-known cheeses. One highly respected and prize-winning cheese-maker remarked to me that 'Stilton production is 5 per cent magic!' Stilton is neither pressed nor heated.

With the exception of one dairy which uses unpasteurised milk, Stilton is made from full-fat pasteurised cow's milk. A starter culture is mixed with the milk which is then pumped into large vats. After about 25–40 minutes rennet is added and the curd sets after about 40–50 minutes. Once the curd is set, it is then cut both vertically and horizontally into long ribbons rather like square tagliatelle or into cubes. The curd is very delicate and great care is taken not to agitate it too much. The curd is left to settle and is then transferred to cookers or drainers where it is left to stand and drain for twenty-four hours before being cut again into blocks and then broken down by hand to pieces the size of tennis balls. Once the curd is drained, it is milled and salt is mixed in by hand. It is very important to get an even distribution of salt throughout the cheese. The milled curd is spooned into 11 kg (25 lb) hoops. These hoops are turned twice a day for five days and the curds compact down, but the cheese still has quite an open texture.

The mould spores may be added to the milk or to the curds. They are a strain of *penicillium Roquefortii*. If the cheese was not sealed, the spores would start to grow at once. To prevent this the sides of the cheese are hand-rubbed with a knife to give an airtight seal. The cheeses are now moved to the cheese store, where they are turned three times a week. After about eight to ten weeks, the cheeses are pierced to allow oxygen into the cheese and so allow the blue veins to grow. The cheeses are graded at about twelve weeks and it is only at this stage that the cheese-makers will be really sure that all their care and hard work has paid off.

Buying guide Look for a cheese where the blue veins are spread evenly throughout the paste. They should, even in a young cheese, provide a good contrast to the creamy yellow paste. When young, the veins will be fairly pale in colour; as the cheese matures, the veins turn to a much brighter blue and eventually to blue green. The paste at the edges may darken slightly to an amber colour with increasing maturity.

Avoid cheeses with a dry, cracked or brownish centre paste or with a badly cracked crust.

Serving Stilton makes an excellent after-dinner cheese. It was traditionally served with port. At one time, it was fashionable to pour the port into the middle of a whole cheese with the top sliced off. The cheese was pierced with knitting needles to help the port penetrate and it was then spooned or scooped out with a special scoop. The practice is now frowned upon. Stilton, like many other cheeses, is moving with the times

and it is now equally popular as a snack or as part of a ploughman's lunch with bread and pickles and maybe a glass of beer.

If really necessary, Blue Stilton will keep fairly well in the fridge. Wrap well in polythene and unwrap and return to room temperature before serving. If you have an area at the correct temperature where the cheese can be stored on its own, larger portions can be covered with a cloth which has been dampened in brine; or if there is a single cut surface only, it can be stored with the cut surface covered.

Blue Stilton wedges can be double-wrapped and deep-frozen for up to three months.

Cooking Grate or crumble straight from the fridge otherwise you will end up with a sticky mass of cheese. Use sparingly as the flavour seems to intensify on heating. Stilton was traditionally potted by mixing with butter, port or brandy and a dash of nutmeg or mace. The mixture was pressed into small pots and the surface covered with melted butter. A similar mixture makes a very good butter for grilled steaks.

Stilton

Stilton soup is fast becoming a modern classic and Stilton tartlets, quiches and vol-au-vents are popular. Other ideas for cooking with Stilton include cheese truffles with biscuit crumbs and nuts, dips with Quark or natural yoghurt, sauces for chicken, veal or pasta and salad dressings for well-flavoured leaves or coleslaw.

History There are some cheese historians who believe that Stilton is the modern descendant of blue goat's or ewe's milk cheese production in the Vale of Belvoir in the middle ages. But the first real evidence of the cheese's existence dates back to the early 1700s, when an Elizabeth Scarbrow was housekeeper to the Ashbys at Quenby Hall. Quenby Hall made first class cheeses which were known first as Lady Beaumont's cheese and later as Quenby cheese. In 1720, Elizabeth Scarbrow married a Mr. Oxton, a local farmer, and she continued to make cheese at home. The landlord of the Bell Inn married one of the Scarbrow daughters and the other daughter married a local farmer named Paulet. Mrs. Paulet continued to make cheeses according to her mother's recipe and they both supplied cheeses to the Bell Inn. The cheese gradually became known as Stilton. Where the recipe originally came from is not known. The cheese became so popular that the enterprising landlord of the Bell Inn was selling Stilton at 2s 6d a pound, a price not to be equalled again until the middle of this century.

SUPRÈME DES DUCS

Semi-soft cow's milk cheese. Fat content 62 per cent

These small French creamery produced cheeses, from Auxerre in Burgundy, have become very popular since they were invented in the early 1970s.

Availability Widely available. Matured for two weeks, it will last another three on the supermarket shelves.

Description Produced in small ovals weighing around 150 g (5 oz) or in larger 200–300 g (7–10 oz) sizes, the cheese has a smooth white rind, a smooth consistency and a mild creamy taste.

Serving Serve as part of the cheese course, with other mild cheeses. It's good after spicy food. Try it with tangerines, nuts or pears.

Cooking Serve sliced as an hors d'oevre, with asparagus, air-dried ham and lamb's or corn lettuce, with a nut oil dressing.

SVENBO

Semi-hard cow's milk cheese. Fat content 45 per cent

A mild cheese from Denmark which is really a kind of Danish Emmenthal.

Availability Widely available, in Denmark only.

Description A flat, cylindrical cheese with a dry, yellow rind which is coated with yellow cheese wax or plastic emulsion. The paste is pale yellow in colour with a number of large round holes, the texture is firm but not hard and easily sliced and the flavour is characteristically nutty.

Variations Large rindless rectangular cheeses matured in vacuum plastic packaging.

Manufacture Manufactured from pasteurised full-fat cow's milk in much the same way as Samsoe. These cheeses carry the Casein and Lur mark (see page 148).

Serving May be served in thin wedges or slices. Wrapped and kept cool it will last for up to two weeks.

Cooking This cheese tends to go slightly stringy on cooking, so it's good on pizzas.

SWALEDALE

Semi-soft cow's milk cheese.
Fat content not available

Sadly, only a handful of farms are now making this lovely English cheese from the milk of Jersey cows reared in the dale itself.

Availability Specialist cheese shops.

Description Produced in millstones, rounds and truncated cylinders of various sizes, this cheese develops a natural rind sometimes with a grey surface mould. The texture is soft, creamy and moist, with a mild, but distinctive flavour and appearance according to the time of the year.

Manufacture The cheese is made with un-pasteurised full-fat milk and is matured for about three weeks.

Serving Serve with other unusual English cheeses as part of the cheese course or on its own, with English apples or grapes, and home-made walnut bread.

History Swaledale cheese was originally made with goat's milk. The recipe for this ancient cheese came over with Norman monks. In those days it was a blue cheese, rather like Roquefort.

TALEGGIO

Semi-soft cow's milk cheese. Fat content 48 per cent

Sometimes known as Talfino, this is a *stracchino* or winter cheese and while the name Taleggio is protected under Italian law, Talfino is not. The cheese takes its name from the small market town near Bergamo in Lombardy and has been marketed as such since the 1920s.

Availability Widely available. Usually matured for about forty days before being sold, some cheeses are matured for a further month or so and these are much prized.

Description Produced in 2 kg (4½ lb), 20 cm (8 in) squares, the cheese has a thin, slightly pinkish-white rind. The paste is white and softly supple with a few small holes here and there. The flavour is milky-mild and slightly fruity. Cheeses made from raw milk are surface-ripened and may still be slightly chalky in the centre when the outside is ripe. The mature cheeses are creamy and more aromatic with an excellent, slightly sour flavour.

Manufacture Mainly made from pasteurised milk, many Taleggio cheeses are now produced by a modern cooked-curd method which produces a cheese more like the typical *italico* cheeses (see page 46). Uncooked-curd Taleggio made from raw milk is a typical rind-ripened cheese with many more organisms on its surface than the factory made cheese. In a good Taleggio the rind is never cracked.

Serving Serve as part of your cheese course or on its own with grapes and biscuits.

Double-wrap in foil and store in a cool place for ten to fourteen days.

History This is one of the oldest soft cheeses and was being made by families for their own use as long ago as the eleventh century. The cheeses were made in the autumn and winter when the cows came down from the Alpine pastures into the villages. The milk was taken from the cows when they were tired – *stracche* in the Lombard dialect – after this long journey. They then came to be called *stracchino* cheeses.

TEIFI

Semi-hard cow's milk cheese.
Fat content not available

This is an unusual Gouda-like Welsh cheese, produced at Glynhoch farm in Dyfed. The cheese-maker served an apprenticeship in Holland, which no doubt accounts for the style of cheeses he chooses to make.

Availability Specialist cheese shops.

Description Produced in 500 g (1 lb), 1 kg (2 lb) and 4 kg (9 lb) fattened balls, rather like Edam, this cheese has a yellow or red wax coating. The paste is elastic, Gouda-like with scattered small holes, and pale yellow in colour. The cheese is quite rich in flavour.

Variations Flavoured with chives, garlic, garlic and onion, celery and garlic, sweet pepper, mustard or cumin seed.

Serving Serve as part of the cheese course, in sandwiches or in a ploughman's lunch with pickles.

Cooking Teifi melts easily and is very good on toast or in a fondue.

Manufacture Produced from unpasteurised, partly skimmed milk with vegetable rennet and low sodium salt.

TÊTE DE MOINE

Semi-hard cow's milk cheese. Fat content 50 per cent

Shaped like little drums, these cheeses are made from only rich summer milk. They were invented by the monks of Bellelay Abbey, in the Bernese Jura, who taught the local farmers how to make them. The cheese is also known as Bellelay cheese.

Availability Specialist cheese shops. The cheeses are matured for four to six months and go on sale in the autumn. Tradition has it that the first cheeses are ready to eat when the first autumn leaf falls. The season lasts until about March.

Description Produced in small 500 g–2 kg (18 oz–4½ lb) drums, the cheeses have a rough, slightly greasy rind. The paste is creamy, straw-yellow in colour, and the flavour quite mild for a 'monks' cheese', but still quite fruity and distinctive.

Manufacture Made from unpasteurised summer milk, the curds are not cooked. The cheese is pressed and stored in cool cellars.

Serving Traditionally the cheese is served in thinly sliced curls – which are cut from the cheese with a special knife called a *girolle* – with pepper and ground cumin. The rind is cut from the cheese to a depth of about 3 cm (1½ in) all the way round. Some people say that this method of presenting the cheese gave rise to the name *Tête de Moine* or 'monk's head'.

TILSIT

*Semi-hard cow's milk cheese.
Fat content 30–50 per cent*

This is another successful cheese which has been widely copied. Tilsit originated in east Prussia in the town of the same name, which is now Soviet Sovetsk. It was first made by Dutch immigrants to the town in 1845, but now it is made all over West Germany, and in East Germany where it is known as Tollenser.

Availability Widely available. Ripening lasts for about six months before the cheeses are sold.

Description The traditional shape for Tilsit is a large wheel but, increasingly, the cheese is being produced in a large loaf-shape which is convenient for electrical slicing machines. The cheeses weigh 3–5 kg (6½–11 lb) and have a thin, natural rind which may be reinforced with a wax coating, or may be absent in vacuum-packed versions.

The paste is creamy-yellow in colour and has numerous small holes scattered throughout. The texture is springy, elastic, but fairly moist and the flavour is mild and delicate, but with a definite taste of its own.

Variations Royalp or Swiss Tilsit is a Swiss version of Tilsit which uses the name Royalp for export. In Switzerland it is usually known as Tilsit. However, it is rather more like Appenzell than German Tilsit for it has fewer, larger holes and is much firmer.

Havarti is the Danish version of Tilsit. Versions are also made in Australia, Sweden, Austria and Poland.

Lower-fat versions are sometimes flavoured with cumin seeds. Bianco is a whiter version of Tilsit.

Manufacture Made from raw or pasteurised whole or skimmed milk, the curds are inoculated with a lactic bacteria starter and curdled with rennet. The curd is cut and cooked before being transferred into perforated moulds. The cheeses are turned often, may be pressed lightly, and then are dry-salted and ripened for a month during which time they are washed regularly with brine. They are then matured for a further five months.

Serving The Germans serve the cheese at any meal, thinly sliced with a cheese slicer. It may also be served with bread and pickles or in open or closed sandwiches. Chunks are a mild alternative for the cheese course.

Double-wrap and store in the warmest part of the fridge for a week, or freeze for a month or so.

Cooking Tilsit toasts well and melts into sauces and soups. Use in slices for toasting or with hamburgers. Grate for use in cheese sauces, flans and potato dishes and dice into salads.

History Tilsit cheese is credited to a Mrs Westphal, who is said to have started making the cheese in 1845.

TOMME DE SAVOIE

Semi-hard cow's milk cheese.
Fat content 25–40 per cent

Tomme which means 'slice' is the generic term for semi-hard cheese and it is used in many parts of France. This one comes from Savoie and Haute Savoie and is made from full or skimmed cow's milk.

Availability Specialist cheese shops and French delicatessens. Matured for two months before sale.

Description Produced in various shapes and sizes, Tomme de Savoie is usually made in 1.8 kg (4½ lb) to 3 kg (6½ lb) fat discs. The cheese has a hard, powdery rind varying in colour from greyish-white to pinkish-brown. The paste is supple, easy to slice, pale ivory in colour and has a few small pea-sized holes scattered through it. The aroma is a little mouldy and the flavour mild and nutty.

Manufacture Made originally on farms or in mountain dairies called *fruitères*, but now mainly in commercial dairies, the cheese is still made according to traditional methods.

The curd is cut into tiny pea-sized pieces and is then drained, turned and salted. The cheeses are then turned regularly, stored at fairly high temperatures and in a very humid atmosphere,

then moved to cool caves which produce the coloured spots on the rind and help to give the cheese more flavour. Sometimes the cheeses are brushed with brandy as they are turned.

Serving Serve as part of the cheese course or slice with other cheeses. Makes very good open and closed sandwiches or it may be cubed and served with aperitifs.

Double-wrap in foil and store in the fridge for up to ten days.

Cooking Tomme de Savoie is a good cheese for toasting and cooking. Use for mildly flavoured *gratin* toppings and in cheese pastries.

TOURNAGAS

Semi-soft cow's milk cheese. Fat content 50 per cent

This is an unusual English cheese which is produced in Somerset and matured in Surrey.

Availability Specialist cheese shops. Matured for six weeks before going on sale.

Description Produced in small discs, the cheese has a washed rind and a creamy ivory paste. The flavour is aromatic, quite sharp and spicy.

Manufacture Two days after it is produced, this cheese is transferred to cheese cellars in Surrey where it is washed regularly in Penshurst wine (which is produced in Kent).

Serving Serve as part of the cheese course, or on its own with water biscuits.

TURUNMAA

Semi-hard cow's milk cheese. Fat content 50 per cent

One of Finland's oldest cheeses, it was made in and around the country's oldest city of Turku. It is now made in factories and sold under a variety of brand names.

Availability Widely available, in Finland only. Matured for two months before it is sold.

Description Produced in 6–10 kg (13–22 lb) drums, the cheese has a rich, smooth texture and a slightly sharp but creamy flavour.

Serving In Finland the cheese is usually eaten sliced for breakfast, but it can be used for sandwiches, grated, or cubed into salads.

TYROLER GRAUKÄSE

Soft blue cow's milk cheese. Fat content 45 per cent

You may come across this unusual cheese in the Austrian Tyrol.

Availability Locally available, in Austria only.

Description Produced in small discs or cylinders, the cheese has blue veining which spreads in from the surface. The paste is often unaffected. The flavour is quite strong with slightly sour overtones.

Manufacture The curds are pressed and the cheese washed regularly with *penicillium* bacteria during the ripening period.

Serving Serve as part of the cheese course or with rye bread and salad.

VACHERIN FRIBOURGEOIS

Semi-hard cow's milk cheese. Fat content 45 per cent

This cheese is often confused with Vacherin Mont d'Or (see next entry), but in fact this Swiss cheese is quite different. Though still very creamy, the paste is much firmer and it has a different kind of rind. It may be made from pasteurised or unpasteurised milk.

Availability Specialist cheese shops. There are two types of Vacherin Fribourgeois. The first, Vacherin à Fondue, is winter-made from a mixture of whole or skimmed milk and is used mainly, as its name suggests, for fondue. The second, Vacherin à Main, is softer, maturing after about three months and is used mainly as a dessert cheese.

Description Produced in flat wheels weighing about 10 kg (22 lb) and with a diameter of 30–40 cm (12–16 in), the cheese has a distinctive yellow-to-brownish rind which is both coarse-textured and greasy. The paste is pale ivory with small holes scattered through it, the flavour is

quite mild, but as it matures the aroma and flavour both strengthen.

Serving Serve as part of the cheese course or in a ploughman's lunch with grapes or apples.

Cooking Use on its own in fondue or half-and-half with Gruyère to make fondue *moitié-moitié*. This cheese dissolves at a lower temperature than usual, so it can be used for a non-alcoholic fondue with water instead of alcohol.

VACHERIN MONT D'OR

Semi-soft cow's milk cheese. Fat content 56 per cent

Despite the fact that a French cheese also carries the same name, this is one of the few authentically Swiss soft cheeses. It is named after a mountain in the south-western Jura where it is made. The dairies are in the foothills of Les Charbonnières and in the valley of Joux so the cheese may also be called Mont d'Or de Joux.

Availability Specialist cheese shops. This is a winter-made cheese, produced when the cattle are inside eating hay, so it is at its best in late winter and early spring. It is not available during the summer months.

Description Produced in flat cylinders in varying diameters from 15 cm (5¾ in) to 28 cm (11½ in), Vacherin Mont d'Or is a mould-ripened cheese and has a white mould rind which ripens to a pale pinkish-brown. The ripe cheese often has two or three waves across the top surface.

The cheese is wrapped in fir tree bark and sold in boxes made of thin pine wood. There is sense as well as romance in this practice, because the cheese can be very runny when it is fully mature.

The paste is very pale with a slightly greenish cast and a number of small holes, and is soft and spreadable when young, ripening to a very runny consistency.

When the cheese first ripens it is a little stronger on the nose than on the palate. The taste is always creamy with a velvety texture and the pine case imparts a slightly resinous flavour to the cheese.

Variation An almost identical cheese is made in France. It has the same name and comes from the French end of the Joux Valley.

Manufacture Made with unpasteurised milk, the cheeses are ripened on pine shelves in cool, damp conditions – the length of ripening depending on the size of the cheese – from a few weeks to a month or two. The shelves absorb large amounts of moisture from the cheeses during this time and they are constantly changed and dried. The workshops of the *affineurs* who ripen the cheeses can be recognised by the mound of boards placed outside.

Serving The traditional way to eat a ripe Vacherin Mont d'Or is to cut off the top rind and to eat the runny cheese out of the centre. In the Jura, people make a complete meal of it with boiled potatoes and cumin seeds. Serve a whole cheese on its own at the cheese course.

Vacherin Mont d'Or should never be refrigerated. Keep it in a cool, damp place. To prevent the cut surface running, press a flat block of wood against it. Eat as soon as possible after purchase if ripe.

VALENÇAY

Soft goat's milk cheese. Fat content 45 per cent

This goat's milk cheese from central France may be farm-made (*fermier*) or factory made (*laitier*). The latter is sometimes known simply as Pyramide.

Availability Specialist cheese shops. Farm cheeses are matured for five weeks and are only available during the summer and autumn. Creamery cheeses are ripened for three to four weeks and are on sale all the year round.

Description Produced in 250 g (9 oz) truncated pyramids, the cheese is coated in wood ash. The paste is smooth and white, the flavour of farm cheeses is fairly mild and delicate, but the creamery produced cheeses are coarser and stronger.

Serving Serve as part of your cheese course or on its own with crusty bread and tomatoes.

VICCALÓN

Fresh soft ewe's milk cheese. Fat content 54 per cent

The name of this cheese, also known as *Pata de Mula,* or 'mule's hoof', probably refers to the shape of the cheese. It originated around Valladolid, near the Portuguese border, but is now made in the provinces of Leon, Zamora, Valladolid and Palencia.

Availability Widely available, in Spain only. This cheese is usually eaten immediately, but it can be left to mature to produce a cheese called Cincho.

Description Usually hand-pressed into an elongated cylinder shape which is oval in section, the matured version carries the characeristic marks of the cheesecloth on its rind. The cheese has a soft white texture and a slightly sour taste.

Manufacture The cheeses are hand-pressed and brined for two or three hours.

Serving Serve with crusty bread and salads. Eat immediately.

VIEUX PANE

Soft cow's milk cheese. Fat content 50 per cent

This traditional-looking French cheese is another mid-twentieth-century invention. It is a large, creamery produced cheese made from pasteurised milk and has a long shelf life.

Availability Specialist cheese shops.

Description Produced in large 2.5 kg (5½ lb) squares, the cheese has an orange-washed rind with a criss-cross marking from the mould. The paste is pale yellow and fairly springy. If left for too long it will start to run slightly. The flavour is fairly full but not really as tangy as the Pont l'Évêque from which it is derived.

Serving Serve as part of the cheese course as a mild alternative, or with French bread.

VULSCOMBE

Soft goat's milk cheese. Fat content not available

These small round English cheeses are hand made in Devon. They are unrenneted and lightly pressed.

Availability Specialist cheese shops.

Description The cheeses are made into 175 g (6¼ oz) lightly pressed cylinder shapes from unpasteurised goat's milk.

Variations With fresh herbs, garlic or peppercorns.

Serving Serve as part of a selection or alone, with figs and a fruity teabread.

WEISSLACKERKÄSE

Semi-soft cow's milk cheese.
Fat content 40–50 per cent

This cheese is quite pungent and often known as Weisslacker beer cheese because the Bavarians, who produce it, like to drink beer with it. It was first produced over a hundred years ago.

Availability Widely available, in Germany only. The cheese may be ripened for up to seven months and sold any time after four to five months.

Description This surface-ripened cheese develops a white shiny surface. The paste is pale in colour with a few scattered holes, the flavour is very pronounced, even in young cheeses, and it increases in strength as the cheese ripens.

Manufacture The cheese is usually made from a mixture of skimmed evening milk and whole morning milk. Rennet is added and the curds are cut into fairly large pieces after an hour or so. The drained curds are placed in moulds, salted and cured in a high humidity atmosphere. The cheeses are placed side by side, and touching, until the surface flora begins to develop. They are then separated and ripened for up to seven months.

Serving Serve with black bread and mugs of Bavarian beer.

WENSLEYDALE

Hard cow's milk cheese. Fat content 48 per cent

This smooth, slightly crumbly, English cheese – Yorkshire's pride and joy – is traditionally served with apple pie. A local rhyme illustrates the point:

Apple pie without cheese
Is like a kiss without a squeeze.

Until the 1920s, this cheese was nearly always blue-veined, but today it is more likely to be white.

Availability Widely available. Wensleydale is generally eaten fairly young at around one to two months' maturation. It does not really improve with age, but the farmhouse cheeses are often eaten a little older, at around three months. Almost all Wensleydale is made in the creamery at Hawes, but there are also some farmhouse versions on sale.

Description Traditional cheeses vary in size from 4–6 kg (9–13 lb) and are drum-shaped. They may be cloth-bound or waxed. The cheese has a thin, dry rind. The texture of Wensleydale is smooth, and fairly crumbly. The paste is white. The flavour is milky with a slightly salt piquancy.

Variation One farmhouse has been experimenting with a return to the use of ewe's milk.

Manufacture Full-fat milk is used. The curds are cut finely and salted and left overnight, unpressed. The mass is then bound with calico and lightly pressed for a few hours.

Serving Fruit cake and gingerbread join apple pie as traditional accompaniments to Wensleydale, but it goes just as well with bread and biscuits in a ploughman's lunch or after dinner. Serve, too, with fresh fruit, like pears and grapes. Eat within a few days of buying.

Cooking Wensleydale cooks very well in most applications. Try it in a dip melted with hot cream or in a savoury crumble topping. *See also Blue Wensleydale.*

WHITE STILTON

Semi-hard cow's milk cheese. Fat content 48 per cent

This is the young Stilton which has not yet started to form its blue veins.

Availability Specialist cheese shops. Matured for about four weeks; if it is left any longer it will blue naturally.

Description Produced in drums the same size, or smaller than, Blue Stilton, White Stilton has little or no crust, a very crumbly texture and is very pale in colour. The flavour is fresh with a slightly sour aspect to it.

Variation Belshire is White Stilton mixed with chives and onions.

Serving Serve as part of your cheese course or in a ploughman's lunch.

White Stilton should be eaten as soon as possible after purchase, though it can be kept, well wrapped, in the fridge for a day or two.

Cooking Use in cooking to give a slightly sour tang to fish sauces or vegetable soups. Use in vegetable stuffings or in filo pastry parcels on its own or with pine nuts or spinach. *See also Stilton.*

YOLO

Semi-hard ewe's milk cheese. Fat content 50 per cent

These French cheeses from Corsica used to be sold under the name of Golo after the village Pont du Golo where they originated. They are now produced in the Lozère under the Yolo name.

Availability Specialist cheese shops and French delicatessens. Matured for two or four months depending on the time of the year.

Description Produced in 2.5 kg (5½ lb) flattish drums, the cheese has a thick brownish-orange rind and a yellow paste, with a scattering of small holes, which slices well. The flavour is quite full and mellow.

Serving Serve as part of your cheese course or slice and serve with a selection of cheeses.

Double-wrap in foil and store in the fridge for up to two weeks.

Cooking Yolo will grate quite well and can be used in a variety of dishes. Try it in soufflés or cheese omelettes.

— *Appendix One* —
CHEESE MARKS

Some countries have introduced cheese marks which are awarded to certain cheeses on a quality basis or which are obligatory for cheeses from certain areas or on cheeses for export. Here are some of the marks you might come across.

DENMARK

All Danish cheeses carry a Casein mark. This is the 'birth certificate' of the cheese and it states where and when the cheese was made. It is made from cheese proteins and is placed on top of the cheese while it is still in the mould. It then becomes an integral part of the cheese. Rindless cheeses carry a special label.

All export quality cheeses with a fat content of 40 per cent or more must also carry the Lur mark. This symbol shows four intertwined *lurs* (an ancient Danish wind instrument used in the Bronze Age). The Lur mark may be included in the Casein mark or may be stamped on to the wrapping. The Lur mark always includes the producer's or exporter's number.

ITALY

Certain hard Italian cheeses carry branded marks on the vertical sides of the cheese to guarantee their authenticity. The cheeses are Asiago, Grana Padano, and Parmigiano Reggiano. The marks take the form of the actual name of the cheese.

Pecorino Romano carries a Casein mark stamped or moulded into the rind of the cheese.

PARMIGIANO·REGGIANO

SWITZERLAND

All Swiss cheeses carry a Casein mark which gives the date the cheese was made and the source. All Swiss cheeses for export are stamped with the Alpine hornblower symbol and with the word Switzerland.

UNITED KINGDOM

There is a variety of quality marks for English cheese. However, many of the smaller producers do not wish to join the official schemes. This is not because their cheeses are not up to standard, indeed some of them may be better!

The English cheese quality mark This mark was introduced in 1983 to pick out home produced cheese of quality. The factory and creamery produced cheesees are tested by graders with many years' experience and the best are entitled to use the quality selected grade mark.

The farmhouse cheese logo This is a quality assurance mark for traditional hard-pressed cheeses including Cheddar, Cheshire, Lancashire, Leicestershire, Double Gloucester, Caerphilly, Wensleydale and Derbyshire.

English farmhouse Cheddar is graded between the ages of sixty and one hundred and twenty days with one cheese from every vat being graded. There are two grades which can be awarded. Only cheeses which reach the top grade are awarded the farmhouse cheese logo. The cheeses are tasted again when they are mature and only those which are still considered to be top grade will be sold with the logo.

English farmhouse Cheshire and Lancashire are graded after fourteen days and the cheeses are awarded one of four grades. Only the top two are permitted to carry the farmhouse logo. The cheeses are tasted again before sale.

The problem with these marks is that, with the exception of Cheddar, the cheeses are graded at such an early age that a great deal may happen before they reach full maturity. The organisers feel that this does not matter because the cheeses are not usually allowed to mature to the extent that they once were. Critics argue that the full flavours of the past are no longer available to the modern generation.

Stilton Stilton is protected by the Stilton trademark which is used by the Stilton Cheese Makers' Association. At the present time there are only five producers who are members of the Association and entitled to produce Stilton and to use the mark.

— *Appendix Two* —
SHEEP'S MILK *and* GOAT'S MILK CHEESES

GOAT'S MILK CHEESES

Widely available
Banon★
Chabichou
Chabi
Chavroux
Chèvre
Haloumi★
Labna★
Pant-ys-Gawn

Specialist cheese shops
Cabecou
Caciotta★
Capricorn
Chevrotin des Aravis
Coleford Blue
Crottins de Chavignol
Mendip
Moorlands
Ribchester
Rigotte★
Sainte-Mauré
Satterleigh
Valençay
Vulscombe

Widely available in country of origin
Aragon★
Caprini★
Montenebro

Locally available in country of origin
Evora★
Malaga
Picadon
Pouligny Saint-Pierre
Selles sur Cher

★ *Also made from ewe's or cow's milk, so check the label.*

EWE'S MILK CHEESES

Widely available
Acorn
Banon★
Etorki
Feta★
Haloumi★
Kefalotiri
Labna★
Roquefort

Specialist cheese shops
Barac★
Beenleigh Blue
Caciotta★
Carolina
Cecilia
Iraty Brebis Pyrénées
Lanark Blue
Manchego
Nepicar
Nuns of Caen
Pecorino
Ricotta★
Spenwood
Yolo

Widely available in country of origin
Aragon★
Burgos
Canestrato
Graviera
Ikiazabal
Kaseri
Liptauer
Requeijao
Roncal
Serra
Viccalón

Locally available in country of origin
Cervera
Evora★
Kopanisti

★ *Also made from cow's milk, so check the label.*

— Appendix Three —
CHEESES by COUNTRY

★ Indicates a mention only: not an entry to itself, i.e. it will be found as a variation of another cheese. See the Index for references to these cheeses.

AUSTRALIAN CHEESES
Cheedam
Pastorello

AMERICAN CHEESES
Albany★
American★
Barrel
Brick
Camosun★
Colby
Coon★
Cornhusker★
Cottage Cheese
Daisy★
Dry Jack★
High Moisture Jack★
Liederkranz
Mammoth
Monterey Jack
Old Heidelberg★
Philadelphia
Pineapple★
Tillamook★
Vermont

AUSTRIAN CHEESES
Smoked Cheese
Tiroler Graukäse

BELGIAN CHEESES
Beauvoorde
Broodkäse★
Brusselsekaas
Echte Loo★
Hervé
Passendale
Père Joseph

Remoudou
Romadur★
St Bernard–Watou

DUTCH CHEESES
Creme de Polder★
Edam
Friesian Clove
Gouda
Kernhem
Leiden
Maasdam★
Nokkelöst
Rembrandt★

DANISH CHEESES
Bla Castello★
Blue Brie★
Danablu
Danbo
Dania★
Danish Blue★
Elbo★
Esrom
Feta★
Fynbo
Gondola★
Grana★
Haloumi★
Havarti
Jutland Blue★
Kefalotiri★
Maribo
Mellow Blue★
Molbo★
Mozzarella
Munster★
Mycella

Rygeost
Saint Paulin★
Samsoe
Svenbo
Tybo★

ENGLISH CHEESES
Abbeydale★
Admiral★
Albany★
Applewood★
Beauchamp★
Beenleigh Blue
Belshire★
Blackwood★
Blue Cheshire
Blue Stilton
Blue Wensleydale
Bressot
Caerphilly
Capricorn
Carolina
Cecilia
Celebrity★
Charnwood★
Cheddar
Cheddington★
Cheshire
Cheviot★
Coleford Blue
Colwick
Cornish Yarg
Cotherstone
Cotswold★
Cottage Cheese
Country Brie★
County★
Cream Cheese

Creamy White★
Cromwell★
Cumberland Farmhouse
Derby
Devon Garland
Double Gloucester
Grosvenor★
Huntsman★
Ilchester★
Lancashire
Leicester
Lymeswold
Mendip
Moorlands
Nepicar
Nutwood★
Oakwood★
Oxford
Penmill★
Pepperdale★
Ribchester
Romany★
Rutland★
Satterleigh
Sharpham
Sherwood
Shropshire Blue
Single Gloucester
Slipcote
Somerset Brie★
Spenwood
Stilton
Sussex Slipcote★
Swaledale
Tournagas
Vintage★
Vulscombe
Walgrove★
Walton★
Wensleydale
White Stilton
Windsor Red

SCOTTISH CHEESES

Arran★
Barac
Bonchester

Caboc
Cheddar★
Claymore★
Crowdie
Dunlop
Dunsyre Blue
Grunddu★
Highland Crowdie★
Hramsa★
Lanark Blue
Langskaill★
Lothian★
Orkney

WELSH CHEESES

Acorn
Caerphilly
Langloffan
Llanboidy
Pant-ys-Gawn
Romany
Teifi

IRISH CHEESES

Cashel Blue
Cushlee
Gubbeen
Merlin★
Milleens
St Killian
Skirrid★
Tipperary

FRENCH CHEESES

Abondance
Baby Bel
Banon
Baraka
Beaufort
Beaumont
Belle Bressane
Belle des Champs
Bleu d'Auvergne
Bleu de Bresse
Bleu des Causses
Bleu de Gex

Bonbel★
Bondon★
Boulette d'Avesnes
Boursault
Boursin
Brie
Brillat Savarin
Cabecou
Calvador★
Camembert
Cantal
Cantalet★
Caprice des Dieux
Carré de l'Est
Cendré
Chabi
Chabichou
Chamois d'Or
Chaource
Chaumes
Chavroux
Chester
Chèvre
Chevret★
Chevrette des Beauges★
Chevrot★
Chevrotin des Aravis
Coeurs
Comte
Corsica
Coulommiers
Crottins de Chavignol
Dauphin★
Demi Sel
Doux de Montagne
Emmenthal
Entrammes★
Époisses
Etorki
Explorateur
Fourme d'Ambert
Fourme de Cantal★
Fourme de Forez★
Fourme de Montbrison
Fromage Blanc★
Fromage Fort de Mont Ventoux★
Fromage Frais
Fromage Vin Blanc★

Gaperon
Gris de Lille★
Gruyère de Comte★
Iraty Brebis Pyrénées
Laguiole
Langres
Le Fournols★
Le Macaire★
Le Roi★
Livarot
Margotin★
Maroilles
Monsieur Fromage
Morbier
Mothe Saint-Heray★
Munster
Neufchâtel
Niolo★
Pavé de Moyeaux★
Petit Suisse
Picadon
Pipo Crem'
Pont l'Évêque
Port-Salut
Pouligny-Saint-Pierre
Pyramide
Pyrénées
Raclette★
Rambol
Reblochon
Rigotte
Rollot
Roquefort
Roulé
Saint Agur
Saint Albray
Saint Bernard-Watou
Saint-Florentin
Saint-Marcellin
Saint-Nectaire
Saint-Paulin
Sainte-Mauré
Salers★
Selles sur Chers
Suprême des Ducs
Tartare★
Tomme d'Abondance★
Tomme d'Aligot★

Tomme de Chevre★
Tomme de Savoie
Vacherin d'Abondance
Vacherin Mont d'Or★
Valençay
Vieux Pane
Yolo

ITALIAN CHEESES

Asiago
Bagozzo★
Bel Paese
Bella Alpina★
Bickaud
Buriella★
Burrini
Butirri★
Cacetto
Caciocavello
Caciotta
Canestrato
Caprini
Chiavara★
Dolcelatte
Emiliano★
Fontal★
Fontina
Gorgonzola
Grana Lodigiano★
Grana Padano
Italico★
Manteca★
Mascarpone
Mozzarella
Pannerone★
Parmesan
Pastorella★
Pecorino
Provole★
Provolone
Ricotta
Stracchino★
Taleggio
Talfina★
Torta San Gaudenzio★
Toscanella★
Vittoria★

GREEK CHEESES

Feta
Graviera
Haloumi
Kaseri
Kefalotiri
Kopanisti

LEBANESE CHEESES

Labna

NORWEGIAN CHEESES

Ekte Gjetost★
Gammelöst
Gjetost
Jarlsberg
Knaost★
Mysost
Pultost
Ramost★
Ridder

SWEDISH CHEESES

Herrgärdsost
Hushällsost
Kryddost
Mesost
Prästost
Ridder
Sveciaost★

PORTUGUESE CHEESES

Evora
Ilha
Requeijao
Serpa★
Serra

SPANISH CHEESES

Aragon
Burgos
Cabrales
Cantabria
Cebrero
Cervera

Entzia★
Gamondeo★
Gamoneu★
Gorbea★
Idiazabal
Mahón
Malaga
Manchego
Montenebro
Orduna★
Pata de Mulo★
Queso Fresco Valenciano
Roncal
Selva
Tronchón★
Urbia★
Viccalón

SWISS CHEESES

Appenzell
Emmenthal
Gomser★
Gruyère
Piora
Raclette
Rasskass★
Royalp★
Sapsago
Sbrinz
Schabzieger
Simplon★
Tête de Moine
Vacherin Fribourgeois
Vacherin Mont d'Or
Walliser★

GERMAN CHEESES

Allgäu Emmenthal★
Bavarian Blue
Bergader Blue★
Bergkäse
Bianco★
Brother Basil
Butterkäse
Cambozola★
Edelpilzkäse
Frühstückskäse
German Blue
Hausekäse★
Kalsterkäse★
Limburg
Münster★
Quark
Pilzkäse★
Romadur★
Tilsit
Weisslackerkäse

HUNGARIAN CHEESES

Liptauer

FINNISH CHEESE

Munajuusto
Turunmaa

— Index —

Acknowledgements

The author would like to record her grateful thanks to the following organisations for their help during the writing of this book.

Asda
Cheeses from Switzerland
Co-operative Wholesale Society
Dairy Crest
Danish Dairy Bureau
Dutch Dairy Bureau
The Farmhouse Cheese Bureau
Food and Wine from France
Food from Spain
Gateway Foodmarkets
German Food Marketing Board
Italian Trade Centre
Jeroboams
Neal's Yard, Covent Garden
Paxton & Whitfield
Safeway
J Sainsbury plc
Tesco Stores Ltd

The author and publishers would also like to thank the following organisations, to whom copyright in the photographs mentioned below belongs, for the loan of transparencies used in this book:

Page 6: The Italian Trade Centre
Page 11: The Dutch Dairy Bureau
Page 14: Cheeses from Switzerland
Page 18: Cheeses from Switzerland
Page 23: The Italian Trade Centre
Page 26: Food and Wine from France
Page 31: The Italian Trade Centre
Page 34: Graham Kirk/Country Living

Especial thanks are due to Jeroboams, 51 Elizabeth Street, London SW1, for supplying many cheeses used in photography. Jeroboams is a specialist in cheese and supplies by mail order (telephone 01-823 5623).

Bibliography
Food and Drink in Britain, *C Anne Wilson*
The French Cheese Book, *Patrick Rance*
Gourmet Guide to Cheese, *Paxton & Whitfield Cheese Club*
The Great British Cheese Book, *Patrick Rance*
The Great International Cheeseboard, *Nancy Eekhof-Stork*
Guide to Cheese, *Androuet*
Guide to Cheeses of France, *William Stobbs*
The Mitchell Beazley Pocket Guide to Cheese, *Sandy Carr*
On Food and Cooking, *Harold McGee*
World Guide to Cheese, *Glynn Christian*